BORN
TO USE
MICS

BORN
TO USE
MICS

READING
NAS'S
ILLMATIC

Edited by MICHAEL ERIC DYSON
and SOHAIL DAULATZAI

BASIC
CIVITAS
BOOKS

A Member of the Perseus Books Group
New York

Published by Basic *Civitas* Books,
A Member of the Perseus Books Group

Books published by Basic *Civitas* Books are available at special discounts for bulk purchases in the United States by corporations, institutions, and other organizations. For more information, please contact the Special Markets Department at the Perseus Books Group, 2300 Chestnut Street, Suite 200, Philadelphia, PA 19103, or call (800) 255-1514, or e-mail special.markets@perseusbooks.com.

Designed by Pauline Brown

Library of Congress Cataloging-in-Publication Data

Born to use mics : reading Nas's Illmatic / edited by Michael Eric Dyson and Sohail Daulatzai.
    p.   cm.
Includes bibliographical references and index.
ISBN 978-0-465-00211-5 (alk. paper)
1. Nas (Musician) Illmatic. 2. Nas (Musician)—Criticism and interpretation. 3. Rap (Music)—History and criticism. I. Dyson, Michael Eric. II. Daulatzai, Sohail.

ML420.N344B67 2008
782.421649092—dc22

2008007435

CONTENTS

REMIXES

FOREWORD

BY COMMON

The year 1994 was pivotal for hip-hop. My second album, *Resurrection*, came out the same year as *Illmatic*, as well as Biggie's *Ready to Die*, Pete Rock and CL Smooth's *Main Ingredient*, Outkast's *Southernplayalisticadillacmuzik*, Gangstarr's *Hard to Earn*, and many other great records too numerous to mention. But that's where hip-hop was during that Golden Age. It was a very fertile period, as the late 1950s to early 1960s were for jazz, or the early to mid-1970s for soul music—when the world seemed wide-open to us then. Hip-hop's incredible diversity reflected that era. And then there was *Illmatic*. You always have to return to *Illmatic*.

I first heard Nas on the 1991 Main Source track "Live at the Barbeque," and I knew, like everyone else, that Nas was an artist who meant something, who was going to change the game. And he didn't disappoint. Because *Illmatic* was brilliant. His lyricism, his storytelling, his control on the mic, that production. *Illmatic* had all the elements, but it was even greater than the sum of its parts. It had that something else—that rawness, that realness, something you could feel but not say, what you might hear on a classic John Coltrane or Curtis May-field record. It came together so flawlessly, so coherently, espe-cially with just ten tracks. When you heard it, you definitely caught a vibe. And when I listen to it now, I still do. But now it's a little bittersweet.

Illmatic came out fifteen years ago and it will remain a clas-sic album, no matter what genre of music you're talking about. And it's aged better with time, because it captured an important moment in hip-hop. In fact, I wrote "I Used to Love H.E.R." in 1994 as a way of expressing how I felt about where hip-hop was at that point and where it might go. Because it was that serious for so many of us. We didn't just grow up with hip-hop; we grew up with hip-hop as hip-hop was also growing, and so that made for a very close and intimate relationship that was becoming more and more urgent—and we all felt it. Our art was being challenged in many ways as the moneymen be-gan to sink their teeth into us. Some of us got eaten alive and others, well, we made it out by the skin of *our* teeth. But barely. We lost Pac and Biggie, Big L and Jam Master Jay, and too many others along the way, many of them our friends and even family members. But through it all, it's an album like *Ill-matic* that keeps us going and reminds us of what's possible.

After *Illmatic*, much was expected of Nas, and maybe un-fairly. But he didn't disappoint. He's one of the few MCs who has continued to put it down consistently, never falling into the easy traps that hip-hop tried to pigeon-hole us into. In his music, Nas was angry without being frustrated, smart but not preachy, and wise but straight up with you—and so you felt him. I like to think he was the round peg that didn't fit the hole the squares created.

People always ask me about hip-hop and the forces that have tried to narrow its creative possibilities. But it's not time to despair because we're in an interesting place right now. Nas called one of his albums *Hip-Hop Is Dead*, and many people either believed it or got upset. I saw it as a call to arms, a battle cry almost. Because if one artist earned the right to say that, it was Nas. And we needed to hear it. That's why this book you're holding is so important. Because with hip-hop definitely in a period of transition, *Born to Use Mics* meets us at the crossroads and forces us to look back in order to chart a course forward. Michael Eric Dyson and Sohail Daulatzai have brought together an impressive group of writers—kind of a cipher in book form—to reflect on *Illmatic* and many of the very serious issues that the album raised and that hip-hop continues to raise. This book you're holding—in case you've missed it—reaffirms that hip-hop matters, that this art form has said and continues to say so much about the world we live in. Read it. And listen.

INTRODUCTION

ILLMATIC: IT WAS WRITTEN

SOHAIL DAULATZAI

As Miles Davis's *Kind of Blue* was to jazz and Marvin Gaye's *What's Goin On?* was to soul music, *Illmatic* is arguably the greatest hip-hop album of all time. It's been fifteen years since *Illmatic* was released, but in some ways, it seems like yesterday. But it also feels like long ago. It's a strange thing—time— especially in the always accelerated world that is hip-hop. On that existential lament "Life's a Bitch," Nas claimed that "time is illmatic," and no doubt it has been. So much has happened since then. And so much has stayed the same.

Coming out at the tail end of hip-hop's "Golden Age" (1987–1994), in the same year as Gang Starr's *Hard to Earn*, O.C.'s brilliant but slept on *Word . . . Life*, Common's *Resurrection*, Biggie's *Ready to Die*, and many other great records, *Illmatic's* subtle and powerful brilliance rests in Nas's detailed descriptions, dense reportage, and visually stunning rhymes of the underbelly of the beast. Like the 1965 landmark masterpiece film *The Battle of Algiers*, which captured the Algerian resistance against French colonialism, *Illmatic* brilliantly blurred the lines between fiction and documentary, creating a heightened sense of realism and visceral eloquence for Nas's renegade first-person narratives and character-driven odes. And like *The Battle of Algiers*, *Illmatic* was about the stories of everyday people caught in the most horrific of circumstances, or as Nas referred to it, "the devil's lasso." Though Nas's narration of life in Queensbridge didn't have the explicit political project and radical liberationist thrust shown in *The Battle of Algiers*, Nas's lyrics captured an urgency and immediacy about life at the tattered edges of the American empire. Through *Illmatic* you could hear the echoes of secret wars and you could see the picture it captured of a particular moment, a photo that revealed, among other things, the brutal reality of the failure of the post–Civil Rights romanticism, the crack war bum rush, that COINTELPRO worked, and that the new prisons caged the rebel that may have proved to be *that* messiah.

Maybe nothing comes closer to embodying *Illmatic*'s dystopic end-time vision than HBO's brilliant series *The Wire*. Arguably one of the greatest epics in any medium, up there with *The Godfather* saga and the *Battle of Algiers*, *The Wire*'s grim yet hopeful pessimism, like *Illmatic*, was layered and complex, refusing judgment yet hard-hitting. On *Illmatic*, Nas was bold but subtle, angry but not alienating, as he rapped from the point of view of a kingpin like Stanfield and a corner boy like Bodie. He wove narratives as mythic as Omar, with his outsider ethos defining a code while defying so much else. And like *The Wire*, Nas did it with a keen eye for the pathos of power, painting a haunting and sometimes redemptive portrait of life in urban America's killing fields.

With all that has happened in hip-hop and in the world for that matter since *Illmatic*'s release, time, and the critical distance that its passage provides, affords us some perspective and gives us an opportunity to look back on *Illmatic*. So we have to wonder, as great an album as it is, how can we continue to see it as relevant? Does *Illmatic* hold some value for us today? Or is it simply a relic, an artifact of hip-hop's "Golden Age" that has nostalgic value for some while eliciting shrugs of irrelevancy from younger audiences?

As the first in a series on great albums, *Born to Use Mics* tries to answer some of these questions while posing some new ones, as we use *Illmatic* as a lens to better understand hip-hop and the history that made *it*, as well as the history that it *made*. But while *Born to Use Mics* is about exploring hip-hop through *Illmatic*, it's also about exploring America through *Illmatic*, reflected and refracted through the prism of Nas's poignant street poetry. *Illmatic* offers us the possibility to explore the landscape, that fertile ground and volatile minefield that gave birth to it: the post–Civil Rights and Black Power era, the Reagan/Bush/Clinton years of white backlash, the shifting sands of race and the emergence of the global economy, the crack era and the formation of an urban police state, the Post-Soul moment in black music, the guerrilla artistry around technology and sampling, the changing marketplace and hyper-commodification of hip-hop, the premillennium tension leading to 9/11, and the Bush II years that followed.

But despite Nas's brilliance, some might ask, why *Illmatic*? Why not Boogie Down Production's *Criminal Minded*, Public Enemy's *It Takes a Nation to Hold Us Back*, or Ice Cube's *Amerikkka's Most Wanted*? No doubt these were great albums, coming at a moment when hip-hop was cutting its teeth on social commentary and refining its ear on dusty breaks, hard snares, and sonic mayhem. But there is something about *Illmatic* that transcends the categories that have ever existed about hip-hop. Something complex about its simplicity, something elusive that we felt we wanted to explore. Straight up though, *Illmatic* is just a dope album, embodying everything that is hip-hop while mastering what matters most: beats and rhymes. It had arguably hip-hop's greatest collection of producers: DJ Premier,

Pete Rock, Large Professor, Q-Tip, and L.E.S. But Nas made the album seem so effortless and flawless. His lyrical prowess was uncanny, his perceptions so wise for someone so young, and his wordplay and rhymes so visual. If *Illmatic* was film, and in many ways it was cinematic, it was at times documentary and fictional realism, melodrama and thriller, noir and sometimes even science fiction.

Part of the reason we chose *Illmatic* was the moment that it was released and the place hip-hop had come to by 1994. You have to remember that from its genesis, hip-hop was both an aesthetic vanguard and a chin check to white America. Before the current babble about the "mainstream" versus the "underground," hip-hop was both—and neither. It was Basquiat smoking a blunt with Marcus Garvey. Cheikh Anta Diop and Rakim building in a cipher. Bunny Lee and Marley Marl fucking with the SP. Harriet Tubman and MC Lyte sharing secrets. And Patrice Lamumba and Pac doing the knowledge. But by 1994, when *Illmatic* was released, things done changed. You have to remember that in 1994 hip-hop was at a crossroads, at the tail end of the "Golden Age," a period of incredible creative and thematic ferment as hip-hop cut its teeth and found its voice both artistically and politically. Hip-hop had its own schools of thought, from street knowledge to the low end theory to everything in between. And consider the incredible artists that came up during that era: Boogie Down Productions and LL Cool J, the whole Juice Crew to the Alkaholiks, Rakim Allah to the Hieroglyphics, Goodie Mob to the Geto Boys, Kane to Cube, D.I.T.C. to EPMD, the wild styles of Organized Konfusion and Freestyle Fellowship, to the Native Tongues and N.W.A., not to mention Common, Ultramagnetic MCs, the Roots, Outkast, Pac, G. Rap, Ice-T, the prophets of rage in Public Enemy, Brand Nubian, and Poor Righteous Teachers, as well the rise of Gangstarr, the Wu Tang Clan, the Boot Camp Clik, Pete Rock and CL Smooth and so many others.

But with all that inevitably came the money men. With hip-hop at the precipice about to go mainstream after the success of Dr. Dre's 1992 album, *The Chronic*, the rise of Bad Boy, and the seemingly scripted, destructive East Coast–West Coast "beef," hip-hop no longer knew the ledge as crass commercialism infected the art so that hip-hop became product placement and commercial jingle, overwrought spectacle and just plain mediocre for the most part. So part of the reason we chose *Illmatic* is that it represents this very important and urgent moment in hip-hop. Looking back, 1994 was kind of the tipping point, where transitions were happening and the ground under hip-hop's feet began to give. That may be hard to understand today, fifteen years later, when hip-hop is everywhere, literally in the ether ready to be wirelessly downloaded. Hip-hop is impossible to avoid now, but back then you had to look for it, which makes that moment of *Illmatic* so important. Jay-Z called *Illmatic* the blessing and the curse for Nas's career. That might also have been true for all of hip-hop too, because in many ways *Illmatic* was either the beginning of the end, or it was the exclamation point on the manifesto that was hip-hop. It's a moment that will never be repeated despite the current recycling of the 1980s and the inevitable cannibalizing of the 1990s that is yet to come.

This gives us an opportunity to look back on *Illmatic* and consider where hip-hop, as a force of black creative expression, has come. In "Jazz and the White Critic," an essay written almost fifty years ago that tragically is still relevant, Amiri Baraka laments that jazz lost its value and significance when it was "stripped of its social context" and emptied of the ideological crucible out of which it emerged: segregation, racial terror, and the creative impulse to resist and create sanctuaries of art and community. In many ways, the same arguments can be made about how hip-hop has been uprooted from its geographic, political, and ideological origins. Even though it has been embraced by the Smithsonian Museum and ironically the Rock and Roll Hall of Fame, that doesn't mean that hip-hop hasn't been uprooted from its history of resistance, emptied of its creative and artistic brilliance, and stripped of the racial and economic context that made its creation a necessity.

If that's the case, *Illmatic* reminds those who forgot or anyone who didn't know. On the vinyl pressing of *Illmatic*, the album is organized not by the typical Side A and Side B, but by "40th Side North" and "41st Side South," the two streets that divide Nas's beloved Queensbridge, the largest housing project in the United States. By dividing the album in this way and centering Queensbridge, *Illmatic* becomes a sonic map, as the album serves as the legend for Nas's ghetto cartography, as he narrates his experiences and those who live in the Queens-bridge housing projects. But even though *Illmatic* is clearly about one place—Queensbridge—it is also about the projects more generally, and the racial and economic forces that create and maintain their existence. The album cover of the young Nasir Jones superimposed on Queensbridge poetically and poignantly reveals not just what poor black life must endure, but also that hip-hop emerged phoenix-like out of the ashes of poverty, segregation, racial violence, and militarized policing that have defined the hip-hop generation. But in an era when hip-pop has become the soundtrack to crass spectacle and hypercapitalism and where MP3s, ringtones, and downloading are making the music so disposable, it's hard not to lose sight of the conditions of hip-hop's genesis, and the ways in which those conditions continue to persist in one form or another.

With *Born to Use Mics*, we've tried to address many of these concerns, and this book is part of an ever-growing body of work that attempts to grapple with the complexity, the diversity, and the brilliance of hip-hop. Books on hip-hop have flourished over the last fifteen to twenty years, as hip-hop publishing has become a powerful force in the literary world. Running the gamut from historical to scholarly tomes, journalistic missives to critical insights, biographies to behind-the-scenes accounts, as well as fiction and poetry to photography and art, books on or about hip-hop are as diverse as the art form itself. With *Born to Use Mics*, we've tried to do something different. Less a behind-the-scenes exposé or "the making of" *Illmatic*, *Born to Use Mics* encompasses the different styles and forms of hip-hop publishing, from the scholarly to the journalistic, the historical to the first-person account, using freestyles and wild styles to wax philosophic on the meaning of *Illmatic*. But the final mix you hold is more than the sum of its parts, as we've brought together an eclectic group of writers, scholars, poets, filmmakers, journalists, novelists, musicians, and combinations thereof who have all grown up with hip-hop and have been deeply connected to it from jump. In essence, *Born to Use Mics* is a literary remix, a cipher in book form as all of these contributors offer up unique and fresh perspectives, as they meditate on the significance of *Illmatic*.

In critically remixing *Illmatic*, we've borrowed and even extended hip-hop's own tradition of interpretation and aesthetic democracy. Clearly sampling forms the very essence of hip-hop. Those breaks and loops taken from old jazz, soul, and funk records and then reinterpreted in new ways are all acts of interpretation. Ahmad Jamal didn't intend for Pete Rock to flip his 1970 gem "I Love Music" for use on "The World Is Yours," and Lee Erwin didn't intend for DJ Premier to take his 1924 track "Thief of Baghdad" and bang out "Represent." Hip-hop's brilliance lies in that interpretive impulse, and that impulse has guided what we're doing with *Born to Use Mics*, only we're using *Illmatic* as the sample and reinterpreting it in a critical way.

The main part of *Born to Use Mics* is structured by the ten tracks that make up *Illmatic*. Each of the writers and scholars on black music, race, and culture who are gathered here takes a song as a jumping-off point, a starting block, to explore themes and ideas that are woven throughout not only *Illmatic* but the fabric of hip-hop culture and the broader world that it is rooted in. Weaving together the personal and the political, critical voices such as Mark Anthony Neal, Imani Perry, Eddie Glaude, Adilifu Nama, Kyra Gaunt, Guthrie Ramsey Jr., and others cover a range of topics, including Nas as a public intellectual, the role of black memory, gender and patriarchy, imprisonment and policing, the politics of "the come-up" for communities of color, the aesthetics of sampling and jazz's influence on hip-hop, the connections between urban America and the Third World, and Nas's implosion of the "mainstream versus underground" debate, just to name a few.

The ten chapters are followed by "Remixes," and like the great remixes done for *Illmatic*, the different contributors are not guided by a specific track but freestyle about Nas and the significance of *Illmatic*. Included here are not only voices such as legendary *Wild Style* director Charlie Ahearn, the brilliant provocateur Greg Tate, solider-scribe dream hampton, *New York Times* music writer Jon Caramanica, novelist Adam Mansbach, and poets Suheir Hammad and Kevin Coval, but we also have some vintage historical pieces, including the original five-mic *Source* review of *Illmatic* by Shortie, the original interview with Nas and others from the April 1994 issue of the *Source*, as well as Bobbito's incredible May 1994 interview with Nas in *RapPages*.

All of these pieces make this project a unique collective insight into the possibilities and pitfalls of not only hip-hop but also the world that we all inhabit. The post-9/11 moment that we now endure has hit the reset button on a whole host of things, erasing so much of what made America what it is, while also centering things that continue to remind us in case we forgot. At its best hip-hop was always that constant reminder, that battle cry that spoke truth to power. In many ways *Ill-*

matic, and hip-hop for that matter, made visible what was not seen, having prophesied so much about where things are at. It had a clairvoyance about America's penchant for militarism and war, an insight into the country's cash rules philosophies, and an omen about the nation's gangster ethos. Using *Illmatic* as our weapon, the contributors to *Born to Use Mics* chronicle and probe that American landscape in that war against oblivion, arguing not just for hip-hop's continued relevance but also for its urgent necessity.

40TH SIDE NORTH

IT WAS SIGNIFIED

"THE GENESIS"

ADILIFU NAMA

Like a bold foreword to a brilliant novel, Nas's sonic prologue "The Genesis" jump-starts his debut album *Illmatic*. Although the track clocks in at a scant one minute and thirty-nine seconds, it is essential for any in-depth interpretation of the artist and his art. The title alone positions the track as foundational and key in understanding Nas and *Illmatic*. The fact that Nas's first recorded MC appearance on Main Source's "Live at the Barbeque" plays in the background of "The Genesis" suggests the first track is referring to Nas's beginning. Case closed, right? Not exactly, because on top of Nas's faintly audible rapid-fire lyrical delivery is a sampled exchange between two male characters from a scene in Charlie Ahearn's brooding cinema verité film *Wild Style* (1982), which is followed by one of the most sinister old-school beats in all of hip-hop, DJ Grand Wizard Theodore's "Subway Theme," also from the film. Not only is the opening dialogue on "Genesis" sampled from a pivotal scene in *Wild Style*, the music played throughout the track is sampled from the film. This is no aesthetic coincidence. Clearly, *Wild Style* is the primary sonic reference and centerpiece of "Genesis." Why? Because *Wild Style* is to hip-hop what Charlie "Yard Bird" Parker's "Cherokee" is to bebop. Required homework for aspirants and aficionados interested in knowing what the music was and what it was trying to be about.

Even though *Wild Style* is periodically referenced or cited in discussions about hip-hop, the film has failed to receive its proper intellectual due, making it woefully underappreciated as the cultural touchstone it represents. Most often the film is mentioned in terms of its trivia quotient as the first hip-hop film. The romantic comedy *Brown Sugar* is an excellent example of how the popular history of hip-hop often trivializes *Wild Style*. The film parallels the contours of a couple's unsung love for each other with the evolution of hip-hop from public park verbal jam sessions to Park Avenue deal discussions. In the beginning of *Brown Sugar* a series of past and present hip-hop luminaries are asked, "When did you first fall in love with hip-hop?" Their separate responses are edited into a clever montage that shows the majority of the different respondents delivering the same historical refrain, "Rapper's Delight," as jump-starting the genre. But as Jeff Chang wonderfully details in his hip-hop tome *Can't Stop, Won't Stop*, the orgy of economic, social, and cultural currents that contributed to the origin of hip-hop cannot be reduced to one seminal song. Instead, a series of serendipitous discoveries, chance meetings, determined individuals, economic setbacks and successes all combined to create this thing called hip-hop, a point best captured in *Wild Style*. Nas draws from this relatively untapped reservoir of hip-hop history by sampling the film in "Genesis" and sonically signifies on the evolution and transformative power and practice of hip-hop.

Wild Style depicts the organic building blocks of the hip-hop generation before it entered the American national pop consciousness. In this sense, *Wild Style* is hip-hop's earliest "home movie" and captures the awkward first steps and formative stages of the varied expressions of hip-hop as an urban folk culture that cobbled together several creative mediums— art, dance, spoken word, and music. This makes *Wild Style* one of the most important films to emerge in the past thirty years. Unlike a host of Johnny-come-lately academics and critics who will eventually end up recognizing the cultural significance of *Wild Style*, Nas is already hip to the fact. *Wild Style* is the hip-hop equivalent to the film *Easy Rider* (1969), which cinematically captures and embodies the counterculture values of the 1960s generation. *Wild Style* combines documentary footage, narrative artifice, and real hip-hop figures to chronicle the underground beginning of a counterculture.[1] Much like the feel and look of the depiction of the Algerian insurgency in the film *Battle of Algiers* (1965), *Wild Style* artfully blends fact and fiction to present another form of violent struggle, a cultural insurrection fought by black and brown youth squaring off against postindustrial decline, combating the failure of America's war on poverty. *Wild Style* records what the postindustrial urban decline of the 1970s would reap in the 1980s, the counterculture of the B-boy and B-girl. But the use of *Wild Style* on "Genesis" goes beyond a simple tactic to imbue *Illmatic* with an aura of old-school authenticity. The sonic vignette comments on the collective memory of the hip-hop community and its real, remembered, and even imagined beginning, as well as the pitfalls of assimilation, the importance of history, and the passing of hip-hop's "age of innocence."

The *Wild Style* cast consists of a who's who of hip-hop pioneers like Grand Master Flash, Grand Wizard Theodore, Fab Five Freddy, and Rock Steady Crew, as well as the king and queen of graffiti art, Lee Quinones and Sandra Fabara. The film is ostensibly about Raymond (Lee Quinones), an outlaw graffiti artist, as he covertly creates spray paint masterpieces on the exterior of New York subway trains under the pseudo-nym Zorro. The film's protagonist, Raymond, is just another Puerto Rican kid looking to find work on the streets of an economically desolate South Bronx. At night, as Zorro, he secretly paints graffiti art across subway trains. The Zorro figure is not just about stealth but personifies hip-hop as an outlaw endeavor to, in the words of Fab Five Freddy in the film, "make things all beautiful and shit." Zorro leaves his beauty marks on subway trains as graffiti murals. These subway trains signify escape to other communities of promise while reminding us, to paraphrase the prolific playwright August Wilson, that there are always "two trains running," one train leaving and one train returning. Hip-hop was the response to this metaphorical embodiment of the cycle of poverty that black and brown youth faced in the late 1970s and early 1980s. It was hip-hop, not Roosevelt's New Deal or Johnson's War on Poverty, that was "the last great social program of the 20th Century."[2]

Nas's use of a pivotal scene from *Wild Style* on "Genesis" exemplifies the above point. Early in the film Raymond is shown climbing into his room through a window after spray painting a subway car and unexpectedly finds his older brother, Hector, lying on his bed pointing a gun at him. Hector, in full military dress, is poised to shoot this "intruder" until he recognizes his younger brother. After the initial shock, Hector vocalizes his disgust over the graffiti art that adorns the inside of his room and the incorrigible lifestyle he believes it reflects. Hector tells Raymond, "Stop fucking around and be a man; there's nothing out here for you!" Raymond responds to Hector's pessimism with, "Yes there is: this!" At that moment the title track drops in to fill the space set up by the sonic cliffhanger. The symbolism embedded in the scene is quite powerful. Raymond's older brother, Hector, is projected as successfully "escaping" the bleak ghetto streets by integrating into the civic mainstream. Hector is the proverbial military man encoded with legitimacy, authority, and military respectability when he implores his younger brother to "stop fucking around and be a man." For Hector, the South Bronx, a borough with rows of abandoned buildings perched over a community littered with high unemployment, is a space that arrests personal and social maturity. Despite his brother's admonishment, Raymond has faith in hip-hop to deliver him from the socioeconomic clutches of what William J. Wilson identifies as the truly disadvantaged, a stratum of urban poor virtually stranded in poverty. For this group of urban denizens, life is confined to the exploration of ghetto postindustrial decay: where the everyday persistence of poverty teaches one to make do with making do. Given this socioeconomic reality, to choose the hip-hop life—the wild style—in the face of a proven route, like military service, to escape such bleak conditions demonstrates a profound commitment by black and brown youth to transform rather than flee the poverty-riddled social space they inhabit.

Historically, escape from ghetto scarcity has been a selling point for the military as a place and vocation that holds the most promise for racial minorities to gain a generic cloak of esteem and economic security. Even though black servicemen and women have found the military an inadequate cloak of protection from savage racism in and out of uniform, it continues to attract black and brown youth today. Whether it's the GI bill, the promise of "being all you can be," funding for college, or expedited citizenship, military service has provided some form of inducement if not hope for a better socioeconomic future for many people of color. The message captured in *Wild Style* and clearly signified in "Genesis" resonates with Chuck D's classic diatribe "I'm a black man. I could never be a veteran" in the song "Black Steel in the Hour of Chaos" more than anything Colin Powell could ever advocate. By Raymond choosing hip-hop in *Wild Style* and Nas choosing this scene to open the "Genesis" track, both texts form an ideological one-two punch that subverts the social symbolism of the military man and the allure of respectability associated with military service. In one fell semiotic swoop both the symbolic status and attractiveness of the military as a conventional means of mainstream social assimilation for racial minorities is replaced in the film. Thus the hip-hop identity of the B-boy and B-girl usurps the promise of respectability and economic opportunity offered by military service.

With the adoption of various monikers like Zorro, Whipper Whip, Grand Master Flash, and Chief Rocka Busy Bee, the black and brown youth in *Wild Style* who choose hip-hop engage in an audacious act of personal self-transformation that defies traditional routes of economic escape. Nas illustrates this point in "Genesis" by sampling Raymond's rebuff of military service in *Wild Style*. Raymond's rejection of his brother's statement "there's nothing out here for you" demonstrates that the formative stage of hip-hop was less about leaving the ghetto and more about transcending the stifling conditions of ghetto life by transforming the street, stoop, and playground into a cultural workshop, a theater of the oppressed. The block was where black and brown youth challenged and transformed their social identity from individual expressions of a disenfranchised socioeconomic racial group to that of a statistically unquantifiable B-boy and B-girl. In this sense, hip-hop, like the blues, expresses what Amiri Baraka characterizes in the seminal volume *Blues People* as a highly responsive and fluid temperament.[3] The music and its adherents, like so many other elements of the black experience, are on the move, migrating, shifting from one register to another, constantly looking for the perfect beat. Hip-hop is a continuation of the politics of racial transformation fermented in the fear, faith, and juju magic of the black experience, a transformation witnessed in those intrepid persons who took the first furtive steps off the plantation and were never dragged back. It was witnessed in those black artists who dared to step outside the restrictive confines of big band swing to play bebop in uptown New York nightclubs as well as the sanctified soul voices that left the orthodoxy of the black church to sing the devil's soul music. And certainly the B-boys and B-girls who broke from the convention of making music with instruments to making new music with old records are examples of this transformative impulse.

Hip-hop, like its bebop predecessor, was about creating community right where you were and adopting a standard of validation based exclusively on black peers, not on what outside critics had to say or what white societal norms dictated. For the postwar bop revolutionaries, Harlem hot spots like Minton's Playhouse and the Three Deuces were the hothouses of innovation and their bandstands the public planning session where radical ideas were etched out in real time. The transformative promise of hip-hop that Nas samples from *Wild Style* is also about radically remaking the cultural landscape with reckless improvisational abandon. Lee, other graffiti writers, break dancers, and rappers in *Wild Style* have the same sort of do-or-die middle finger to the stark conditions of urban poverty that bebop gave to mainstream American musical conventions. Both would ultimately alter the sonic and cultural landscape of America. Consequently the birth of bebop and hip-hop mirror each other and if Monk, Dizzy, Bird, and Miles had been born several decades later they would have been B-boys rocking the most vicious styles. For caustic critics of hip-hop and diehard fans of jazz like Stanley Crouch, who chide the cultural relevance of a music made by and bought by what he would probably consider a loose consortium of knuckleheads, such a statement must sound like blasphemy.

Yet the popular embrace and identification with the "hood" found in much of hip-hop echoes the bebopper's strident commitment to make the music relevant for those who were insiders to the culture. Nevertheless, for the hip-hop Horatio Algers who extricate themselves from "slangin'" dope on the boulevard to spitting rhymes onstage and in the studio, their odyssey of upward social mobility known as "the come-up" has not endowed these black men (and a few women) with the same aura of artistic admiration or racial respect heaped on minorities that crawl out of the well of obscurity and make it up the ladder of success. Instead, the opposite has often occurred with both black and white political quarters sounding the alarm that hip-hop is corrupting American youth in general and young black folk in particular. However, by sampling the confrontation scene between Raymond and Hector in *Wild Style*, Nas reaffirms in "Genesis" the transformative power and practice of hip-hop not only for himself as a young man making his way out of one of the largest public housing projects in America, Queensbridge, but for all the nameless B-boys and B-girls who tried to do the same. Nas is also aware of the cultural double standard that persists with hip-hop's racial image when it comes to black American success stories and confronts it with a subversive élan in the "I Can" video off the *God's Son* release.

In the video Nas has the slogan "I Am the American Dream" plastered on his chest. By wearing that shirt, Nas confronts the topic of young black men being identified as America's nightmare.[4] The first time I saw this video it immediately brought to mind the classic black-and-white footage of early civil rights protesters who wore placards suspended from their shoulders declaring "I Am a Man" to symbolically attack the perception and practice of referring to black men as "boy." Nas's statement shirt is performing similar symbolic work. It signifies that the black and brown youth who have pulled themselves up by their own Adidas (or Nike) shoelaces vis-à-vis hip-hop and go from "ashy to classy" are in keeping with the rags-to-riches narrative that has come to define the American Dream, even though they are often stigmatized and denied the esteem and status of representing it. In previous decades the hard-fought and won upward mobility demonstrated by scores of African Americans served as proof that the American Dream is ripe for anyone who possesses enough determination and talent. Rightly or wrongly these black women and men bore the burden of representing the race and were conscripted as "race men and women" to lead the good fight against racism. A substantial part of what made them candidates for this platform was that their personal narratives reflected a high degree of self-reliance. The net effect of their personal success dovetailed with the collective American mythology of rugged individualism and meritocracy in ways that made them a "credit to their race." Black entertainers like Sidney Poitier, Jackie Robinson, Bill Cosby, and, at its most radical, Paul Robeson embodied this title and represented a connection between an upright image and gaining the respect, rights, and privileges commensurate with first-class American citizenship.[5] The key contrast between hip-hop's narrative of success and social transformation and the civil rights generation's narrative of upward mobility is that hip-hoppers do not equate social mobility with escape but embrace the ghetto as a site and source of social identity. Unlike the civil rights generation, securing a spot in some suburban oasis is not a significant part of the hip-hop aura of ghetto authenticity. The ideas and imagery found in hip-hop magazines and rap videos to a large extent depict ghetto fantasies of "thug life" success in which a black or brown protagonist is shown surrounded by his "crew" on the mean streets they rap about trying to desperately escape. Moreover, the willingness to express beliefs and engage in behavior associated with the ghetto has blossomed into a hip-hop sensibility that informs a multitude of black and brown youth today. Hip-hop, for better or worse, has facilitated the transition from middle-class respectability to ghetto authenticity as the predominant black racial paradigm.

For this cohort, what white America and "decent" black folk think about them is not all that important. Consequently hip-hop refuses to accept black middle-class notions of appropriate racial representation or adopt white liberal conceptions of racial decorum. For the hip-hop generation it's not about representing the race or adhering to strict codes of morality. It's about being "real" in representing hip-hop, and if that involves profanity, weed-induced philosophies, an aggressive social posture, the glorification of violence, and coarse sexual politics lifted from everyday experience, then so be it. For hip-hop the issue is not over content; anything is fair game for discussion (maybe even doing). To hip-hop's credit this sensibility has lessened the artificial and often idealized separations between "the good, the bad, and the ugly" aspects of the black and brown experience. Consequently, stringent and bifurcated notions of the sacred and the profane have been jettisoned for a messy and fluid assessment of right and wrong. The prototypical example of this sensibility is heard on Nas's "Thug Mansion," also off the *God's Son* release, where the late rapper Tupac Shakur—who encompassed the moral polarities of saint and sinner—is featured rapping about the people he "kicks it wit" in heaven.[6] For the hip-hop generation, it's no longer about holding the moral high ground to compel white acceptance or even God's grace. In the cosmological lexicon of hip-hop, even gangsters get to go to heaven.

These contradictory polarities of hip-hop are brought to bear on "Genesis" when Nas must restrain one of his partners from unknowingly trashing the featured track from the film. Nas counters the unwitting rejection of the track by conferring legitimacy to the track as "the shit," a classic example of the inverse play on language in black culture where bad means good. But on an even broader level it demonstrates a contradiction: those who consider themselves the most adamant adherents of "real" hip-hop can also be the least knowledgeable. When this is the case, only an appeal to history and memory are capable of bridging contradictions between status and taste. The significance of history and memory in hip-hop is signaled on "Genesis" when Nas implores his crew to stop burning phillies (a cigar-like marijuana joint). The connection is further amplified on "No Ideas Original" from the controversial *Lost Tapes* release where Nas states: "If niggas could look inside my mind . . . go to the center and enter with caution past the brain cell graveyard where weed is responsible for memory losses." The allegorical point of Nas's admonishment on "Genesis" to "stop burning phillies" and the loss of memory on "No Ideas Original" speak to the meaning and place of memory in hip-hop more than any type of antidrug diatribe ever could. Consequently, the link between smoking weed and memory loss is not an analytical fluke but a significant metaphor for the vulnerable position historical memory has had in hip-hop and by extension black culture.[7]

Nas throws the hip-hop generation into the cultural fray by showing that hip-hop nation is susceptible to cultural amnesia, a point made when *Wild Style* is unwittingly rejected by one of his peers on "Genesis." When Nas admonishes his hip-hop peers about the importance of memory, he echoes many members of the civil rights generation who have also critiqued the hip-hop generation for forgetting and therefore being unable to appreciate and uphold the legacy of struggle and sacrifice by the civil rights generation—dismantling the legal scaffolding of institutional racism. Although the hip-hop and civil rights generations are presumed to be at opposite ends of the political spectrum, this generational breach is not as dire or distinct as some have proclaimed.[8] The time and conditions of the contemporary moment are different, but the rules of generational engagement remain relatively unchanged. Each generation responds to the social conditions of its time in its own particular fashion. For the first wave of civil rights advocates, peaceful protest and freedom songs made sense, but for the subsequent black student generation, direct civil disobedience and black power chants were deemed more appropriate for confronting institutional racism. Many civil rights advocates fail to recall the rupture that occurred between the old civil rights bulwark and the new direct action student activists of the 1960s black freedom movement. The classic example of this generation divide is beautifully captured on the critically acclaimed *Eyes on the Prize* documentary series when Dr. Martin L. King and Stokely Carmichael (later known as Kwame Toure) walk side by side articulating divergent approaches to the specter of violent intimidation waiting for them as they marched toward Jackson, Mississippi. Here is an example of two generations of black folk caught in the same crucible of southern racial discrimination and violence yet advocating different remedies to the situation. Admittedly, Nas's use of *Wild Style* to comment on the place of memory in the hip-hop generation is more socially obscure than the ideological schism that became of the civil rights versus black power generational conflict. Nevertheless Nas's use of *Wild Style* suggests that the rejection of tradition by the hip-hop nation is not the result of an uncritical acceptance of nihilism but a lack of historical memory.

Certainly the lack of historical memory is endemic across the generational spectrum and if we are to be honest the real and symbolic rejection of traditional means of upward social mobility by black and brown youth is problematic. Case in point, the popular gangsterism of today's hip-hop undercuts the notion of acceptable means for black folk to achieve material success. Unfortunately, however, for too many black and brown youth the dream of success as outlaw rapper or just plain outlaw outweighs the more tangible and substantive opportunity to experience success in virtually any nine-to-five profession. Although today's thug/gangster is similar to Raymond's antihero status in *Wild Style* it has become a clichéd symbol of status quo defiance that arrests the imagination and stifles potential. In *Wild Style*, the source of identity for a growing segment of black and brown youth was as B-boy and B-girl, but for many, now it is as thug/nigga or gangster/bitch. Whether true or concocted, the hip-hop gangster identity is a million miles away from *Wild Style* in tone and style. This troublesome development, however, is not a detour or dead end but merely a bump along the road. It means some aspects of hip-hop as social critique are more difficult to relate to and even more difficult to find. But one thing remains certain. Hip-hop is political and popular, both vulgar and progressive. At its best it is the continuation of the African American oral tradition of preserving and transmitting suppressed, censored, and ignored narratives of racial resistance and struggle not shown in corporate media or discussed in the halls of political power.

A striking example of a black counter-narrative in action is the unauthorized remix of Kanye West's "Gold Digger" single and retitled "George Bush Don't Like Black People" by the hip-hop duo K-Otix. They were inspired by Kanye's comments on a live telethon where he proclaimed: "George Bush doesn't care about black people." The remix lyrically characterizes the dire circumstances that poor black folk in New Orleans faced in the aftermath of Hurricane Katrina and the failure of the Bush administration to effectively address the calamity. Despite such flashes of political subversiveness much of hip-hop has shifted from critical social allegory to senseless spectacle, rendering it virtually meaningless as social critique; too often it is an obscene cliché of black-on-black violence, material desire, and male sexual fantasy. These elements were also present in the formative stages of hip-hop but formed only a part of what fueled the music and shaped the message. Like a Romare Bearden collage, the best of the music expressed, with urgency, the disjointed and hard angles of the struggle to find dignity in making a way out of no way and the brutal consequences of violence, pain, and the unbridled embrace of nihilism when the effort proves unsuccessful. This is Nas's relevance and his gift to the hip-hop genre.

In the same way Marvin Gaye's sonic masterpiece "What's Going On" expresses a myriad of social concerns that demanded change or Stevie Wonder's poignant racial narrative "Living for the City" captures the public imagination with socially biting material, *Illmatic* is similarly situated in the genre of hip-hop. With *Illmatic* hip-hop witnessed the birth of an urban griot telling hard-boiled tales of ghetto alienation and triumph like a spoken-word version of a Chester Himes novel. Unfortunately, critics and dilettantes alike have misread the portraits of pain and passion found in Nasir Jones's ghetto pulp fiction as tawdry tales meant to fulfill the cheap thrills that all pulp fiction promises. Rather, the urban motif Nas verbally paints throughout *Illmatic* signals how the world of *Wild Style* has gotten bleaker, darker, and more intense. Competition between crews was no longer for the bragging rights, cheap champagne, or exciting and easy sex exemplified by Busy Bee's rap victory and celebratory party in *Wild Style*. In the age of *Wild Style* black and brown youth were concerned with audaciously claiming public space, not with freedom songs, picket signs, and closed fists aimed toward the sky but with boom boxes, cardboard dance floors, and colossal graffiti murals scrawled across public facades. This first wave of the hip-hop generation re-created community in underground clubs, decorated its living space with graffiti art, and celebrated the body with aggressive street corner style and stances à la Black Panther Party machismo. The culmination of this is articulated in Joseph Simmons's classic line, "I cold chill at a party in a B-boy stance."

Admittedly, many listeners will view "Genesis" as a conversational prologue to the main event. But some will decode the cryptic sampling of *Wild Style* and understand it as a challenge and admonishment to the staunchest adherents and practitioners of hip-hop to bear witness not only to the beginning but in many ways the end of hip-hop's age of innocence. "The Genesis" demonstrates that Nas is a purist and wants to remind the hip-hop collective that they are too if they would only remember and recognize it. This is a theme that Nas returns to in subsequent releases that give praise to various hip-hop luminaries. What Nas did with "Genesis" on *Illmatic* is amplified on *Street's Disciple* with the track "U.B.R." (Unauthorized Biography of Rakim). Nas chronicles the life and times of Rakim, a lyricist approaching the status of a living hip-hop deity for his verbal prowess and who is known as the "god of the microphone." This is a fitting tribute from Nas, given he makes a point to define himself as God's son.

Although Nas's body of work brilliantly illuminates the vulnerability beneath the bluster of too many young black men trapped in the shadow world of underclass poverty trying to make a dollar out of fifteen cents, Nas faces fierce criticism and even ridicule for offering up a premature autopsy of hip-hop nation with the declaration that hip-hop is dead. Maybe Nas is wrong. Maybe hip-hop is not dead. But for me hip-hop is at the least a zombie, a walking corpse like the ones in George A. Romero's *Night of the Living Dead* (1968), and in this sense I share Nas's lament over the seemingly lifeless state of hip-hop today. The brooding street poetry, poignant portraits of life and loss along with "live by the sword die by the sword" inner-city street justice laid over beats and breaks found in Nas's work have too often been replaced with racial clichés like Hollywood's take on ghetto strife presented in the

MTV-backed film *Hustle and Flow* (2005). Then there is the pornographic pop art of hip-hop music videos littered across much of today's hip-hop landscape in the early rounds of the new millennium. What started out as a sophomoric appreciation of the African American and third world female form has mutated from provocative eye candy to raw objectification, with a black woman's femininity reduced to the circumference and bounce quotient of her behind. Scores of hip-hop music videos now pay dubious homage to the memory of Sarah Bartmann (the Hottentot Venus).

Still, hip-hop has experienced tremendous growth despite a series of debatable achievements. At the moment hip-hop is the proverbial irresistible force that has yet to meet the immovable object. Like a Las Vegas gambler on a runaway winning streak, hip-hop continues to "double down" and wager its relevancy on the popular acceptance of new hedonistic spectacles and their ability to outsell the previous sonic craze. Given that hip-hop is merely one brand among many jockeying for position in a multibillion-dollar music industry, it is not surprising that instead of bringing into bold relief the spectacle of American excess, both economically and sexually, many hip-hop artists have uncritically embraced and promoted it. Yet this excursion through the economic underbelly and soft-core pornographic side of hip-hop demonstrates how hip-hop is alive (although maybe not well) and animated enough to take economic directions from American consumer capitalism. "Bigger is better" and "sex sells" continue to be the market mantras of American capitalism, and hip-hop as industry and product has come to the same conclusion. As a result, like the late Liberace, with his glittering candelabras and flamboyant suits, much of hip-hop has become simultaneously sensationalistic and mediocre, controversial yet predictable, over-the-top and underachieving.

Against this backdrop, Nas draws on his stature as one of the top lyricists in the hip-hop pantheon to exhort the hip-hop nation to become better.[9] Nas's struggle over what images and ideas represent blackness threatens to consume his art, but this struggle is neither new nor unique. Hip-hop has now matured to such an extent that evaluating where the line between pandering to the public for pop hits and genuine social expressions begins and ends becomes increasingly difficult.[10] Is true hip-hop about staying underground or selling millions of units? The chopping block of American popular culture is as strident as it is fickle when it comes to categorizing black genius, and Nas continues to let experience be his teacher as he fights for his own place of recognition and respect in the hip-hop pantheon. There was the public war of words against Jay-Z, the edict that hip-hop is dead, and now the controversial title of his next release with the n-word as the prominent catchphrase. In the wake of hip-hop's meteoric commercial rise, I view these events as examples of an aesthetic war between emergent notions of hip-hop street credibility and tradition against hip-hop modernism as command of mainstream popular culture. This tension permeates Nas's body of work as well as the hip-hop cultural landscape and, in my judgment, will continue to fuel the internal struggle that Nas seems compelled to share with the public as he attempts to reconcile his old-school B-boy sensibilities with new-school counterparts that demand homage to market forces. I only hope that the most public expression of this internal struggle, the Nas and Jay-Z beef, is remembered or replicated as the aesthetic war that it was and not as a hip-hop preamble for a black-on-black turf war over reputation and revenge. The lesson to learn from their rivalry is that such skirmishes are to be expected when true artistry is at stake. Socially relevant black art always involves a clash of attitude and outlook over the feelings, conditions, hopes, and aspirations of the group it comes to represent, not just the artist it is associated with.

Because of the seminal nature of *Illmatic*, his hip-hop opus, Nas will forever face the daunting task of repeating the genius of it.[11] An inconsequential debate persists as to whether or not subsequent releases have sacrificed lyrics that reach the bourgeois and rhymes that rock the boulevard for more listener-friendly dance hooks that merely move the crowd and images designed to titillate the masses. For me, each subsequent release was never about duplicating *Illmatic* but extending the themes presented in *Illmatic*—an unapologetic internal dialogue on racial politics and pride, sex and salvation, inner-city violence and moral relativism—to a broader audience. All of Nas's releases, whether they fell short of, matched, or surpassed the creative synergy of *Illmatic*, compel independent analysis. The only caveat is that the admiration, criticism, and overall mystique surrounding Nas stems from his first release. Nas, however, is still up to the challenge of matching if not surpassing the benchmark he set and struggling against being consumed by his own precocious genius. He has done this by offering a series of controversial statements and images in his desire to not only remain relevant but make us listen to the clarion call of history. For example, on *Street's Disciple* the track "These Are Our Heroes," Nas castigates a range of black public figures for their pseudo-blackness and servile political capitulation; on "Where Are They Now" along with "Carry On Tradition," both off of *Hip-hop Is Dead*, he challenges hip-hop nation to remember the past by invoking a litany of old-school rappers and waxing nostalgic about what was. By naming names, Nas pulls the hip-hop audience back to the center of the ongoing debate over black role models, black authenticity, and social memory and dares the listening audience to be neutral. As if this were not inflammatory enough, on the cover of *Street's Disciple* he has himself holding the center seat of a hip-hop rendering of the *Last Supper*. Nas: the self-proclaimed hip-hop savior ready to resurrect the dead? Agree or disagree with the message and by implication the prophecy. In the final analysis, whether you decide to take heed or ignore, you best listen.

A REBEL TO AMERICA
"N.Y. STATE OF MIND"
AFTER THE TOWERS FELL*

SOHAIL DAULATZAI

MICHAEL CORLEONE (in Cuba, 1958): I saw an interesting thing happen today. A rebel was being arrested by the military police. And rather than being taken alive, he exploded a grenade he had hidden in his jacket. He killed himself and he took a captain of the command with him.
GANGSTERS: Those rebels, you know, they're lunatics.
MICHAEL CORLEONE: Maybe so. But it occurred to me. The soldiers are paid to fight. The rebels aren't.
HYMAN ROTH: What does that tell you?
MICHAEL CORLEONE: They can win.
Godfather II, 1974

It's really no surprise that DJ Premier—hip-hop's greatest sonic architect—who literally defined a sound, an era, and a movement, was central to *Illmatic's* making. With his affinity for the boom bap and his deep crates, Premier's golden touch was no doubt showcased on Nas's brilliant debut album.

* For Mahmoud Darwish, and all the others who are blamed and held like hostages.

On "N.Y. State of Mind," one of the samples Premier uses is "Flight Time"—the opening track to Donald Byrd's 1972 album, *Black Byrd* (sorry, Preemo!!). It's an appropriate sample, if for no other reason than "N.Y. State of Mind" has such a bananas beat—vintage Preemo laying down an ill tapestry of sound. But it's also nice conceptually because the opening to Byrd's "Flight Time" begins with the sounds of an airplane taking off, and though we don't hear this part of the record that was sampled, it's absence on *Illmatic's* second track provides a kind of haunting beginning to "N.Y. State of Mind." Because without that sound of the plane taking off, Premier's use of "Flight Time" almost implies an inability to flee, to escape the New York that Nas is about to meditate on, grounding the young Nasir—and serving to create a heightened sense of claustrophobia just as the brooding bass line (sampled from Joe Chambers's "Mind Rain") builds and the eerie piano stab signals Nas's impending soliloquy of chaos "straight out the fuckin' dungeons of rap." Throughout the song, Nas's dystopic vision continues to hint at this claustrophobia in his descriptions of the labyrinth that is the Queensbridge projects, whether it's his overt references to being "held like hostages" or later with "each block is like a maze, full of Black rats trapped." In the bleak sci-fi world Nas creates of his beloved Queenbridge, the sufferation continues, but it's also emblematic of so much more.

Seven years after the release of *Illmatic*, on 9/11, as those planes crashed and the towers fell, Nas's hook—"I think of crime when I'm in a New York state of mind"—proved to be prophecy, echoing as if in a dub chamber, as empire state building was unleashed again with terrifying fury. Crime was definitely in the ether, as the globe holders were in a New York state of mind. But then again, so were the rebels.

When it happened, my first thoughts were, please don't tell me it's us. But that's what they said. My sister was in Paki-

stan at the time, near our family at the Afghan-Pakistan border, and the first thing I thought was that she's got to get out
of there. The rest of my extended family? They had no choice,
trapped between borders drawn in their blood, but not by
them. And I knew that it was about to go down—again.

But then again, war is not new to them there. The cinematic imagery that Nas uses throughout *Illmatic* to describe
the violent and desperate streets of New York sounds like
home to me. For the past thirty years, not including the previous centuries that were marked by British occupation, foreign
invasion, murder and mayhem, the Cold War was won and lost
at that border, while the very essence of the "War on Terror"
rages there now. During this time, drugs were run, guns were
drawn, and gangs and cliques were everywhere, repping their
colors, from the Red Army to mujahideen fatigues and now on
to Yankee pinstripes. All as war continues to loom. And when
the Cold War ended there, the civil one popped off, only to be
topped by the "good war" of the post-9/11 era. In the midst
of it all, newer gangs and cliques formed, as Afghan kids recy-
cled the remnants of Cold War shrapnel like Bronx kids did
samples. Turning something into something more.

In fact, *Illmatic* was released right around the time the civil
war in Afghanistan began, and Iraq was still under the jackboot of an American henchman, as the violence of the sanc-
tions placed on Iraq began to take their toll. KRS-One had just
rapped about "Black Cop" in American ghettos. To me, his
brilliance was also a commentary on American proxy war in
the post-Vietnam era, where brown cops like Saddam and the
Saudi royals policed the ghettoes of the Third World for their
Yankee masters.[1] The capo regimes claiming countries as corners for their American dons, because as Nas says in "N.Y.
State of Mind," "crews without guns are goners."

Immediately after 9/11, in that moment of heightened
fear and impending doom, the media onslaught began, as the

two minutes hate got cut and mixed into a loop where collective history and selective memory got blurred. So much was lost, and also gained, in those desperate moments, as reality got remixed amid a Dali-esque landscape of pop art and spectacle. To generate a coherence or sense of community to the chaos that was ensuing, the American media broadcasted images from countries all over the world—in Europe, Israel, parts of Asia, Africa, and Latin America—where people held up signs that said "We Are All New York," a global empathy for the victims of the attacks and for America itself. With those signs, the world was also saying that not only are we all potential victims of "terrorism," but also that the whole world will rally around the flag of the United States to bring those responsible to "justice."

But when the American media flashed these images, their meaning and implications were slippery, because with this came the implicit suggestion that not only does New York represent America, but also that New York represents the world. This idea about a kind of American universalism, that America stands in for or represents the world, did not start after 9/11, though. We can go back more recently to that mid-1980s liberal pop music orgy masked as benefit known as "We Are the World." But it goes back even farther than that—to the establishment of this republic on native soil, an idea that is central to the very identity of the United States and its melting pot dream. As the logic goes, because people from nations all over the globe come here to start anew, the United States represents the diversity of the world and is in fact a microcosm of it. With this diversity then, the United States is a global citizen, containing the world, so that the idea of "America" becomes a universal one.

The implications of this have been profound because America has viewed this as a kind of mandate to justify American expansion and supremacy in world affairs. But it also springs from something more deeply rooted within the national psyche, because from its very beginning, America has seen itself as an expansionist power, with Manifest Destiny its mantra and violence its redeemer. What stood between the fulfillment of the divinely ordained belief of Manifest Destiny and the violence necessary to make it happen was the frontier—a powerful trope in American history that divided white "civilization" from native "savagery." Out of this idea of the frontier sprang the very genesis of the idea of America—that through the establishment of "civilization," a distinctly American identity would emerge that was about strength, rugged individuality, and a so-called democratic spirit.

But when the Pacific Ocean was reached and the genocide of Native peoples was almost complete, the "closing of the frontier" at the dawn of the twentieth century created a crisis about how America would define itself. What happened then was that the frontier thesis was exported abroad so that American expansion into Cuba, the Philippines, Puerto Rico, and Guam—just to name a few—would continue the project of Manifest Destiny as "savages" were "civilized" through conquest and control, continuing the formation of this distinctly American identity. So it's important to view American supremacy throughout the world—then and now—as intimately connected to this history, that America's sense of itself as a microcosm of the world, as universal, is one way of justifying and romanticizing a deeper impulse of imperialism.

As "America's city," New York has in many ways been the beneficiary (if not the engine) of American imperial expansion, holding a unique place within the American imagination. Like Gil Scott-Heron's poignant song letter to the Big Apple entitled "New York City" where he laments, "I don't know why I love you, could be you remind me of myself," America has had a similarly conflicted yet sympathetic relationship with the city, where New York is seen as both the blessing and the curse, the American Eden and the forbidden fruit. In America, New York is the shining city on the hill and the apocalyptic inferno. It's loved as the epitome of the cosmopolitan body politic but loathed for us dark hordes that flow through its veins. It's hailed as the paragon of elite high culture and feared for the graffiti-tagged walls that write back in wild styles. New York is the Gilded Age and the iron cage, the World Trade Center and the planes.

Just as in Scott-Heron's song where the narrator and the city are connected not despite but because they share contradictions and corruptions, frailty and beauty, tragedy and triumph, America and New York City share a similar affinity and fate. Whether it's culturally, through the rhetoric of diversity and pluralism, with Ellis Island and Lady Liberty as seductress, or economically, as the center of high finance with the market bulls on Wall Street, or politically, with 9/11, where New York stands as Ground Zero and the genesis and symbol for the "new" America in the "War on Terror," New York is clearly "America's city," embodying so much of what the country is, wants to be, and even fears. And because of American global power, America's city becomes the "city of the world," a moniker New York has proudly repped.

Less a celebration of it though, Nas's "N.Y. State of Mind" sounds more like a eulogy for the Big Apple, with 9/11 being the headstone that reads, "We are all New York." But let's not get it twisted, because when those towers fell and the world collectively read the epitaph, it missed the fact that New York has always been the world, and the world New York—that urban quagmire of fiber-optic violence that Nas poetically reveals in "N.Y. State of Mind." No doubt New York has been the city of the world, and after 9/11 it still is, but only now more ominously and with more foreboding. Because as America continues to make the world in its own image, with its footprint expanding and entrenching itself globally, its imprint is everywhere: entertainment as war, torture as porn, Bin Laden's mix-tapes hitting the streets worldwide. All over in this fantasia, throughout the shantytowns and outposts of empire, skull and bones fill mass graves as the killing fields have become theme parks, a brave new world built as a cross between Disneyland and the West Bank. In fact, in the last days lament that is "N.Y. State of Mind," Nas suggests that New York might just be that—a state of mind—something that's not geographically bound, that's borderless, amorphous, asymmetrical, ephemeral, dangerous even, if in the wrong heads. In essence, the song is a dystopic allegory for American global power. Because it's that New York state of mind that Nas refers to that is also an American state of mind—it's what's made America become the world, and the world become America. It's a state of mind that is both domination and resistance, the prison house and the inmate rebellion. It's the seat of imperial power and the guerrilla war, the shock and awe and the Falluja response. It's the white noise and the black remix, the huckster's dollar and the hustler's fifteen cents. Either way, that dynamic, that tension, makes that New York state of mind that Nas names a gangster's paradise, a rebel's hell.

Every Ghetto, Every City

Using the Queensbridge housing projects as a microcosm, Nas's "N.Y. State of Mind" is a bird's-eye view, a series of close-ups and cutaways that not only allows us to imagine the land-mine-littered landscape of the globe under American power—but also to see the connections between the forces that have devastated urban centers in the United States and those that are destroying lives throughout the Third World. A vicious geography of violence that connects Queens to Kabul, Abner Louima to Abu Ghraib, and Pelican Bay to Guantanamo Bay. This cartography of American power that links the tenements and townships of urban poverty in the United States with the empire's slums abroad is a violent mix and political logic where urban communities (read: black and brown) in the United States and the Third World as a whole are viewed as a threat to both domestic and global stability, whether it be the fear of "crime" here or "terrorism" from there, "gang wars" here or "civil wars" there. In both instances, urban communities here and the Third World as a whole are seen as being on the margins of "civilization" but at the center of many of the debates about the dangers and threats they pose to America, "democracy," "peace," "freedom," and so on.

Hip-hop itself emerged from these geographies of violence, where the Third World meets the First, that mash-up of Jamrock and Planet Rock, and Nas's "N.Y. State of Mind" vividly captures what has taken shape since. Because in bridging the gap and embodying the street swagger of Kool G Rap, the metaphysics of Rakim, and the revolutionary lumpen philosophies of Ice Cube, Nas and "N.Y. State of Mind" in many ways unified the disparate threads of urban rebellion that were conflagrating from hip-hop's street corner ciphers. That state of mind, as much as it was New York, also spoke to the blues wails echoing in South Central L.A., Southside Chicago, and Houston's Fifth Ward, not to mention the casbah of Algiers, the *favelas* of São Paulo, and the prison house of Gaza. Because to see "N.Y. State of Mind" as solely a Gotham City saga is to limit its power, meaning, and impact. Let's be real, though; it definitely reclaimed hip-hop's mantle for New York and staked a defiant claim after the West Coast redefined the genre with its gangsta poetics and choruses of crack tales. But "N.Y. State of Mind" is also bigger than that because Nas didn't just describe a world, he laid out a worldview, so that "N.Y. State of Mind" is not just hip-hop's official anthem—no diss to Flash's "The Message," Public Enemy's "Fight the Power," or Wu

Tang Clan's "C.R.E.A.M." It's also that global clarion call to prayer for hip-hop's believers worldwide because it's a chilling track that harrowingly describes and imagines with such surreal imagery, with so much noir discontent and even more fuck-you ambition, the fragile and tenuous lives of ghetto dwellers, shantytown residents, and war-torn refugee camp denizens of a new world order fraught with defiance and dread.

That dread, so ambiently woven through "N.Y. State of Mind," makes the song a kind of message in the bottle sent down the ether for all those who heed its warnings, brilliantly revealing and anticipating how important geography and place would become in a deeply interconnected global economy. In fact, with *Illmatic*, Nas married sound with geography, making *Illmatic* in essence a sonic map. On the vinyl pressing of the album, *Illmatic* replaces the traditional Side A and Side B division with "40th Side North" and "41st Side South," respectively—the very streets that form the geographic boundaries that divide the Queensbridge housing projects, the largest public housing development in the United States. Unlike Big Daddy Kane's classic 1989 album *It's A Big Daddy Thing* that was divided by "Homiside" and "Suiside" or Ice Cube's 1991 magnum opus *Death Certificate* that was divided by "The Death Side" and "The Life Side," Nas's use of geography as the primary framing device for *Illmatic* suggests that like himself and so many others, poverty, segregation, and project living are deeply imprinted upon the experiences of black and brown communities, as Nas said in an interview in 2001: "When I made *Illmatic* I was a little kid in Queensbridge trapped in the ghetto. My soul was trapped in the Queensbridge projects."[2] For sure *Illmatic* is a poignant ode about *a* place—Queensbridge—but it's also a meditation on *the* projects and the forces of poverty, neglect, and racial injustice that mark not only project life throughout the United States but the shanties and slums the world over. Even though Nas literally and thematically frames *Illmatic* around the Queensbridge housing project, that shouldn't narrow our point of view and focus us only on Queensbridge, or only on projects in the United States for that matter. Instead it should broaden our perspective and give us a powerful glimpse into the ways that *Illmatic* suggests to us that we understand how the politics of place and the violence of geography help us to make sense of what has taken shape in our midst, as capital flows freely across borders, and the militaries and the police target specific places and the people who live there in violent and devastating ways.

In fact, that is how hip-hop's "official" history has been told, that it's a product of the postindustrial condition: the movement of industry and capital away from urban centers across America's borders, a process that devastated urban communities in the United States, that, when combined with white flight, political scapegoating, and repression created these grimy conditions and pockets of poverty that birthed this thing called hip-hop. All that is true. But this "official" history on hip-hop usually ends there. *Where* does the capital go? Why *there*? And what impact does it have on those places?

It's important to understand how these geographies of violence are connected and related in the global economy because for far too long many have believed that what happens here, be it in Detroit, New York, or L.A., has little or no bearing on what occurs in other cities like Kingston, Lagos, Delhi, or even Baghdad. Instead it's important to know that American society—its consumption, its economic structure, its political maneuvering, its very being—is dependent on the exploitation of the countries and the peoples of the Third World, and that poverty in U.S. urban centers is partly due to the movement of factories abroad, which did not enrich these countries or their people but exacerbated poverty both in the United States and in the Third World.

Hip-hop's history is deeply interwoven within the fabric of these massive global forces. Four years before *Illmatic* was released, America rode the pale horse triumphantly as George Bush I quoted the dollar bill and declared a new world order just after the Cold War ended. As the "end of history" was claimed and capitalism was seen as triumphant, the rhetoric of "globalization" in the mid-1990s was reaching a fever pitch at the same time that the "information superhighway" and the Internet were being touted as the utopian ideal that would bring the world closer together, shrinking the geographies of distance and making the world a "global village." In 1994, the same year *Illmatic* was released, the landmark North American Free Trade Agreement (NAFTA) between the United States, Canada, and Mexico was passed—a trade agreement that not only benefited American banks while devastating industries and workers, but that also sparked the Zapatista rebellion in Chiapas, Mexico, against Yankee imperialism. What is important to recognize is that these terms—"globalization," "free trade," "open markets," and so on—have all been code words for further extending and deepening America's global reach in a new era when the Cold War ended. As the world's only superpower, America in the 1990s wanted to accelerate the profound violence and despair in the darker nations of the world by continuing to thwart the national liberation struggles in Africa, Asia, the Middle East, and Latin America—as the vulture capitalists feasted on the national carcasses of the Third World seeking natural resources, cheaper wages, and nonunion labor, making bootstrap capitalism and jackboot militarism the law of the global economy.

What does that have to do with hip-hop? A great deal, because hip-hop itself emerged out of this global economy of fluid capital and massive repression. Its deep roots to the Third World are not just in its connections to the rebel music of dub reggae and sound system culture that emerged out of

Jamaica in the 1970s. We also have to be real about where hip-hop is at now and how it got to be here: I mean, all the gear, technology, and whatnot that hip-hop is connected to—the jeans, shirts, lids, kicks, throwbacks, cell phones, PDAs, mp3 players, the whole nine. *Where* are these products being made and *who's* making them? And what *price* are they paying? I mean, the diamond trade (and not just the "conflict" ones) is only one way that the hip-hop generation is connected to other spaces of conflict. What about SUVs and the flashy whips? Where is the oil, better yet, *how* is the oil getting here? And *whose* blood is being spilled for that oily silence? I'm just saying, not only did hip-hop emerge out of the global economy, but it—like all of American society—is now deeply entrenched in it too, making for some really ill and awkward alliances with global corporate power, blood money, war, and repression in the Third World.

These global realities and the new landscapes of power that have emerged as a result of the global economy are deeply intertwined with hip-hop's own history. So if "N.Y. State of Mind" serves as an allegory for understanding how American power connects the violent geographies of ghetto communities in the United States with the Third World, *Illmatic* brings us back to the segregation and poverty of the projects in the United States as a starting point. Centering the role of geography, *Illmatic*, and "N.Y. State of Mind" in particular, provides a lens for us to see how the United States responded to the urban communities here that were devastated due to the fluid movement of capital across borders—responses that created and enforced repressive laws that violently policed and controlled the devastated communities and regions left in its wake. Because in many ways, this is not only hip-hop's story, its genesis, if you will—but also the story of how America has continued to be America.

Criminal Minded

Blame Reagan for making me into a monster/Blame Oliver North
and Iran Contra/I ran contraband that they sponsored/
Before this rhyming stuff we was in concert.
—JAY-Z, "BLUE MAGIC"

Coming out at the tail end of hip-hop's Golden Age, in the same year as Gang Starr's *Hard To Earn*, O.C.'s brilliant but slept on *Word . . . Life*, Common's *Resurrection*, Biggie's *Ready to Die*, and many other great records, *Illmatic*'s subtle and powerful brilliance rests in Nas's detailed descriptions, dense reportage, and visually stunning rhymes of the underbelly of the beast—his renegade first-person narratives and character-driven odes an epic scribble and scream in a time when powerful forces in America used poverty, policing, and prisons to deal with an urban America that they saw as the frontier for the new politics of fear in an era of global capital.

Maybe nothing comes closer to embodying *Illmatic*'s dystopic end-time vision, or its visceral eloquence, than HBO's brilliant series *The Wire*. Arguably the greatest epic in any medium, up there with *The Godfather* saga (no, not Part III) and the *Battle of Algiers*, *The Wire's* grim yet hopeful pessimism, like *Illmatic*, was layered and complex, refusing judgment yet hard hitting. On *Illmatic*, Nas was bold but subtle, angry but not alienating, as he rapped from the point of view of a kingpin like Stanfield and a corner boy like Bodie. He wove narratives as mythic as Omar, with his outsider ethos defining a code while defying so much else. And, like *The Wire*, Nas did it with a keen eye for the pathos of power. What *Illmatic* laid bare more poignantly than any other hip-hop album before it or since was not only the brutal chaos of urban America's apartheid, but also the increasingly seamless line between the project and the prison—a line that got blurrier over the last quarter century before the release of *Illmatic*, and even more so since then, a direct by-product of the radical rightward shift of the political center in America over the last forty years.

This shift can in many ways be directly traced to the political fear and social anxiety connected with the city and urban America, deeply held fears about racial others that both the Democratic and Republican parties were central in creating and benefiting from throughout the 1970s, 1980s, and 1990s. In fact, Nas's "N.Y. State of Mind" not only offers the opportunity to understand what the city has meant within the American imagination before and especially during the rise of hip-hop, but it also gives a better sense of how hip-hop emerged and how it used the city as its canvas, as its foil, and its muse. "N.Y. State of Mind" is not just about *a* city—New York; it's about life in the city in general, its possibilities but mostly its pitfalls, as Nas's sonic noir reveals the labyrinth that is life in urban America. That's what makes "N.Y. State of Mind" so powerful. But as much as it is an anthem for hip-hop's rebels and ghetto dwellers, "N.Y. State of Mind" is also a eulogy for the city itself, signaling the demise, decay, and death of a city—maybe even a country—that once was, despite its hollow claims to the contrary.

But that's not how it always was. During America's rise as an economic and global power in the nineteenth and twentieth centuries, the city was assumed to be the center of American political, economic, and social life. Cities were the engines of prosperity and progress, the citadel for art and commerce, the mecca for all that was modern, forward thinking, and sophisticated. But all of that changed by the mid- to late-1960s. Because as capital left the city and crossed borders in the second half of the twentieth century, the city came to embody and represent something very different. In order to displace the fears caused by global capital, America's decline was not seen as due to the larger contradictions in capitalism, but instead due to the moral decay and degeneracy that the city—and its inhabitants—supposedly represented, as racial anxieties and economic insecurities continued to form the twin towers of American political logic. Almost overnight, but definitely over time, as a result of repression, white flight, and eroding local tax bases due to corporate flight across borders, the city was demonized to embody fear, danger, and crime in the mainstream imagination—all of which were code words for a full frontal assault on the black and brown communities that lived there, as the prison population in the United States skyrocketed 500 percent between 1970 and 2000.[3]

How did it get to this point? Well, while Lyndon Johnson's Great Society programs in the mid-1960s claimed to address the condition of the nation's cities, it wasn't until the mid- to late-1960s that the city began to radically change and morph into what it represented during the birth and reign of hip-hop. In the late 1960s, under the banner of law and order, Tricky Dick Nixon and his goon squads, including the FBI and their local police proxies, used covert programs such as COINTELPRO as well as other "legitimate" means to destroy the political unrest that was taking place all across urban America. With hundreds of urban uprisings setting American cities ablaze that sent smoke signals of black power rising, Nixon used his "law and order" mantra to mobilize what he called the Silent Majority (his white constituencies) to generate the political will and national consensus he needed to destroy the Black Panthers, US, and other black (and brown) liberation and antiwar organizations. As black communities challenged policing, poverty, and American imperial desire around the world, Nixon repeatedly returned to the hook of "law and order" amid his gangsta raps about Vietnam, as he desperately tried to contain the domestic unrest that ultimately made America's colonial aggression in Vietnam untenable.

As the 1970s wore on, the rhetoric of crime continued to capture the national imagination. New York, and specifically the Bronx, came to symbolize urban decay—the ashes out of which rose the phoenix of hip-hop. All over America, the movement of factories abroad exacerbated the conditions set in motion by Nixon's politics of aggression, so that as tax bases and economic opportunities shrank, both federal and state governments began to shift their focus away from education and infrastructure toward the eradication of crime, as budgets for policing fattened and more punitive laws (such as the notorious 1973 Rockefeller drug laws) were passed in order to calm the national fears about crime in the city. This onslaught is much of the reason why the city, the area code, and even the block live and breathe within the hip-hop canon. Because as hip-hop licked shots back at the forces allied against it, it didn't put the city on the map. It just made the city the proscenium, the mythic stage on which its sound and fury would be unleashed. That it was a child of the Black Arts movement of the late 1960s and early 1970s is no surprise, because it was at this point that urban centers—coded as black—were firmly within the sight lines of a white America hell-bent on creating what Nas refers to in "N.Y. State of Mind" as that "maze full of black rats trapped."

While Nixon's right-wing agenda and call for law and order had a not-so-subtle racist bass line, it wasn't until Ronald Reagan was elected in 1980 that the white backlash that had been bubbling throughout the 1970s finally boiled over. I mean, let's not forget what Reagan was really about, despite the pomp and circumstance of his monarchical funeral. A searing and telling moment occurred on August 4, 1980, as Reagan chose to launch his presidential campaign in the small town of Philadelphia, Mississippi. As the symbolic first stop on his campaign for the White House, Reagan's choice was a harbinger of things to come, as this was the town where in

1964 civil rights activists Michael Schwerner, Andrew Goodman, and James Chaney were murdered by white supremacists in what became at that time a national and even international cause célèbre. In his speech there in 1980, Reagan openly declared, "I believe in states' rights," a not-so-subtle support of the southern segregationist mantra that dates back to slavery and had became a white rallying cry against the Civil Rights movement. This was essentially the flip side to Reagan's deeply coded attack on "big government" and distrust of D.C. that echoed throughout his campaign and tenure as president, as his appeal to not only conservative whites but also working-class whites (known as Reagan Democrats) tapped into a rich vein of white resentment against the perceived gains of the Civil Rights and Black Power movements.

What made Reagan so appealing was that he assuaged white folks' deepening fears of American decline in the shadows of Vietnam, the post-Watergate discontent, the economic stagflation of the 1970s, and the Iranian hostage crisis of 1979. What Nixon began under the banner of "law and order," Reagan repackaged as part of his "Morning in America" crusade. Mourning in America indeed, especially for urban centers and minorities, as Reagan's far right-wing politics and attacks on civil rights gains went big-time under the lights of the new Hollywood–Beltway axis, as his "War on Drugs" and "War on Crime" slogans played like blockbusters, as he used "welfare queens," "crack dealers," "gang wars," and "illegals" as supposed threats to domestic order and the very essence of America. Reagan manipulated these ideas brilliantly as a resurgent whiteness retook center stage with a vehemence, pitting hardworking Americans (read: white) against the "criminal" element in the cities, who were not only accused of draining the resources of hardworking taxpayers, but were also seen as a moral failure and a collective shackle on America's feet.

In Reagan's doublespeak, the inner cities kept America captive and prevented the nation from reaching its destiny, but Nas later on in "N.Y. State of Mind" defiantly claimed that it was black folk who were the ones "held like hostages," the ones who lived where the "nights were jet black," and the ones who had to face down the barrel of that gun that American power emanated from. That potent symbol of American democracy, while metaphorical, was also literal, as the militarization of urban centers through massive policing violently increased. Nas poetically captured this omnipresence of violence on "I Gave You Power" on his second album, *It Was Written*, a powerfully cinematic track where he raps from the perspective of a gun—a song that drips with the irony and tragedy of how black men are viewed as violent weapons and a menace to a society that saw urban America as both the blackdrop to, and the frontline of, the coming apocalypse. The theater of war that the projects were the stage for signified a great deal, but as gums kept flapping, the guns kept clapping, and Nas and his soldier-scribes in hip-hop detailed the war zones unfolding in their midst. As Nas says on "Represent," "the killer coppers even come through on helicopters," suggesting the battleground surveillance and captive power that was being unleashed on project denizens. On "N.Y. State of Mind" he tragically observes that "cops could just arrest me, blaming us," all of which made his "reminiscing about the last time the task force flipped" deeply tragic in its poignancy.

Even after Reagan left office, his legacy and deep Hollywood connections strengthened the complicity between the bright lights and the Beltway—as the sequels provided by Bush I and then Clinton about the hysteria of the inner cities tapped deeper into that rich vein of race in America. Both Bush I and Clinton continued to use "crime" to generate political capital as the media matrix continued to provide the agitprop needed. Bush I grabbed the mic from Reagan and spat the same rhymes, using Willie Horton to get elected and the Los Angeles uprisings of 1992 to get reelected. And though Bush failed, Clinton's "tough on crime" policies resulted in the largest increases in the prison population of any president in American history. If Clinton was a friend to black folks, imagine the enemies, as he passed the repressive 1994 Violent Crime Control and Law Enforcement Act, which among other things added $30 billion to build more prisons and 100,000 more police officers to the streets.[4] This was indicative of a larger pattern in which huge cutbacks in education and infrastructure were met with drastically increased funding for the formation of an urban police state and massive increases in prison building, as the organized confusion of Reaganism addressed the symptoms and not the causes of urban poverty under the government's extinction agenda.

Hip-hop responded to these downpressor men and their policing and prisons in profound and even prophetic ways. It was in this climate of criminalization that hip-hop essentially cut its teeth throughout the 1980s and 1990s, as it coupled its demand for recognition with a righteous indignation that bore witness to the devastations occurring in its midst. In this climate, it's no surprise that what would become the prison industrial complex was front and center within the hip-hop imagination. "One Love" on *Illmatic* poignantly deals head-on with the prison system, and Nas makes reference in "N.Y. State of Mind" to the fact that the "island is packed"—meaning Rikers Island, New York City's largest jail, a place that Kool G Rap memorialized in song ("Rikers Island") and where Public Enemy performed to promote their landmark album *It Takes a Nation of Millions to Hold Us Back.*

Clearly the rhetoric of crime (or the "War on Crime" or "law and order") was the consistent mantra that successive presidents since Nixon have used to not only displace the anxieties caused by massive economic shifts in the global economy, but also to mobilize political constituencies and militarize urban communities. Nas's claims then on "N.Y. State of Mind" of being the "smooth criminal," his embrace of Scarface and Al Capone, and the hook that he "thinks of crime when he's in a New York State of Mind" are more than what some have called "bad nigga" posturing or even a kind of self-destructive romanticism—as many claim about hip-hop in general. Instead, that embrace of crime lays bare how "crime" as a category is used to police and control. What does that mean? Well, it's thought that in order to fight crime, more laws must be passed in which more activities are considered "criminal," so that more potential "crime" is created. In essence, by creating the category of crime and expanding what can fall under that category, politicians are in fact creating more potential "criminals" and then spending vital resources to violently police and incarcerate whole communities. Much like the category of "terrorism" that is used today, it's a politicized term that, as more laws are passed, more activities are falling under the rubric of "terrorism," so that more "terrorists" are potentially created to be dealt with by all kinds of violent and torturous means. Consider the passage of H.R. 1955—the Violent Radicalization and Homegrown Terrorism Prevention Act of 2007—which was passed in the House by a near unanimous vote and is awaiting Senate approval. It defines "terrorism" and radicalization so broadly that a range of activities (protests, speeches, writing, etc.) can fall under those categories, creating more potential "terrorists." Whether it's the "war on crime" or the "war on terror," these terms become a way of stigmatizing, branding, punishing, and even killing those accused through "legal" means such as the death penalty and torture.

While the category of crime (or "terrorism") is used to stigmatize and punish some, it defines the rest as legitimate—so that there are "legitimate" forms of economic and political activity, and "illegal" ones. This is not only what Nas implies when he dreams of the "legal luxury life" but also what the great gangster films poetically revealed: that the law is inherently corrupt(ible), and that what is considered "legitimate" or "criminal" is an act of power, not justice. And so when Nas "thinks of crime" in "N.Y State of Mind," he not only brings into bold relief the contradictions in American society but reveals the utter lawlessness by which it is governed—the law a fiction made real by brute power. Nas gives texture and moral complexity to these figures who would easily be dismissed as evil—letting the listener or the American public know that, as Michael Corleone in *Godfather II* says to Senator Geary, "we're both part of the same hypocrisy."

Nas may be talking about the streets in and around Queensbridge in "N.Y. State of Mind," but that same code of the streets governs Wall Street and Washington, D.C. In a country where cotton money still generates inordinate wealth, where the financial markets are built on the exploitation of the world's poor so that blood money is the middle-class dream, the question of what is "legitimate" is almost absurd. Nas pulls the romantic and egalitarian rug out from the Ellis Island dreamscape and Lady Liberty as "the city never sleeps, full of villains and creeps," stripping naked the lie and ripping the veneer off of New York as that cosmopolitan dream, because for him to "think of crime" when he's in a New York state of mind suggests that New York itself is criminal—the city not just corruptible but corrupt. A powerful suggestion, but who can argue with him? Just ask Diallo, Louima, Sean Bell, and so many others.

Streets Is Watching

The explosion will not happen today. It is too soon . . . or it is too late.
—Frantz Fanon, *Black Skin, White Masks*

By the time *Illmatic* was released in 1994, hip-hop had already struggled for exposure in a world where film, television, and even black radio dismissed it. Chuck D's claim that hip-hop was the "Black CNN" only told part of the story because hip-hop was more than that—it was pirate radio and guerrilla cinema, talking book and subversive theory, political theater and radical public art. But after 1992, when Dr. Dre rolled up *The Chronic* and revealed how high hip-hop could get, the paranoia set in, or maybe it was an awareness that the mind fuck that is hip-hop had begun. From New York to L.A., and places in between, the rags-to-riches fantasies that marked early East Coast hip-hop gave way to a grams-to-Grammy ethos that continues to dominate hip-pop. As dark alliances formed and coca crops got imported to local blocks, the vivid tales and documentary realism of street life couched as sonic fantasy got put on wax, eerily coinciding with hip-hop becoming more profitable and palatable to suburban voyeurs. Stakes were high for ghetto youth and corporate thugs as coffins and coffers got filled, so that once again in America, black death equaled white wealth.

It's this kind of profane mathematics that made the cinematic tales of early hip-hop burn with such urgency. In Los Angeles, with his militaristic policing getting cover from Reagan's policies, police chief Daryl Gates was the perfect cross between Bull Connor and Dirty Harry, and one of the main overseers to the state of California, which has the biggest prison system in the industrialized world, holding more inmates than France, Britain, Germany, Japan, Singapore, and the Netherlands combined.[5] If the Twin Towers in New York stood as that city's symbol of power, L.A.'s equivalent is not the Hollywood sign but the world's largest prison known as the Twin Towers Correctional Facility. So it's no surprise that N.W.A.'s 1988 song "Fuck Tha Police" dropped amid the frontier justice of L.A.'s ganglands. The song radically redrew the borders between nihilism and rebellion, and it functioned as a political theater of the oppressed, a courtroom drama that put the L.A.P.D. on trial for *its* vigilantism. As the lyrical force behind N.W.A., Ice Cube continued to blur the lines between celluloid, wax, and prophecy during his solo career, so that when he lyrically laid to waste Chief Gates on *Death Certificate* in 1991, it was both collective redemption and Hollywood fantasy, Nat Turner and Sweetback coming back to collect some dues.

In New York, similar things had been brewing. In fact, liberal New York Democratic Governor Mario Cuomo (1982 to 1995) added more prison beds than all the previous governors in the state's history combined.[6] From its genesis, hip-hop responded to and even anticipated the social decay unfolding in front of its eyes with Grandmaster Flash's prophetically titled 1982 song "The Message." With its documentary reportage and its existential poignancy about "the edge," hip-hop tried to keep its head and protect its neck as later Rudolph Giuliani and his partner in policing, William Bratton, implemented their repressive "broken windows policy." With tracks like Kool G Rap's "Streets of New York" extending Flash's realist aesthetic and Public Enemy's anthem "Black Steel in the Hour of Chaos" giving brothers in prison ideas, hip-hop was broadcasting sound bites of hope and bulletins of rebellion. KRS-One's 1993 song "Sound of Da Police" was the fire to "Fuck Tha Police" brimstone, as hip-hop continued to scream against the silence that was being imposed.

Though *Illmatic*'s response to these conditions didn't lay out the political theory of KRS-One or Public Enemy, or the brash street knowledge of N.W.A. or Ice Cube, Nas clearly crafted his own unique vision. By 1994 though, it seemed that hip-hop had already been there and done that. But when Nas verbally samples N.W.A.'s *Straight Outta Compton* with his opening lines in "N.Y. State of Mind," coming "straight out the fuckin' dungeons of rap," Nas placed himself, and *Illmatic* for that matter, underground, much like Freeman in Ivan Dixon's classic 1973 rebel film, *The Spook Who Sat by the Door*. Though *Illmatic* was a highly anticipated release, far from under the radar, Nas's taking it back to the "dungeons of rap" was also a kind of exorcism or purging ("where fake niggas don't make it back") that was at the very least trying to claim a different aesthetic of resistance and rebellion that was all too aware of hip-hop's newfound mainstream potential due to the gangster tales and spectacle excess of L.A.'s mean streets. Because if N.W.A.'s "Fuck Tha Police" was hip-hop's declaration of war, then "N.Y. State of Mind" will stand as the battleground blueprint for the impending insurgency, as Nas complemented N.W.A.'s bravado by weaving intricate visuals that detailed the trap doors, rooftop snipers, street corner lookouts, and paramilitary zones of the urban matrix.

In many ways, "N.Y. State of Mind" named something that already existed long before *Illmatic*, and long before hip-hop even. Yeah, other MCs, from Tragedy to the Geto Boys to Ice-T and so many others, were all dealing with Mr. Charlie in one way or another. Nas distilled it to its gritty essence—drawing the battle line in the concrete and perfectly capturing that grimy urban dreamscape of late-twentieth-century America. With Illuminati looming, *Illmatic* was that mind's eye, and Nas was that clairvoyant who held the mic like a camera, as his jittery shots, rack zooms, and sweeping long shots were combined with the stark tones and warm hues of his dense lyricism and epic storytelling, so that the "compositions of pain" he inflicted, or felt, were the perfect response to the silent weapons for the quiet wars being fought all around him.

Nas's black dadaist imagery on "N.Y. State of Mind" doesn't simply describe a world, it lays out a worldview so that his portrait of a young man "who ran like a cheetah with thoughts of an assassin" also evokes the possibility for him that hip-hop, *Illmatic*, and his epic street poetry are a means of escape from the apartheid of project existence. Whether literally through economic opportunity, or momentarily through imagination and fantasy, Nas suggests (or is it hopes?) that hip-hop and its sights and sounds will traverse and transcend the violent boundaries imposed on it and the people whom hip-hop represents. For despite the end-times energy that is so much of *Illmatic*'s fury, Nas lyrically sends smoke signals to those in other shanties and townships that, even though "it's time to start the revolution," hip-hop is also a way of staking a defiant claim to believe that, just maybe, as he says on *Illmatic* in reference to *Scarface*, the world is yours—despite the sufferation that you endure in the shitstem.

This possibility of transcending one's existence can mean a lot of things, and hip-hop forged its own theosophic vision with its psalms and surahs, where cats sparked Buddha to get enlightenment, Moses sought freedom carrying the ten crack commandments, where Black Jesuz would return with creased Dickies and locs, and Muslim gods stood in the cipher believing I Self Lord And Master. Hip-hop's own visions were a means toward navigating more traditional theological ideas about transcendence. For example, some claim that divinity exists beyond this world and so to transcend it—to leave this world or escape from it—means to reach God. Immanence, on the other hand, suggests that God exists *in* this world, not beyond it, so that all we have to do is to see the multiple ways in which divinity manifests herself. But in the sci-fi netherworld of "N.Y. State of Mind" at least, Nas doesn't suggest that divinity lives beyond this world or within it, only that in his mind's eye of the storm she is nowhere to be found. Before *Illmatic*, we had already heard of the cat who "went to hell for snuffin' Jesus." But with *Illmatic* he came back, only to return there to drink "Moet's with Medusa." The poet-warrior known as God's Son and the contemplative Nas of "Heaven" didn't come until later. If the child in the brilliant third verse of Flash's "The Message" was "born with no state of mind," the profound existential dilemma facing the colonized that Fanon grappled with about nature or nurture, essence or existence, do we make the world or does it make us, is almost a moot point. When "life is parallel to hell" and one "must maintain," Nas reveals in "N.Y. State of Mind" how that "edge" Flash warned about may have been reached and the Rubicon already crossed, as the brazen prodigy on *Illmatic* was too immersed in the earthly devastations of Queensbridge, in the fact of his blackness and all the horror that entails in Amerika.

But with songs on *Illmatic* like "The World Is Yours," Nas is also the secular prophet whose street scriptures decree that redemptive suffering is a trap. And maybe that's why Nas, like black dreamers and realists before him, have sought escape and resistance as a means of redemption—escape from the slave plantation, from the South, from segregation and the ghetto, from prison, and even escape from this thing called America. This escape from racial violence had many landings—Indian territory (black Seminoles), Mexico (Jack Johnson et al.), Central America (Edward Wilmot Blyden), Cuba (Robert Williams, Eldridge Cleaver, Assata Shakur), Mecca (Malcolm X), Europe (Dexter Gordon, Langston Hughes, Paul Robeson), outer space (Outkast, Parliament Funkadelic, Sun Ra), and of course Africa (W.E.B. Du Bois, Geronimo ji-Jaga Pratt, and many more). All of these places came to embody escape and respite of some kind, if not the possibility of freedom itself. And hiphop also imagined that possibility; check Jeru The Damaja's "Jungle Music," Rakim Allah's "The Ghetto," and Reflection Eternal's "Memories Live"/"Africa Dream," just to name a few.

For the intelligent hoodlum Nasir bin Olu Dara, escape later on meant leaving the Bridge and New York, wishing he could either "flap wings and fly away to where Black kings in Ghana stay" ("You're Da Man"), or escaping this world altogether—"this world's my home but world I would leave you" ("Heaven"). In a world overwhelmed with a New York state of mind, that kind of escape may be the only option available. But Nas would never let us off the hook that easily. That's why Nas, the seeming nihilist, the eternal skeptic, who exists in a world too tortured and too traumatic, closes "Heaven" with a kind of Five Percenter Muslim-inspired teaching, that for the true and living, heaven, or salvation, is in one's own heart and one's own existence, not in the corrupt world that we have to endure.

So maybe that's why Nas is so concerned with saving hip-hop—or should I say resurrecting it? Because for him, it serves as a kind of secular salvation. Whether he is the messiah or simply wants to call attention to the Rapture that will signal hip-hop's rise, why does it matter? I mean, maybe it should die. Isn't that what was said about jazz—that it was dead? And wasn't it hip-hop—both in sampling and in spirit—that jazz, funk, and the blues for that matter were reincarnated as? Maybe this is just some sort of natural cycle of black creative genius—what Amiri Baraka calls the "changing same." Maybe, maybe not. But if hip-hop, according to KRS-One on *Edutainment*, is the "last voice of Black people," then maybe what troubles Nas isn't so much that hip-hop is dead, but that in this modern-day Babylon, it's the fire and urgency that hip-hop represented that is no more. Because now hip-hop is the blessing and the curse, the meal ticket and the hand that feeds. Lying somewhere between a dream and a disappointment, it's the form and not the function, the dollar that don't make sense. Hip-hop used to be the migrant; now it's the checkpoint. It went from being rebellious runaways to House.Negroes.In.Charge. Hip-Hop went from the Molotov to the cocktail, from the sound and fury to signifyin' nothing. And if that's the case, then God save all our souls.

But that's what makes Nas's attempt at salvation so vital in these last days, because hip-hop licked shots at the ideas and images of black people being beamed from media conglomerates and spit it back to them, bringing the theater of war to wax by writing themselves into existence and imagining their own liberation, where black people went from wretched of the earth to cream of the planet. Spanning the continuum of black creative genius, encompassing rage, hope, deliverance, and what Aime Cesaire calls "poetic knowledge," hip-hop was insurgent cultural war, and if it's still that, then peep the strategies and tactics of every kind of guerrilla war in history and you'll see that they're won or lost by the range of their attacks, the diversity of their methods, and the conviction of their beliefs. Let's just hope it ain't too late . . .

TIME IS ILLMATIC

A SONG FOR MY FATHER, A LETTER TO MY SON*

3

GUTHRIE P. RAMSEY JR.

When I first heard "Life's a Bitch," I froze. I connected it to my father's death in 1994, the year the song came out. Dad died at the age of sixty-nine, a ripe old age for black men of his generation. But it was not simply the themes of fatalism and nihilism among black males that provoked the connection. After Dad's funeral, we ate, danced, and played cards at a relative's house. The song that jumped off the party happened to be the Gap Band's "Yearning for Your Love," the sample on which "Life's a Bitch" is based, and a song that lyrically could not be further in tone and tenor from "Life's a Bitch." In the private community theaters of black culture and in the more public forum of hip-hop sampling, the recording was still doing important cultural work some thirteen years after its release. Our communal gathering spontaneously elected in this theater of mourning to transform the recording into a blues-stomping, cathartic affirmation of life

---

* Dedicated to G. P. Ramsey Sr. (1924–1994) and R. G. Ramsey (b. 1984).

before the unflinching face of death's reality—themes that are central to "Life's a Bitch." The Gap Band track will always "mean" this to me. And whenever I hear it on the radio or in a club, it transports me back to that bittersweet moment in time.

Nas's recording "Life's a Bitch" is a song of its time, rich in its multiple layers of historical, social, and cultural dialogues. But the song also resonates profoundly with the past; it anchors itself in the moment while reminding us that powerful musical statements often select past materials and knowledge for use in the present and hope for the future. My own experience of this piece, as we will see, is all about the fruitful dialogic meanings that are inspired by digital sampling and how it could be a model and inspiration for intergenerational relationships among fathers and sons, mothers and daughters, and ancestors and progeny more generally speaking.

The time was 1994, the year the recording appeared, a watershed moment in hip-hop cultural production; many say it was the genre's shining hour. Although hip-hop was in its pre-bling stage, consumerism, commercialism, and critiques of black access to capital—especially as they concerned contemporary black masculinity—emerged as thematic tropes in the music. Like the bebop moment in the mid-1940s, hip-hop's mid-1990s aesthetic seemed poised to succeed at the unlikely mix of musical experimentation *and* commercial viability. Today it is remembered nostalgically as "the year hip-hop was reborn," the days when "hip-hop was an art form," or "hip-hop's last great year." Indeed, Nas's *Illmatic* stands as an artistic emblem of that moment: thematically complex, immaculately, eclectically, even delicately produced, and rich in layered textures and colors: a hip-hop version of Miles Davis's signature work, *Kind of Blue* (1959), if there ever was one.

The poet Gwendolyn Brooks once proclaimed during the black arts movement of the 1960s and 1970s that it was no longer a "rhyme time." But rhyming returned with a vengeance in hip-hop culture, and performed in semi- to nonmelodic declamation, otherwise known as rapping, it became a key sign of authenticity for two generations of listeners to date. Around 1994, hip-hop was marked by a growing and self-conscious eclecticism that was regionally oriented across the black, urban archipelago. The group Outkast hailed from the South, Notorious B.I.G. from the East, Snoop Dogg from the West, and Da Brat from Chicago (smack dab in the middle of the shit, she once proclaimed), forming a dynamic and creative landscape.

In 1994 we also saw the appearance of another emblem of hip-hop culture: the publication of Tricia Rose's landmark study, *Black Noise: Rap Music and Culture in Contemporary America*, the first book of its kind, one that thrust hip-hop into the academic world of postmodern ideas. Rose's work helped to initiate another space for experimentation and commercial efficacy in hip-hop. Following her lead, hip-hop scholarship and its cousin "journ-academic-criticism," a rich blend of academic cultural theory and journalism, have blossomed. Hip-hop bibliography, blog-ography, and other forms of mass-mediated commentary have exploded across libraries, bookstores, and the internet.

More than a decade later, "black noise" is a veritable cottage industry, spawning a growing field of pundits, academic specialties, and book deals in and through which blackness is explained to a consuming public fascinated with it. This critical community praises Nas's work as a towering artistic statement. And its status as artistic invention has not prevented it from spilling over into lived experience, into other domains of culture. A telling turn in hip-hop exegesis, for example, occurred at the nexus between hip-hop musical practice and the realm of its study.

This junction has been a rich if sometimes controversial one. When scholar Mark Anthony Neal coined the term "Thug-NiggaIntellectual" to describe the social contradictions some black male intellectuals experience, he apparently borrowed from the linguistic flair and penetrating poetics of MCs such as Nas. And scholar-preacher Michael Eric Dyson's penchant for breaking into sing-song rap lyrics to illustrate points during formal lectures and sermons is now legendary. For his part in this dialogic, Nas has been criticized for reading way too many books for an MC. This anti-intellectualism can cut both ways, as scholars such as Cornel West, Kyra Gaunt, and Cheryl Keyes have been criticized for engaging hip-hop culture too seriously in the first place—either as participants or as "objective observers." Many of the nation's most respected hip-hop critics, I should mention, hold PhDs or are otherwise impressively pedigreed or very gainfully employed. Thus the social energies permeating hip-hop's critical establishment and hip-hop's musical community have mixed, exchanged, and blended. Each of these aspects of the hip-hop enterprise set high benchmarks for both the music and its study. I am proposing here that these kinds of dialogues—social, musical, emotional, and scholarly—can illuminate the impact of the song "Life's a Bitch."

The song's birth year was steeped in music industry drama. Something was definitely in the air: Nas's debut was a part of something larger. Debates about artistic authenticity and commercialism in popular music, hip-hop culture, and black identity raged in 1994—on the recordings, in the trade press, and on the street. In that year, for example, jazz star Branford Marsalis released a recording under the name Buckshot LeFonque. Originally a pseudonym for another genre-busting jazz musician, Julian "Cannonball" Adderley, the project was an eclectic mix of hip-hop, jazz, rock, R&B, and all manner of pop. Marsalis and his collaborator, the producer DJ Premier, defied the generic marketing categories that typically order taste and the cash register in the music industry. As one of America's most familiar faces in entertainment because of his previous stint as the musical director of the *Tonight Show* band, Marsalis thumbed his nose at the industry by recording music that experimented and toyed with generic expectations. Definitely an "in your face" move, the project was highly successful artistically but challenged its own status as a commodity in the conservative, nonprogressive marketplace. Thus it did not gain commercial support. Why was a "jazz musician" doing this, the market seemed to ask. Also in 1994 Prince waged his famous battle with Warner Bros. over the financial and artistic control of his work. It disintegrated into a full-scale war of words and symbols. Prince's public struggles with the corporation became an important symbolic and subversive act that brought into high relief and subsequently critiqued his artistic output as commodity.

Remember that although hip-hop music is a distinct entity, it is also part of the music industry writ large. That Nas's work appeared in the context of these other highly visible black musicians' responses to artistic freedom is significant. The struggles in which Prince and Marsalis found themselves embroiled surely washed through and resonated within other genres of music. Since hip-hop was not created in a historical vacuum—a critique of black culture since the Enlightenment—could we also assume that Nas's music, this singular musical statement, could also be read as rubbing against the grain of industry expectations? Is this, in part, the reason for the unique outpouring of critical acclaim that was inspired by the *Illmatic* album? Was this hip-hop's response to the strange bedfellows of art and commerce?

As interesting as it is to speculate about these larger cultural matters, getting at the meaning of a piece also demands taking into account the deeply personal ways in which listeners

engage music. In this regard, I am fascinated with the changing senses of authenticity in black musical communities across
time and place. Despite claims to the contrary, ideas about
what is "real" or "authentic" or "correct" are not historically
static but are always on the move. And how one interprets
these authentic moments is always a direct function of who is
doing the analyzing. As a forty-something black American,
I've lived, experienced, and negotiated, on a personal level, a
number of musical styles and what they were supposed to
mean in the public sphere: jazz, Motown, traditional and contemporary gospel, black art music, pop, soul, funk, fusion, and
now hip-hop. I have experienced these musical styles as social
markers of a constantly moving, forever searching, and always
challenging idea of "musical blackness." With that said, the
fact that generational misunderstandings arise about musical
taste, meaning, and identity should not be surprising. This has
been the case since Plato. Interestingly, it seems that bringing
into high relief the social and political divisions of a "community" is precisely the cultural work a musical piece is intended
to do. At other times, music resonates and engages dialogues
across generational boundaries. "Life's a Bitch" is one such
recording, in my view.

Some of the markers of authenticity, however, are embedded deep in the musical organization of the piece, a point that
is often overlooked in hip-hop criticism. Fortunately musi-
cology's toolbox, together with analysis of the poetry, can
unpack the rich dialogue swimming below the surface of the
truth claim of the lyrics. The formal plan of the song features
six large structures that are unified by a two-measure gesture
loop throughout the recording (example 1). Despite this rather
simplistic design, the song packs lots of rhetorical and thematic information. The mode of delivery moves from spoken
dialogue in the introduction, a rapped refrain featuring AZ,
two verses divided between as many rappers, and an ending

with a muted, subdued trumpet solo in the coda. The brief refrain or hook is not sung but rapped, positioning it formally as a dialogue between traditional popular song and rap music conventions. The trumpet solo is an obvious nod to jazz and stretches the envelope of generic expectations in hip-hop.

Example 1. Formal plan of "Life's a Bitch"

Introduction	Verse 1	Refrain	Verse 2	Refrain	Coda
Spoken	AZ rap	AZ	NAS rap	AZ	Olu Dara solo

As I stated above, the song's rhythm track is sampled from the Gap Band's 1981 R&B hit "Yearning for Your Love," a song that lyrically could not be further in tone and tenor from "Life's a Bitch." But as we will see below, context, history, and memory can radically change what meanings are conveyed in songs for listeners. The formal qualities of these pieces share a basic rhythm track, which encourages the connection between them for someone of my generation. ("Life's a Bitch" is an example of sample-based hip-hop, the art of which is the sole focus of Joseph Schloss's book *Making Beats: The Art of Sample-Based Hip-Hop*, 2004, an academic study in the intellectual lineage of Tricia Rose's *Black Noise*. *Making Beats* is pitched as a statement that explores the relationship of its subject matter to the academy.) As far as my ear can discern, Nas's piece ignores the introduction of the earlier recording and employs throughout the entire piece a two-measure loop lifted from the opening bars of the first verse.

The two-measure passage comprising the sample is revealing. It contains all of the timbral components of the original but with major shifts in the sonic field. The ostinato bass line is placed more prominently in the field, unleashing it as foreground, freeing it in same manner that bebop moved drummers from timekeepers to major components of the modern jazz enterprise. While the keyboard and drum parts remain intact, the repetitious rhythm guitar line is dropped in favor of the residue of a single note from the lead guitar, perched together with an even higher-pitched string sounding far above the field. This arrangement clears midrange space for the dense narrative that will be performed by the rappers AZ and Nas, even as it provides an ominous accompaniment to the gripping drama that will unfold.

If the pleas that Charlie Wilson, the Gap Band's lead singer, makes in "Yearning" express the frustration of unanswered adoration in the kind of virtuoso performance that has made soul vocals the lingua franca of global pop, AZ and Nas achieve a similar result but on hip-hop terms. Again, these respective authenticities are striking when contrasted. Wilson's cultural work takes place in the context of a song with few lyrical complexities, depending largely on his husky yet flexible delivery, spattered with well-placed melismas for its rhetorical power. The form of "Yearning" comprises a looping verse section, a harmonically different chorus, and a bridge providing further harmonic contrast. As I mentioned, Nas's rhythm track is decidedly simpler. It's basically a two-bar loop, yet one cannot imagine a denser narrative packed within its three and a half minutes. Let's turn now to the poetry.

Although "Life's a Bitch" features two rappers with distinct delivery styles, they do not participate in the typical male braggadocio that has marked the performance realm of the genre since its beginning. In the song's introduction, we hear a conversation between two male comrades participating in a seemingly ritualistic division of spoils.

> **[AZ]** Aiyyo, wassup wassup, let's keep it real, son.
> Count this money, ya know what I'm sayin?

[Nas] Yeah, yeah.

[AZ] Aiyyo, put the Grant's over there in the safe, ya know what I'm sayin?

[Nas] Yeah, yeah.

[AZ] Cause we spendin' these Jackson's.

The Washington's go to wifey, you know how that go.

[Nas] I'm sayin, that's what this is all about, right?

Clothes, bankrolls, and hos, ya know what I'm sayin?

Yo, then what man, what?

AZ opens the song proper with a powerful missive detailing the life philosophies of a young thug whose understanding of status and manhood are, not surprisingly, tied to the acquisition of money. While he portrays this mantra as a function of his upbringing in the ghetto, we know that to "stack plenty papers," as he puts it, is to participate in the all-American, middle-class dream of upward mobility. He credits his money-oriented mentality to a street ghetto essence that guides him through the challenges of life and the paper chase. Although his young peers are imprisoned or dead, he vows to live the dream for them until his own inevitable death. On the one hand, his game is one marred by a stunning fatalism and not of hope: "keepin' it real, packin' steel, gettin' high, cuz life's a bitch and then you die." But on the other hand, our protagonist is assured that at the very least, his thievery will allow him to leave a little something behind for those who survive him. The lyrics for verse 1 follow:

Visualizin' the realism of life and actuality

Fuck who's the baddest, a person's status depends on salary

And my mentality is, money orientated

Others such as myself are tryin' to carry on tradition

Keepin' the effervescence street ghetto essence inside us

Cause it provides us with the proper insight to guide us

Chorus

Life's a bitch and then you die, that's why we get high

Cuz you never know when you gonna go

Life's a bitch and then you die, that's why we puff la

Musically, AZ demonstrates in his verse the rhetorical dexterity that earned him status as a well-respected MC. The urgency of his delivery is mostly a function of his sixteenth note, drumlike subdivision of the loop. Together with a vocal quality that strains at the top of his range, the rhythmic character of the piece puts the listener on edge, especially because it is staged within a rather tame rhythm track. One of the most rhetorically rich moments occur in this verse on the words "cause yeah," "now some," and "dough, so" (in bold below) because they break the verse's hypnotic effect with their stress on weak beats. The irregular placement of these gestures adds to the musicality of the whole. Other similar moments happen on the lyrics "all gotta go" and "keepin' it real, packin' steel, gettin' high" when AZ delivers them in a sing-song manner; the notes he sings create tension with the underlying harmonies of the rhythm track.

I'm destined to live the dream for all my peeps who never made it

cause yeah, we were beginners in the hood as Five Percenters

But somethin' must of got in us cause all of us turned to sinners

Now some, restin' in peace and some are sittin' in San Quentin

Even though, we know somehow we *all gotta go*

but as long as we believe in thievin' we'll be leavin' with some kind of

dough so, and to that day we expire and turn to vapors

me and my capers'll be somewhere stackin' plenty papers

Keepin' it real, packin' steel, gettin' high

Cause life's a bitch and then you die

After the introduction's dialogue, the verses that Nas and AZ split can be interpreted as the voices of an inner dialogue between different aspects of one protagonist's searching consciousness. He wakes up on his twentieth birthday reflecting on the uncertainties of manhood. One side of him accepts the fate of an involuntary "ghetto essence inside us," the other uses his experiences earlier in life as a stepping-stone to a higher level of consciousness. In Nas's verse the resolve of fatalism morphs into a more mature understanding of life and the consequences of choices. This comparison is perhaps more feasible because Nas's verse lacks the echo effect that surrounds AZ's verse and gives it a more ethereal quality. Nas's rhythmic rhetoric is richer and more nuanced than AZ's here. With its less emphatic delivery, the mood conjured is more contemplative than reactionary. Nonetheless, two gestures on the words "got rhymes" and "once I" hint at a musico-rhetorical connection between the two verses as Nas performs them similarly to AZ by accenting weak beats. Nas's work has been hailed for its lyricism, a depiction surely meant to describe both the weight and inventiveness of his words and the rhythmic and timbral rhetoric moving them through time. This is evident in verse 2.

> I woke up early on my born day, I'm twenty years of blessing
> The essence of adolescent leaves my body now I'm fresh in
> My physical frame is celebrated cause I made it
> One quarter through life some god-ly like thing created
> **Got rhymes** 365 days annual plus some
> Load up the mic and bust one, cuss while I puffs from

The coda of the piece with its jazz inflection brings the piece full circle. In a musical environment that, as noted above, was rich in intragenre dialogue, this piece does not disappoint. Nas's father, Olu Dara, plays a plaintive, poignant solo on muted trumpet, providing a sonic link to work by the late

Miles Davis in the 1980s. This intergenerational dialogue between father and son is but one in the recording—we also hear
it between jazz, hip-hop, and R&B, and between two aspects of
the protagonist's consciousness. Dialogue is fundamental to
appreciating sample-based hip-hop. Listener competence—
based on personal experience—always determines how clearly
one will hear the conversation.

As noted above, when I first heard the recording I connected it to my father's death in 1994. When I strolled
through the funeral home where his remains lay, I saw in room
after room corpses of black men around his age and some even
younger. African American men have the highest death rate
and lowest life expectancy of any other racial and ethnic
group, male or female, in the United States. According to the
National Center for Health Statistics, homicide tops the list for
leading causes of death for African American men between the
ages of eighteen and thirty-four, and is the fourth leading
cause for African American men between the ages of eighteen
and sixty-four. If you are lucky and survive being "one of the
number," African American men also rank higher than other
groups for death by AIDS, heart disease, and prostate, lung,
and colon cancers. These dismal statistics are linked to unemployment rates for black males, a fact that negatively impacts
access to quality health care in this country. These statistics
suggest that life, death, and the borrowed time in between
should be a central concern to black men of all generations in
America. Nas's work underscored hip-hop's important role as
social commentary; it showed how a musical form can be just
as engaged and relevant as scholarship.

Beyond the social sharing among these statistics among
black men, cultural practice also functions in the dialogue of
my interpretation. During the mid-1970s to mid-1980s, I considered myself primarily a jazz head, a musician somewhat

narrowly focused on the postclassic bop mainstream jazz world. I was raised in a musical environment in which jazz was but one of many parchments in a sonic mosaic that included gospel, rhythm and blues, and soul. Yet a taste for jazz, as I think back, was an important way in which younger males in the family experienced a spiritual connection to older Ramsey men and to others of their generation. So deep was my Uncle W.J.'s identification to jazz, for example, that his funeral service was filled not with traditional Christian hymns and choral music but with the sounds of hard bop. It was authentically "him." To this day, I can't hear some stomp-down blues played by an organ, guitar, and drums trio without thinking of my family's departed patriarchs. These kinds of connections extend into my professional life as someone who analyzes music; I as much as anyone make very strong identifications with sound organization. We all make meanings through a complex web of personal history, memory, and subjectivity.

I referred earlier to the connection between the piece and my father; I end with a meditation on my son, a quiet and articulate man whose speech combines the southern drawl of his Chicago beginnings, the New England clip of his formative years in Boston, and the edgy force of his coming-of-age years in inner-city west Philadelphia. As of this writing he is in his early twenties, his "physical frame celebrated 'cause he made it." Although his father is a scholar and jazz musician, hip-hop forms the soundtrack of his life. In our dialogues, I've learned of his budding interest in a music career as a producer, the challenges of life, his anxieties over losing peers to violent death, and the vexed relationship between all-American manhood and capitalism, among other themes articulated in "Life's a Bitch."

Recently he revealed that during a college music appreciation course, a lecture on the twelve-bar blues form spurred a memory of me teaching him as a youngster to play the blues as part of our daily routine practicing his Suzuki cello lessons. He dumped this activity at age twelve with the declaration, "Dad, I'm an outside kind of boy." But I know that if he pursues one of his dreams of hip-hop producing, inevitably he'll discover my vintage vinyl collection, dig in my crates, and perhaps stumble onto some of my father's favorite recordings and complete the circle.

As Nas taught us in 1994, the year Pops died, time and musical dialogue are both *Illmatic*. Life's a bitch.

"IT'S YOURS"   4

HIP-HOP WORLDVIEWS
IN THE LYRICS OF NAS

We are all savages in the pursuit of the American Dream.
NAS, INTERVIEW BY MIMI VALDES IN
ORIGINS OF A HIP-HOP CLASSIC

Nobody said you have to be gangstas, hos/Read more,
learn more change the globe.
NAS, "I CAN"

n Brian De Palma's 1983 classic remake of the film *Scarface*
the line "the world is yours" functions as a powerful refrain
reappearing across the screen as the digitized text signaled
on an airborne blimp and then as the text encircling the globe
of a statuesque sculpture in the palatial home of the film's
enigmatic antihero, Tony Montana, also known as Scarface.[1]
For the film's protagonist, "the world is yours" functions much
like a recurring gangsta refrain. Deep in his gut, Tony feels
entitled to the world and everything in it. As a dispossessed
Cuban immigrant/refugee, Tony Montana's negotiation of
racial and economic oppression in the face of the extraordinary

bling of the capitalistic American Dream serves to inspire an entire generation of hip-hop citizens who identify with both Montana's plight and his lethal drive to achieve economic power and privilege by any means.

The fourth track on Nas's classic debut album, *Illmatic*, is entitled "The World Is Yours." The song exemplifies his lyrical genius, especially as it continues to reflect and represent the complex desires and challenges of the hip-hop generation.[2] Beneath the surface meaning of the title is a canny reflection of Nasir Jones's views of the world from the poignant perspective of his beloved Queensbridge projects. A corollary to this point of view is an accompanying heartfelt *racial romanticism* often gestured toward in the lyrics of hip-hop culture but rarely so eloquently captured as it is in the lyrics of "The World Is Yours."[3] The theme of these Nas lyrics is equivalent to hip-hop's version of the American Dream; also known as the "come-up." This represents the aspirations of inner-city African American culture, the idea that even oppressive, violent challenges do not prevent everyone from transcending poverty. Moreover, the come-up experience produces narratives that inspire others to follow nontraditional paths, so that dispossessed folk know that there is a path for them when all mainstream opportunities are closed. Consider Biggie's "Juicy," which begins, "It was all a dream/I used to read Word-Up Magazine." B.I.G. allows all of his listeners to revel in his own come-up, a move from "ashy to classy," from crack dealer to multiplatinum recording artist. The specific connection to dreaming of being a rapper allows the "juicy" come-up narrative to resonate with listeners whose only hope of getting out of the ghetto may be some form of superstardom provided by entertainment or sports. The come-up comes by way of education most readily and regularly, but in order for the narrative to be omnipresent among young black and brown folk it must have that heroic element. The come-up narratives form the critical architecture of the most popular hip-hop worldviews. Consider Jay-Z's "Can't Knock the Hustle" or Outkast's "Elevators," and we begin to hear how potent the come-up narrative is within hip-hop culture. The list of these narratives is extensive, and they don't all have happy endings. They do, however, offer the possibility of overcoming lack of opportunity and the resulting poverty. Think Ice Berg Slim, Too Short, Nicky Barnes, T.I., A.I., Tupac, and of course Nas, whose poetic narrative witnesses to the goings on of the inner-city neighborhood. And his skills are so adept, his verbal ability so prophetic and now legendary that his come-up narrative is distinct from the normalized hustle narratives we see and hear regularly. Still, the pimps, ballers, hustlers, dealers, and other underground figures (like legendary MCs) are heroes of the folk in much the same way Scarface (the movie character) has become a hero to the hip-hop generation.[4]

For the hip-hop generation, especially young black and brown men who face poverty and lack of opportunity, *Scarface* the film has "long been embraced as a contemporary example of a postimmigration attempt at pursuing the American Dream."[5] What immediately distinguishes Nas's world from De Palma's is that this motif functions in hip-hop discourse as call and response rather than as the one-sided text messages in the film. This is a signal distinction; Nas's worldview through the "The World Is Yours" call and response discourse practices the most central component of the African American oral tradition.[6] Producer (and MC in his own right) Pete Rock samples T-La Rock's vocals from the old-school classic "It's Yours" at the onset of the track and periodically throughout. But immediately following the "It's Yours" sample, Pete Rock begins the hook by singing the question, "Whose world is this?" To which Nas immediately replies, "The world is yours. The world is yours." Pete Rock then replies, "It's mine. It's mine. It's mine," followed by a return to the T-La Rock sample "it's yours" before the sequence repeats itself. You can only appreciate this audio collage by listening to it repeatedly. Nas's "The World Is Yours" is a critical riff on De Palma's *Scarface*. By posing and answering the question (even as it simultaneously quotes common themes from hip-hop history à la T-La Rock), it opens discussions of lack (of economic opportunity) and desire (for material possessions) to all of his listeners and by extension an entire generation of black and brown people living in oppressive urban conditions.[7] This idea is a come-up because it invites listeners to claim an ownership stake in the world around and beyond them. "The World Is Yours" as a come-up narrative had and (still has) the potential to reshape the mindset of young people trapped by impoverished inner-city life. If the world is yours, then the block cannot be the limit of your physical realm. Through the words of this song you are invited to see the world beyond your marginal existence.

"I sip the Dom P, watchin' Gandhi til I'm charged/Then writin' in my book of rhymes all the words pass the margin." With these lines Nas begins to outline his worldview in verse. While this view specifically references a peaceful yet revolutionary history, it is also overwrought with a sense of prophecy and altruism almost tending toward contradiction. A resident of the Queensbridge projects sipping champagne is inherently ironic, but that straightforward irony (if such a thing exists) is complicated by Nas's ideological muse—Mohandas Gandhi. If, as the hook and the title of this song suggest, Nas borrows the phrase "the world is yours" from De Palma's *Scarface*, one of the most violent films produced in the postmodern era, he then turns almost immediately in his lyrics to a more nuanced inspiration for (non)violence in the film genre. One would be hard-pressed to find two film protagonists more opposite in ideology and action than Gandhi and Scarface. Released in 1982 (one year before *Scarface*) and starring Ben Kingsley (in brown-face), *Gandhi* is a remarkable film chronicling the world's most successful nonviolent or, as Gandhi himself would describe it, noncooperative revolution.[8] For Nas, juxtaposing these two films or even reveling in a bottle of Dom Perignon as he watches *Gandhi* are for the most part not contradictory. This type of juxtaposition signals what scholar Imani Perry has revealed as "reunion" in hip-hop culture.[9] The film is important to Nas's worldview because it highlights a central component of Mohandas Gandhi's philosophy that "suffering is a necessary condition for progress."[10]

Nas's perspective here underscores a similar patience with the challenges of postindustrial urban living even as he looks toward revolutionary, nonviolent inspiration for the lyrical articulation of his worldview. When he embraces the awesome potential of such a revolution and makes a personal connection to the figure of Gandhi, the margins of his book of rhymes and, by signifying extension, the margins of society—to which Nas and his audience have been regularly relegated—become incapable of containing or restricting his lyrics. Hence "*all* the words pass the margin[s]." Nas's lyrics have clearly passed beyond his humble Queensbridge origins. As a scribe he can take solace in the fact that his words have the ability to pass beyond his marginal beginnings and are even capable of extending across the globe influencing young people the world over. The margins also serve as a metaphor for urban youth relegated to the margins by being forced to work within clearly defined legal, economic, social, and political parameters (i.e., margins). Some of these urban youth embrace a worldview that captures their marginality while simultaneously challenging it. Thus they love the neighborhood—hood, block, or street—but at the same time they are willing to achieve the American Dream of economic success by any means necessary, the come-up in full view. We want what you got and we are prepared to get it any way we can. In strange ways this notion of the come-up is more American than the American Dream.

Interestingly enough, Nas returns to the Gandhi reference in his later work on the *God's Son* album. In the appropriately titled "Book of Rhymes," Nas flips through an imagined old rhyme book providing listeners with snippets of unused lyrics over the course of his career. In this stream-of-consciousness type of flow Nas quips, "Gandhi was fool/nigga fight to the death/the U.S. Army teaches the price of conquest." This line does not necessarily contradict Nas's earlier inspiration from the nonviolent revolutionary detailed in the first lines of "The World Is Yours." On the contrary, in his continuing artistic outline of a worldview, this new perspective on Gandhi reflects the paradigmatic shift in post–cold war U.S. foreign policy since the release of *Illmatic.* As the United States has become more aggressive in its global domination, Gandhi's nonviolent tactics have lost some of their inspirational luster from Nas's perspective.[11]

In an insightful alignment with the principles of perseverance, revolution, and suffering hinted at in the lines discussed above, Nas in the initial verse of "The World Is Yours" draws a striking analogy between his love for hip-hop culture and the oft-referenced crack epidemic (a very specific form of suffering) in urban communities, referred to regularly in rap music. He refers to himself as "the fiend of hip-hop: it's got me stuck like a crack pipe." The significance of this reference resides in the impact of crack cocaine on inner-city communities across the United States. With its well-documented addictive effects on individuals and its equally well-documented destructive effects on communities, crack cocaine has irrevocably changed urban economies. According to scholar and cultural critic Mark Anthony Neal, crack cocaine overdetermined the underground economy of black urban life after the civil rights era in the wake of economic depression and rising unemployment. "Crack cocaine was a unique drug; its emergence exemplified the paradox of consumptionist desire in the midst of intense poverty."[12]

This crack fiend analogy reverberates in a number of ways. The paradox to which Mark Anthony Neal alludes is addressed in this song through its inviting discussion on economic empowerment (an admitted oversimplification of the "world is yours" theme) and its suggestive referencing of said economic empowerment through the drug (crack) trade. Nas simultaneously challenges and negotiates this paradox by claiming his addiction to the culture of hip-hop, an addiction to which his audience as well as the contributors to this volume can attest. Yet as we acknowledge and accept our fiendish love for hip-hop culture through this line, we must also acknowledge and accept the violent and ravishing consequences of crack cocaine on our communities and on the individual addict's and dealer's souls.[18] At least according to the narratives of ex-crack dealers and various rappers who bear witness through their lyrics, the decision to sell crack in urban neighborhoods is largely influenced by an utter lack of opportunity and the ubiquitous material desire among poor folk in an American capitalistic society. Thus when Nas likens himself to a fiend, he is also signifying on an uncontrollable desire for material sustenance in an impoverished postindustrial environment; an economic environment that lacks jobs, proper education, and/or models of economic success outside of sports, entertainment, and the underground economy, which features various forms of hustling including selling drugs. This is the social and cultural context out of which the come-up by any and all means necessary is the most plausible paradigm for success. Even if one's comeuppance requires an apparently nihilistic approach to the community (which by necessity must suffer the consequences of the crack trade), the ends (i.e., the come-up) always justify the means (selling poison to the community). Economic empowerment in these cases means something very different from black-owned businesses and black patronage. In Nas's world, economic empowerment positions us all as fiends, whether that unchecked desire is for crack, for culture, or for money and material possessions.

Consider another lyric from another song on *Illmatic*, aptly entitled "Represent," where Nas wonders, "Somehow the rap game reminds me of the crack game."[14] Other artists and figures of hip-hop culture make these allusions and usually use the crack game as a metaphor for the music industry's relationship to hip-hop (e.g., Biggie's "Ten Crack Commandments" or Kanye West's "Crack Music"), commonly referred to as the rap game. This crack game/rap game metaphor has become one of the most compelling staple concepts of the hip-hop worldview and is the general undercurrent of the come-up narrative in rap music.

This first verse, already rich in worldly sociopolitical viewpoints, resolves itself in a simple but traditional blues stanza:[15]

> I'm out for presidents to represent me (Say what?)
> I'm out for presidents to represent me (Say what?)
> I'm out for dead presidents to represent me.

Here Nas and Pete Rock re-engage their call and response performance; this time Nas posits a statement before and Pete Rock asks for clarification after. The form of these lines mimics typical blues lines of verse that repeat themselves in lines 1 and 2 and then ultimately resolve in line 3, a repeated line with a slight signifying difference.

The signifying difference here (the distinction between presidents and *dead* presidents) captures the central tension between hip-hop artists who are continuously challenged by an American Dream type of success with accompanying capitalistic pursuits (i.e., economic success translated as selling out the community) and an audience within hip-hop culture that desires its own economic success but occasionally connects economic empowerment to political representation. The suggestion that Nas is "out for" presidential representation expresses the political frustration of millions of black and brown urban folk who are struggling with the burden of the civil rights legacy in an era of confused electoral voting systems and political leaders who exhibit open disregard for the hip-hop generation and its as yet untapped voting power.[16]

The lyric is so politically potent that it demands both the question (say what?) and the repetition. A president who would represent Nas would be forced to redress the economic disparities of late capitalism (or globalism) and the wretched conditions of so many postindustrial urban neighborhoods manifest in the residential conditions of project living. "Black communities . . . have the appearance of cities recently at war: dilapidated housing, gutted buildings, pothole-filled streets, and little economic activity."[17] No president could genuinely relate to these conditions unless he or she actually lived through them. Nas, in much of his work, invites us to do so. He reveals "the bleak reality of ghetto life" without removing hope from the equation of ghetto existence. "The World Is Yours" is both dark and bright. In it Nas seeks to report on the dark realities to which he has been exposed even as he offers up an ethos— of claiming the world as one's own, which smacks of hope and possibility.[18] Not getting caught up in the darker side of life is an important quality to Nas's lyrical work, and the theme of optimism or positive possibility is also a component of the worldview articulated through Nas's artistry in general. If those who listen to "The World Is Yours" can accept their stake in Nas's words and by extension their personal stake in the world around them (an antinihilistic proposition to be sure), then they are better prepared to accept Nas's more complex request for presidential representation of the socially invisible residents of the urban environment.

Just in case presidential representation of project residents seemed far-fetched to the average 1994 hip-hop listener (as was most probably the case), *dead* presidential representation offers a signifying blues/hip-hop response to the material conditions that so readily (and violently) separate the haves from the have-nots. The term "dead presidents" is a complex (and often oversimplified) reference to American money—the stuff of which most American dreams are made. It is complex because while it functions as a synecdoche for cash money (i.e., it refers to money as the representation of the deceased presidents depicted on U.S. dollars), it also bears in its black English or Ebonics meaning an abstract delight in the death of American political leaders. The suggestion here is that if living presidents won't represent me, dead ones will. Nas's aspiration to dead presidential wealth is common among his audience, and this aspirational sentiment reflects many of the life-changing pitfalls of inner-city youth who decide to engage in illegal drug trafficking, thievery, and prostitution. In addition, however, the term "dead presidents" always engages the fundamental political question of presidential representation even as it gestures toward financial and economic gain.[19]

The notion of dead presidents also signals and gestures toward a kind of a death of politics, or at least a death of protest politics expressed by an earlier generation, à la the civil rights generation. The aforementioned abstract delight taken in the death of American presidents also suggests a critical commentary on protest politics, mass marches, and the political/electoral system in general. This critique differentiates the hip-hop generation worldview from a civil rights generation worldview. The civil rights worldview challenges the American political system to own up to its promise of equality and access to the American Dream. The hip-hop generation, especially because it came of age in the post–civil rights era, fundamentally questions the viability of the system itself. In fact, the hip-hop generation's worldview considers electoral politics, protest movements, and the like as inherently futile; if

Dr. King and Malcolm X could not achieve equality for black folk, maybe it is not an attainable goal.[20] The pitfalls of this kind of reasoning are readily apparent, but so are the advantages when one considers the fact that the combination of the underground economy (illicit drug trade, prostitution, etc.) and the hip-hop sector of the music industry ultimately account for more jobs in some inner-city neighborhoods than any socially acceptable alternative for poor dispossessed young black men.

The lyrics of "The World Is Yours" are often directed at the material living conditions (i.e., economics) of project residents who are sometimes forced out of their meager homes and other times brutally policed and under surveillance within them. "The high visibility of such housing [federal housing projects], with its distinct architecture that privileged more efficient use of urban space over livability and the concentration of the black poor within such spaces, increased notions that such communities were socially isolated from mainstream life and thus to be feared and neglected."[21] Our fear and neglect of project residents establish social conditions in which nihilistic attitudes can thrive unchecked. Glimpses of nihilism rear themselves in the middle of the second verse as Nas laments "dwellin' in the Rotten Apple, you get tackled/Or caught by the devil's lasso, shit is a hassle." But this theme shifts eventually to an older generation ("old folks") who pray to Jesus and soak their sins in "trays of holy water." For the older generation, seemingly, the challenges of the Rotten Apple are diminished through religious tithing. But ultimately Nas reaffirms his faith (or contradicts himself) in suggestions of his own redemption and resurrection through his daughter and son. "My strength, my son, the star, will be my resurrection/Born in correction all the wrong shit I did, he'll lead a right direction."

In the third and final verse, Nas fully engages the nihilism so often cited as central to the ideological inner workings of the inner-city thug mentality. Yet he does so with such a clear focus on his interior self that the nihilism is nearly masked in his lyrical revelry.

> I'm the young city bandit, hold myself down single-handed
> For murder raps, I kick my thoughts alone get remanded
> Born alone, die alone, no crew to keep my crown or throne
> I'm deep by sound alone, caved inside in a thousand miles from home
> I need a new nigga, for this black cloud to follow
> Cause while its over me it's too dark to see tomorrow

Somehow, by the time Nas's narrator gets to his third verse a deep sense of alienation and singularity have crept into the lyrics. "Born alone, die alone . . . I'm deep by sound alone." In this verse, Nas's narrator is overwhelmed by the singular nature of his existence in the inner city. These themes of urban alienation emphasize an in-depth sense of nihilism in this narrator's voice; thus he needs a "new nigga, for this black cloud to follow."

The long-standing discussion of nihilism in the black urban communities of the hip-hop generation has been given voice in spirited exchanges between Dr. Cornel West of Princeton University and Dr. Michael Eric Dyson of Georgetown University. In *Race Matters* West suggests that nihilism, the lack of hope, care, and most of all love are eroding what's left of the cultural infrastructure of the black community. According to West both the liberal and conservative perspectives on the challenges facing the black urban poor miss the key issue: black nihilism. For West, this nihilism includes "a profound sense of psychological depression, personal worthlessness and social despair."[22] These feelings are rampant in black America, according to West, and some of them are represented in the lyrics of hip-hop music in general and in the worldviews articulated through Nas's artistry. Yet nihilism is only part of the worldview expressed in "The World Is Yours." In response to

West's analysis, Dyson proffers the following: "As an explanation for what ails us, nihilism has severe problems. First, nihilism is seen as a cause, not a consequence, of black suffering."[23] In all three verses of "The World Is Yours," the audience is witness to a multifaceted worldview that includes sociopolitical and economic critique, spiritual and generational reflections, and finally a meditation on the kinds of urban alienation that tends to produce the hopelessness of nihilism in the inner city, a world powerfully detailed on Nas's debut record. Whether nihilism is a cause or a consequence of black suffering (and in some ways it must be both), its thematic presence in the worldviews of hip-hop culture underscores once again the prevailing mind-set behind the desire to come-up in a world where opportunities are lacking yet material desire is ever-present and growing. If we understand nihilism as a cause of the will to come-up by any means necessary, then we miss the consequential relevance of project living, eroding public educational systems, and the emergence of powerful underground economies. We need both perspectives (those of West and Dyson) in order to fully engage the complex worldview expressed in Nas's *Illmatic*.

"*Illmatic* is a hip hop classic of the first order. Nas's poetic lyrics are some of the most poignant words ever to describe the postindustrial urban experience. . . . Songs like 'Life's a Bitch (And Then You Die),' 'It Ain't Hard to Tell,' and 'The World Is Mine' [sic] will forever be held up as hip hop standard-bearers."[24] Of course Todd Boyd is referring to the "The World Is Yours," but this oversight and/or psychological slip is instructive for how listeners of the worldviews expressed by and through "The World Is Yours" themes experience the lyrical influence of the song from its call and response phrasing to its collage-like sampling of T La Rock's refrain: "Its yours." Even in the midst of articulating a dispossessed, economically, and spiritually challenging existence, "The World Is

Yours" poetically and musically deconstructs these challenges by repeatedly answering the (whose-world-is-this) call: "It's mine, it's mine, it's mine." Thinking of the song title as "the world is mine" is therefore not necessarily an editorial or technical misunderstanding. Instead, this renaming suggests the deeper themes of and the (at times) contradictory principles within Nas's lyrical genius, especially as they are expressed on the album *Illmatic.*

The music video for "The World Is Yours" offers additional insight to this discussion. It is one of only two music videos in Nas's cinematic career to be shot in black and white.[25] The video features Pete Rock playing piano while the scenes scroll through a montage of Nas reciting his lyrics interspersed with glimpses of random people, young, old, and of various ethnic backgrounds. The video suggests an existential empowerment (i.e., who can take ownership of the world) that extends far beyond Queensbridge public housing. Viewers experience this connection between the project housing of New York City and the rest of the world through a refracted televisual screen. The scenic transitions visually challenge the claustrophobia and economic entrapment of inner-city, postindustrial living. People from Nas's 'hood (or any hood for that matter) are visually treated to the interconnectivity of their physical locale and lived experiences with locales and life experiences of other people around the world.

Nas's artistic connection as an inner-city African American youth with the Latin American refugee-turned-outlaw antihero from De Palma's *Scarface* is powerful because they both challenge the physical boundaries of poverty and lack of economic opportunity that the federal housing projects have come to emblematize. The video signifies on the film directly in one of its earliest scenes where Nas is in a large Jacuzzi smoking a cigar. A beautiful woman primps and preens herself at a vanity table situated in the background. *Scarface* fans will recognize this music video scene as a direct sample of Tony Montana in his luxurious bathroom in the film. Although the scene reflects a certain amount of material success (and excess) for Nas's character in the music video, in the film the scene is rife with the tension that success brings. Tony Montana is at odds with his wife, Elvira (played by Michelle Pfeiffer), and his underworld business partner and closest friend, Manny Ribera (played by Steven Bauer). He is also at odds with himself. Montana's success has brought him all of the trappings of our material world—the beautiful girl, the lavish house, expensive cars, and more money than he can spend. Yet this material success leaves him wanting something more substantive out of his existence. Surely Nas is aware of this fact even as he shoots the scene for this music video. The nuances of material success are also not lost on Nas's hip-hop audience. Yet the message (the world is yours) resonates because it is communicated personally here from Nas to viewers in the video as well as us, the viewers out in the world. This is ultimately a message of liberation and empowerment to which Nas's lyrics and video eloquently gesture.

Finally, though, Nas's narrator leaves us contemplating his "chipped-toothed smile" in the midst of the aforementioned challenges and reflective discussions. This seemingly flippant reference at the end of his last verse returns to positive themes in the hip-hop worldview detailed in other parts of the song. Nas's chipped tooth has been repaired, but in the early days it signified the "brutally truncated opportunities" of the inner-city residents Nas so effectively represents. Indeed, in this last verse, where he asks his audience to "check the chip toothed smile," Nas's narrator bops down city blocks, smiling amid "the problems of the world today." The smile flies in the face of the alienated, nihilistic narratives articulated earlier in this same verse. But his dental imperfection is a stark reminder of those challenges, in spite of which the narrator's smile still shines. These themes also gesture toward Nas's next lyrical work explicitly wrestling with signifying notions of the world and the worldviews that are inspired by such artistry.

"*It Was Written* doesn't have the underground aesthetic and lyric-driven genius of *Illmatic*. Then again, Nas's persona went from 'Nasty Nas's to 'Nas Escobar.' His aesthetic and lyrical shift underscores his transformed identity, from ghetto projects denizen whose hard-core themes were wed to high concepts if idiosyncratic articulations of urban weltanschauung, to a more traditionally identified hustler/gangster whose aspirations to the high life are filtered through conventional if compelling narratives of upward mobility linked to spiritual and moral aims fueled by racial romanticism and altruism."[26]

Dyson's assessment of the differences and distinctions between Nas's first and second albums puts into bold relief the conceptual transitions and developments of Nas's worldview as it develops throughout his musical repertoire. In the lead (and most popular) single from *It Was Written*, "If I Ruled the World" (featuring the enigmatic Lauryn Hill), the lyrical reflection of Nas's transformed identity is readily apparent. Gone is the chipped-tooth smile, literally and figuratively, as Nas trades the panoramic view from his Queensbridge projects for a top-of-the-world perspective that only the tallest skyscrapers of Manhattan can provide.

In his running commentary throughout the DVD *Video Anthology, Vol. 1*, Nas explains to viewers his desire to shoot a video in locales other than his beloved neighborhood of origin. When the music video lens is shifted from Queensbridge to Manhattan, Nas's artistic persona undergoes a transformation through which new worldviews emerge. In "If I Ruled the World," Nas envisions a racialized existence pulled tight by the dual binds of white supremacy and lack of economic opportunity. To remedy this tension he fantasizes a world where all of his people are rich, wear designer clothes, elude the justice system, and have no need for contraceptive devices. "Just some thoughts for the mind/I take a glimpse into time/watch the blimp read: The World Is Mine." The fantastical nature of Nas's lyrics in this song has the radical effect of outlining a vision of the world ruled by platinum-era hip-hop heads.

The hook/refrain, "if I ruled the world," revisits Nas's confidence for all of us in "The World Is Yours." The conditional "if" suggests that maybe the world is not ours. Maybe we can only claim ownership of the world in which we live through fantasy-like narratives represented in "If I Ruled the World." The ultimate effect here may still be the empowerment of his listeners: if you ruled the world, what would you do? Better still, if disempowered black and brown people ruled the world, what would it look like? Nas's listeners are invited to contemplate the world in which we live and what might be different if the powers that be were not.

The key image of the song derives from the following line: "I'd open up every cell in Attica, send 'em to Africa." Throughout the chorus Lauryn Hill and Nas trade vocal riffs and verses that include references to "freeing all of my sons," thereby challenging the prison-industrial complex that eagerly incarcerates poor young men and women of color. These are powerful suggestions for the hip-hop audience, but the concept of freeing convicts and releasing them to Africa smacks of an immature, racially romantic (and maybe just plain stupid) idea. The challenge to the prison system and its traditional classism and racism is completely lost by sending African American convicts to some contrived notion of freedom in the motherland. That being said, these lyrics also reimagine the possibilities of redemption and repatriation. Africa most likely would not benefit from an influx of convicts. However, a deeper connection between African Americans and Africans would be revolutionary in both the United States and Africa. Consider as well the political energy connected with Attica, especially during the prison uprisings of the early 1970s. Prisons, especially from the perspective of an inner-city griot like Nas, house some of the most revolutionary figures in black and brown cultures. There is no one way of hearing and interpreting these very controversial lines. They are deliberately delivered for multiple interpretations, which is the most important concept to extract from them.

The lyrics examined here only hint at the more sophisticated and better formed notions of racial romanticism articulated in Nas's worldview through his music. If the come-up narrative is one idea in Nas's worldview, then the romantic themes of race operate as a sort of background to this idea. Nas's references to Africa may be informed by a nostalgia that is historically misinformed through the history of American slavery and underdeveloped because black folk had for many centuries been unable to revel in the positive cultural and civil resources of their native pre-American existence. "Black culture has an extraordinary romance with aspects of Kemet, the Egyptian name for Africa, and with black kings and queens and the like because racial romance was denied to blacks as a condition of our oppression."[27] The come-up narrative of getting money at the expense of your black and brown brothers and sisters apparently contradicts the undercurrents of racial romance in Nas's lyrics. Nas has consistently straddled these apparent oppositions throughout his career. Upon further reflection, the Afrocentric conscious designation is not so diametrically opposed to the gangsta-bling designation of rap lyrics. The come-up narrative deconstructs these oppositions, resolving itself in a worldview where the slim hope of economic success inspires an audience that readily identifies with the Afrocentric racial romanticism in Nas's narrative genius. Racial romanticism here inverts the impoverished status of black folk by pointing to a history of cultural and material wealth. It helps construct a community that exists outside of the confines of the inner city, where poverty, violence, and drug abuse abound. In this deconstructed model of lyrical artistry, upward mobility becomes a form of political resistance even if it is essentially reflected in the narrative of capital and economic success so central to the American ethos. This unstable form of political resistance (i.e., getting rich through illegal and at times destructive means) requires the balancing effects of racial romance in order to form a collective consciousness through which the heroes of the urban folk can come to terms with the awful effects of their come-up. These themes come together in Nas's lyrical and visual performances. As a result he may be the most influential and, yes, the best MC of all time.

The evidence of Nas's racial romance originates in the various world-is-yours discourses, but it takes several visual cues as well. Consider the pharaoh-like cover art of the *I Am* and *Nastradamus* albums and, even more poignantly, Nas's character, Sincere, in Hype Williams's visually stunning film, *Belly*. Sincere leaves behind a life of crime and unmitigated violence to start a new life with his partner (T, played by T-Boz) in Africa. Some critics and viewers dismiss *Belly* as unbelievable urban fantasy primarily because both of its protagonists, Tommy and Sincere (played by DMX and Nas respectively), escape the violent hell of inner-city life by joining a black nationalist movement (DMX) and relocating to Mother Africa (Nas). As unbelievable as these narrative outcomes may seem (especially in the context of more traditional nihilistic resolutions to hip-hop gangsta/hood films), the worldview expressed through these outcomes powerfully articulates the significance of racial romance to the ideological health of hip-hop's collective consciousness.

The ending of *Belly* stands as a singular inspirational (visual) voice amid a sea of images and lyrics with nihilistic negative outcomes in hip-hop hood films. "As Tommy, Sincere, and

T come full circle (Tommy to accept the spiritual and political teachings of the film's spiritual leader, Reverend Savior, and Sincere and T to follow their dreams of getting out of the 'hood and moving to the motherland ...), [Hype] Williams has given us an alternative definition of the new Black youth culture."[28] According to Bakari Kitwana, the new black youth culture resists nihilism and embraces semblances of traditional social responsibility most often associated with the civil rights generation.

Lyrically, Nas renders this messaging most effectively through his 2003 single "I Can" from the *God's Son* album. "I Can" reflects a more sophisticated but still racially romantic depiction of Africa. "It was empires in Africa called Kush/ Timbuktu, where ever race came to get books/To Learn from black teachers who taught Greeks and Romans." "I Can" insists on the presence of opportunity even in absence of opportunity and hope for the generation of children following in Nas's demographic footsteps. Essentially the theme of "I Can" is that young black boys and girls need to reclaim their regal African history in order to excel in their dismal present and look forward to a hopeful future. The fullest potential of this racially romantic optimism is suggested theoretically as Nas signifies on "Be" and the *B* in "B-boys and B-girls" (as in the opening lines of each of the three verses in "I Can"). He says "Be, B-boys and girls listen up." There are many ways a listener might interpret this first "be." It may just be repetition for lyrical effect, but my sense is that Nas gestures toward a sort of existential command "to be" and by extension "to be black." Being black is best understood through the connections Nas makes in "I Can," one of his most powerfully crafted come-up narratives sans the gangsterism and consumerism but with the addition of a pronounced Afrocentric sensibility. This interpretive hearing is underscored by the rich connections between B-boys and hip-hop culture. B-boys or B-girls are the essential performers from early moments of hip-hop culture who danced to the manually looped breaks of old soul and disco records. Breakin' (or break dancing) along with poppin'/pop locking were early foundational forms of dance. Break dancing derives its name from the break beats that drove the music and culture at the outset. But B-boying and B-girling took on more meaning and significance within the culture of hip-hop and today are known as guardians of the culture. By lyrically connecting existential "be" with the *B* in B-boy, Nas masterfully captures the social force of hip-hop culture and its most inspiring by-product: sociopolitical agency in the lives of young people. Thus in the same ways that B-boys *are* hip-hop, Nas invites his listeners to *be* black.

With its imagery of queens and kings, its historical references to great nations on the continent of Africa and their relationship to hip-hop youth, "I Can" represents a lyrical development in Nas's worldview, especially in the come-up narratives of the world-is-yours songs and themes. The theme of racial romanticism in "I Can" has in many ways displaced the most nihilistic undertones of the economic come-up. Nas does not advocate getting money by any means; instead, he advocates getting cultural knowledge by all means necessary": "read more learn more, change the globe." The naïveté reflected in freeing prisoners and sending them to Africa is also gone. Given the time and artistic space to develop his thinking, Nasir Jones has cultivated a complex and fluidly unfolding worldview that contains all of the nihilism, Afrocentrism, and undying hope in the hearts and minds of the hip-hop generation. Although any number of other Nas joints ("Doo Rags," "One Mic," "These Are Our Heroes") continue to explore the various ideas operating in the lyrical world of Nasir Jones, "The World Is Yours," "If I Ruled the World," "Belly," and "I Can" provide the clearest lyrical diagram of the come-up and racially romantic pride in the worldviews present throughout Nas's body of artistic work.

CRITICAL PEDAGOGY COMES AT HALFTIME

NAS AS BLACK PUBLIC INTELLECTUAL

5

MARC LAMONT HILL

Despite its placement in the middle of the album, "Halftime" in many ways represents the beginning of the *Illmatic* legacy. Nearly three years before Columbia Records released *Illmatic*, Nas made hip-hop history by stealing the show on Main Source's classic 1991 posse cut "Live at the BBQ" featuring Joe Fatal, Akinelye, and Large Professor. The subsequent buzz from Nas's verse ("Verbal assassin, my architect pleases/When I was twelve, I went to hell for snuffin' Jesus") prompted 3rd Bass's MC Serch to recruit him for the soundtrack to *Zebrahead,* Anthony Drazan's low-budget race movie.[1] Nas responded with the Large Professor-produced battle track "Halftime," a strong lead single on an otherwise forgettable album. Through a clever mix of braggadocio and sharp lyricism, the artist still officially known as "Nasty Nas" created an underground hit and a national buzz. "Halftime" was so well received that it was also placed on *Illmatic* in order to secure sales as well as please loyal underground fans. Although the musical value of "Halftime" is significant, it is dwarfed by the larger implications of the song and the *Illmatic* album within the public sphere. As Nas's first official single, "Halftime" marked a watershed moment in his career and in the cultural life of a generation, signaling Nas's first full-fledged foray into the world of black public intellectuals.

Throughout the *Illmatic* album, Nas performs the most critical function of the public intellectual: linking a rigorous engagement with the life of the mind to an equally rigorous engagement with the public and its problems.[2] While not as pensive or contemplative as some of *Illmatic*'s more celebrated tracks like "One Love" or "Life's a Bitch," "Halftime" is in many ways a more precise representation of Nas's intellectual project, as it brings together two allegedly irreconcilable camps within the hip-hop community: "conscious" and "commercial." Although these terms are wholly artificial and insufficient for understanding the complexities of artistic identity, they serve as useful tools for understanding the current division of labor within hip-hop's cultural landscape.

Within hip-hop culture, the terms "conscious" and "commercial"—as well as others like "political" and "mainstream"—are assigned to rappers in ways that divide them into discrete categories. Through these terms, artists develop public identities that shape the ways they are understood and engaged by various audiences. In addition to prefiguring artist-audience relationships, such divisions are often based on superficial criteria. For example, despite the relatively apolitical nature of their work, groups like The Roots and A Tribe Called Quest are hastily branded "conscious" or "political" because of their avant-garde music and aesthetics. On the contrary, the political critiques and philanthropy of "mainstream" rappers like Jay-Z and Ice Cube are often overlooked or dismissed. Within this superficial framework, hip-hop political consciousness is reduced to a thin politics of fashion and speech that privileges bourgeois bohemianism over engaged social critique and concrete action.

The construction of a conscious/commercial divide also undermines a sophisticated and evenhanded analysis of all hip-hop artists. Too often, commercial figures like Jay-Z and Ice Cube are classified as mere rappers who are only worthy of critical attention in order to expose the troubling dimensions of their music. On the other hand, "conscious" rappers like Talib Kweli and Mos Def are romantically viewed as legitimate cultural workers whose work should be analyzed based on artistic merit. Such distinctions are highly problematic, however, as they obscure the complexities and contradictions that operate within every artist's body of work. For example, Jay-Z has written songs that critique the American invasion of Iraq ("Beware of the Boys"), post-9/11 race relations ("Ballad for the Fallen Soldier"), and the nation's response to Hurricane Katrina ("Minority Report"); in his solo and group projects, Ice Cube has consistently critiqued police brutality ("Fuck Da Police"), black Christianity ("Heaven"), and white supremacy ("The Nigga Trapp"). Talib Kweli and Mos Def, on the other hand, have both appeared on songs that deploy homophobic language ("REDEFinition," "The Rape Over"). By ignoring such work or dismissing it as the exception to an otherwise useful rule, we squander valuable opportunities to enrich our understanding of hip-hop identities, as well as the forces that help constitute them.

No hip-hop artist better spotlights the poverty of the conscious/commercial divide than Nas, whose refusal to fit neatly into either category provides the basis for his artistic identity.[3] Unlike most rappers, Nas has a thoroughly equivocal relationship to both the commercial and conscious sectors of hip-hop culture. Despite his commercial leanings, Nas openly moves between each space in ways that defy the dominant logic and practices of hip-hop. As opposed to his counterparts, Nas's movement between the conscious and commercial realms is not understood as a momentary departure from his "true" artistic self, such as when hard-core rapper Jadakiss released the politically charged single "Why." Instead, Nas is viewed by fans and critics as the rare artist who can traverse the boundaries of each territory with equal skill. This artistic ambidexterity is acknowledged by Nas himself on songs like Kanye West's "We Major," where he uses a guest verse to deliberate about whether to write a verse about "44s or Black Christ," "big paper or the Black man's plight." This type of public rumination, which occurs on a track with Kanye West, whose artistic identity also embodies this tension, combined with his conclusion that "both flows would be nice," demonstrates Nas's intentionality and comprehension of his position.

Despite the public's recognition of Nas's modus operandi, many view his fluid artistic identity as a shortcoming rather than a virtue. This discomfort with Nas surfaced during his well-publicized feud with Jay-Z, who pointed out Nas's alleged contradictions in his 2002 title track "Blueprint 2":

> You can't give cred to anything dude said
> Same dude give you ice and you owe him some head . . .
> Is it "Oochie Wally Wally" or is it "One Mic"?
> Is it "Black Girl Lost" or Shortie owe you for ice?[4]

Like many hip-hop observers, Jay-Z viewed Nas's penchant for releasing radio-friendly songs like "Oochie Wally Wally" and "You Owe Me" as directly contradictory to the content of his socially conscious songs like "One Mic" and "Black Girl Lost." Jay-Z's critique of the moral and ideological contradictions within Nas's music is accurate, particularly with regard to the consumerist and misogynistic impulses that animate his commercial releases. Still, Jay-Z's comments also reflect a deep suspicion of Nas's authenticity as a conscious artist based on his location within the commercial marketplace.

Suspicions regarding artistic authenticity are animated by a belief that "real" art cannot exist in the capitalist marketplace. As a result, artists who move from the margins to the center of the commercial sphere are often viewed as "sellouts" whose work no longer honors the spirit of the craft. While this claim is true in certain cases—such as the underground-turned-pop group Black Eye Peas, for whom such a choice was deliberate and unabashed—it cannot be held as a universal truth claim about commercially successful artists. Conversely, it is equally problematic to view commercial marginality (i.e., lack of sales) as an index of artistic integrity or quality. Such an approach is deeply problematic, as it overestimates the extent to which artists choose not to operate within mainstream circles, and it romanticizes the underground as a space untouched by the same corporate capitalist forces as mainstream spheres. An excellent example of this reality is the rap group The Roots, who are often viewed by critics and fans as exemplars of authentic and untampered artistry. Despite their reputation for self-imposed marginality within the hip-hop community, the group has written multiple singles (e.g., "You Got Me," "Break You Off") expressly aimed at mainstream radio audiences and mass sales. Additionally, the group's label, Def Jam, is owned by Universal Music Group, which has more than a 25 percent market share in the music industry. As such, the group not only willfully operates squarely within the capitalist marketplace but helps promote and finance pop acts (like Black Eye Peas) that are also under the Universal Music Group umbrella. This is not to suggest that The Roots are less authentic than popularly imagined, but that any sophisticated notion of authenticity must consider the ways in which artistic identities are crafted in relation to pervasive forces of global capitalism.

In classifying Nas as an intellectual, we must reconsider the possible sites where intellectual work occurs. In the case of Nas, it becomes necessary to look beyond formal locations such as universities, think tanks, and literary circles, and look to the highly contested domain of hip-hop culture. While many critics and scholars have argued the intellectual merit of hip-hop culture and its practitioners (in many ways this has been the unifying thread of contemporary hip-hop studies), much of their work has relied on a narrow conception of hip-hop that distinguishes it from rap. Within this limited and limiting framework, debates about Nas as an intellectual can only be resolved after first determining where he fits along a hip-hop/rap continuum that is often used to evaluate hip-hop artists. This framework enables fans, artists, and critics to mimic the elitist postures of earlier European traditions by creating high/low distinctions within the culture.[5] Through these distinctions, "rap" (low culture) becomes shorthand for the most problematic aspects of hip-hop culture (commercialism, sexism, violence, etc.) and "hip-hop" (high culture) is represented as a space for genuine artistry and political consciousness. These divisions also facilitate the cooptation of black art by corporate interests and parasitic (read: white) cultural forces through all too familiar divide-and-conquer tactics. An excellent example of this is the growing overrepresentation of suburban and bohemian whites within the conscious fan base, as reflected in retail consumption and concert attendance. As in the case of jazz, such trends allow ostensibly highbrow hip-hop to be dislocated from its original cultural homes and appropriated by whites and bourgeois intellectuals. Additionally, these high/low distinctions prevent us from recognizing the intellectual merit of ordinary people and popular culture.

The dilemma Nas confronts is not peculiar to him or to other black cultural workers who initially gain popularity with the general public. Those who are intellectuals by profession (i.e., professors and researchers) but begin to encroach upon the popular territory typically reserved for actors, athletes, and politicians are equally derided for their activities inside and outside of academe. Figures like Michael Eric Dyson and Cornel West, two of the most visible and influential black public intellectuals of the late twentieth and early twenty-first centuries, are met with great skepticism from those outside of the academy who question the authenticity of their organic links to community, as well as from their academic colleagues for departing from traditionally narrow and technocratic standards of academic productivity and rigor.[6] An example of the academy's intolerance with black intellectuals came in the spring of 2002, when Cornel West became embroiled in a public feud with Harvard University president Larry Summers over West's public intellectual activities, particularly his involvement with the 2004 Al Sharpton presidential campaign, appearance in the latter two *Matrix* films, and release of a spoken-word poetry (not hip-hop!) album.[7] Summers argued that such activities were unbefitting a Harvard University professor, and that West should focus exclusively on writing peer-refereed publications.

Similiar to Nas, intellectuals like Dyson and West are victims of a vicious turf war, which demands that one choose between the academy and the outside world. The stakes of this war are grounded in the assumption that "real" intellectual activity is naturally incompatible with popular culture. In short, intellectuals cannot be celebrities and celebrities cannot be intellectuals. Analogous to the artificial conscious/commercial divide within hip-hop culture, this Manichean stance is underpinned by Western capitalism's emphasis on specialization over versatility, narrowness over proteanism. Within the logic of this purist ethic, academic work (as well as the academic herself) is compromised by an engagement with real-world problems. Again, like the conscious/commercial binary, such a belief obscures the ways in which the academy's walls are inevitably porous, infiltrated by myriad political agendas, ideological commitments, and relations of capital that constitute its very existence.[8]

This shortsighted stance was exemplified in 2002 when neoconservative scholars John Patrick Diggins, Gertrude Himmelfarb, Hilton Kramer, and Irving Kristol threatened to boycott an academic conference on Sidney Hook after being notified that Cornel West was added to the list of participants. When questioned, Diggins responded that he was "concerned about whether [West] has any point of view in matters of philosophy." He also added that "one would have to read at least 20 of [Hook's] books. Cornel West is such a celebrity intellectual, I don't think he'll have time for it."[9] In addition to evincing the racist paternalism that governs collegial relations with many black intellectuals, Diggins's comment speaks to a pervasive sense that an intellectual cannot "return home" after entering the realm of popular culture. Despite being perfectly qualified to speak on Sidney Hook—in addition to being the only trained philosopher on the panel—in his book *American Evasion of Philosophy* West provides a substantive, critically lauded treatment of Hook's work—West's status as a public intellectual was viewed as a professional demerit that denied him access to the very spaces that he was accused of abandoning.

The punitive treatment black intellectuals receive for functioning outside of the ivory tower is not only an outgrowth of narrow-minded romanticism, which can be excused as misguided idealism or naïveté, but also a tradition of repressing particular strands of intellectual activism. It is within this tradition that Cornel West's public support of Al Sharpton, Edward Said's demands for an end to the Israeli occupation of Palestine, and Noam Chomsky's critiques of American imperialism are treated as extracurricular and inappropriate while the pro-conservative activities of public intellectuals like Alan Dershowitz, John McWhorter, or Diane Ravitch are excused or critiqued solely on the basis of ideas. This disparity in treatment speaks to the ways in which intellectuals who work in the interest of black and brown communities are policed in an effort to transform them into "coopted progressives" rather than "intellectuals in exile" who are in the academy but not of it.[10]

Among progressive scholars, a narrow view of the life of the mind is also informed by an outmoded conception of the public intellectual that does not adequately consider the potential of popular culture as a legitimate site for transformative intellectual work. For example, Michael Eric Dyson's immediate and effective rejoinder to Bill Cosby's neoconservative critiques of the black poor beginning with his 2004 "pound cake" speech was largely linked to his ability to operate within the same spaces that Cosby used to offer his commentary.[11] Rather than merely responding within left-wing academic circles (which generally held Cosby's critiques to be facile, stale, and uninteresting except to the extent that they were linked to his celebrity status), Dyson occupied the same public venues that Cosby used to preach his hostile gospel of individual responsibility. By appearing on national television shows ranging from *Nightline* to *Rap City* and writing his best-selling book *Is Bill Cosby Right? Or Has the Black Middle Class Lost Its Mind?* Dyson was able to leverage his fame and media access in ways that countervailed Cosby's dangerous rhetoric.

While these examples demonstrate the dangers of prima facie rejections of public intellectual work, it is equally important not to ignore potential pitfalls. For Nas as well as traditional academics, access to mainstream audiences can become an end in itself, transforming them into celebrity rather than public intellectuals. Instead of functioning as an engaged cultural worker, the black intellectual is then reduced to, at best, a glib and detached cultural critic or, at worst, a politically promiscuous spokesperson for an imaginary constituency. As the work of Nas (as well as Dyson and West) suggests, however, such outcomes are not inevitable. Instead, the conditions of public prominence can be manipulated in ways that yield concrete benefits for the people represented by public intellectuals.

For both Nas and traditional academics, it is the relationship between the popular and the political that constitutes both the form and content of black public intellectual work. In his essay on Nigerian political musician Fela Kuti, Mark Anthony Neal introduces the term "celebrity Gramscian" in order to (post)modernize Gramsci's conception of organic intellectuals as the "thinking and organizing element of a particular fundamental social class."[12] As Neal argues, it is necessary to expand our definition in order to account for those organic intellectuals who utilize their fame in order to further a particular political agenda.[13] The notion of the celebrity Gramscian is extremely important for understanding the black public intellectual.

Although Neal accurately cites explicitly political (or at least politicized) hip-hop figures like Talib Kweli, Common, and Mos Def as examples of celebrity Gramscians, these artists are hampered by the mass public's general ambivalence or unawareness in relation to their music. Despite receiving sustained critical acclaim for their albums, none of the artists have attained platinum sales (the contemporary benchmark for mainstream hip-hop success) for their efforts, which, along with limited radio airplay and smaller concert venues, has undermined their ability to reach mass audiences through their music. Also, despite the "raced" nature of their music—all of the artists openly draw from black musical traditions and openly write their music for black audiences—the primary consumers of their live and recorded music are not African American.[14] On the contrary, Nas's consistent platinum sales and largely urban black fan base are a testament both to his ability to successfully move across the commercial and conscious worlds and to his efficacy as a celebrity Gramscian.

As Grant Farred argues in his book *What's My Name*, the nexus between the popular and the political within black intellectual spaces is linked to the vernacular tradition.[15] Through this tradition, which is rooted in an engagement with the popular, we are able to understand how a wide range of figures engage in intellectual activity. For Farred, Bob Marley's music, Muhammad Ali's "trash talking," Stuart Hall's theory, and CLR James's writing, despite their disparate ideologies and vocational locations, can all be seen as legitimate intellectual production that operates in the interests of their respective communities. With regard to Nas, the site of intellectual labor is rap music, which is steeped in the hip-hop vernacular traditions of storytelling and signifyin'.[16] Through his music, Nas engages in rigorous intellection in the form of cultural criticism and public pedagogy.

Like other black public intellectuals, Nas uses the public sphere as a space for critically engaging pressing social issues of the day. While Nas's cultural critiques are often conveyed through explicitly political songs like "I Want to Talk to You" and "New World," such commentaries have typically failed to garner critical approval or commercial attention.[17] On the contrary, Nas's most successful work has emerged more comfortably through the practice of lyrical storytelling. Through his lyrical representations, Nas functions as an informal ethnographer by consistently offering an on-the-ground counternarrative of day-to-day ghetto life.

Unlike intellectuals who operate within traditional academic spaces, Nas faces a unique burden of authenticity when engaging in his storytelling practices. In addition to personal stories, Nas's music also includes third-person narratives and autobiographical fiction. Although these are common Western literary devices, they conflict with hip-hop's authenticity fetish, which demands that artists "keep it real," or rap exclusively about personal experience. Within this context, to be "real" is to participate in particular practices (violence, drug use, etc.) or to have access to specific experiences (poverty, absentee parenting, etc.) that have become normalized within the hip-hop context. As such, Nas's stories must also withstand intense biographical scrutiny in order to qualify as legitimate. Jay-Z's critiques from the diss record "The Takeover," where he accuses Nas of merely witnessing the ghetto as a spectator rather than "really living it," reflect this sensibility.[18] While Jay-Z's allegations, which allude to Nas's vivid *Illmatic* narratives (he later references the "Tec on the dresser" from "Represent"), are intended to expose Nas for his alleged lack of authenticity, they also speak to Nas's uncanny ability to accurately represent his surroundings.

Since Nas functions as a black public intellectual, the value of his lyrical narratives cannot be reduced to their coherence with narrow and arbitrary standards of authenticity, but on their ability to relocate previously overlooked stories from the margins to the center of public consciousness. For example, Nas makes a reference in "Halftime" to the "foul cop that shot Garcia." While Nas's lyrics suggest a level of intimacy with the situation that (if we are to believe Jay-Z) he uses to deliberately overstate his ghetto affiliations, the truth of Nas's story is subordinate to its political potential. In fact, an obsession with the "realness" of the narratives (i.e., if Garcia actually existed, whether or not Nas knew him, and if a cop actually shot him) is counterproductive, as it directs attention away from Nas's implicit claims about police brutality as a common feature of urban life.

Skepticism about the stories of the relatively powerless is not restricted to hip-hop culture, as many academics, politicians, and everyday citizens remain wary of individual stories out of deference to dominant (often called "generalizable," "scientific," or "objective") narratives about the world. In the case of the aforementioned reference to Nas and police brutality, many critics would argue that Nas's individual experiences are atypical and therefore cannot be used to refute accepted claims about the day-to-day practices of police in urban spaces.[19] It is, however, the matter-of-fact manner in which Nas references police brutality (he devotes only one line to the event and does nothing to suggest that it was unusual) that underscores its commonness. By presenting police officers as routinely and unsurprisingly violent, Nas is able to offer an important counternarrative to the dominant belief that in urban America police are agents of order and justice, rather than terror and repression.

Like many hip-hop artists, Nas's stories are rooted in what Murray Forman calls the "extreme local," which refers to hip-hop culture's focus on specific cities, neighborhoods, area codes, and housing projects.[20] It is through the extreme local that Nas is able to spotlight and humanize ghetto suffering by appending names and faces to otherwise distant and abstract narratives about urban ghettos. Queens, New York, and more specifically the Queensbridge housing projects, is the primary setting for Nas's stories. This narrative commitment to the extreme local is immediately demonstrated in the first verse of "Halftime," where Nas "shouts out" (verbally acknowledges) the "forty side" as "the place that has given me grace." By locating himself within his neighborhood, Nas is able to engage in what Michael Eric Dyson calls "Africeture," or the practice of people of African descent writing themselves into existence.[21] In this case, the residents of Queens and its surrounding area are given narrative life through Nas's rhetorical gestures. The connection between "Africeture" and the "extreme local" is critical for understanding Nas's vocation as a black public intellectual. By placing the lives and experiences of particular communities within the public sphere vis-à-vis his storytelling practices, Nas is able to account for people who historically have been rendered anonymous. Through this act, Nas crafts a new counternarrative of black existence for his generation.

Despite growing scholarly discussion of the role and function of modern black public intellectuals, little direct attention has been paid to the *pedagogical* dimensions of their work. As critical educators have argued, pedagogy, the practice of teaching and learning, is not exclusively or even primarily confined to formal schooling or official subjects such as English or mathematics. Instead, the entire social world serves as a classroom in which particular beliefs, values, identities, and stories are sanctioned at the expense of others. Through this broader understanding of education and pedagogy, we are able to understand how public intellectuals function outside of the classroom as public educators for their respective constituencies. There is hardly a better example than Nas, whose work reflects the particular importance of "public pedagogy" for black communities, as well as the unique role of hip-hop artists in articulating and informing public discourse.

Due in large part to the persistence of structures, both legal and de facto, that have limited or completely obstructed their access to quality formal education since slavery, black people have often looked outside of schools for learning.[22] In addition, those who have had the benefit of formal schooling often depend on out-of-school educations in order to earn a "dual degree," or a supplemental education designed to ward off the disingenuous, disempowering, and dehumanizing aspects of the official school curriculum.[23] The sites for black public pedagogy have been various counterpublic spaces such as churches and mosques, barbershops, and black bookstores.[24] Within these locations, black people have been able to share alternate forms of knowledge and affirm their fundamental humanity within relatively safe and supportive communities.[25]

The centrality of out-of-school learning is critical to an analysis of Nas's work as a public intellectual. Although he dropped out of school in the eighth grade, Nas's musical corpus reflects a high degree of literacy that is indebted to an intellectual tradition largely ignored by formal schooling. Like many other rappers, Nas demonstrates a familiarity with a black intellectual canon that is transmitted primarily outside of school.[26] This canon includes the radical black Islamic traditions, such as the Nation of Islam and the Nation of Gods and Earths (Five Percenters), as well as black nationalist traditions like the Black Panthers. The most prominent intellectual vein in Nas's work comes from what can be broadly called the Afrocentric intellectual tradition, which informs the most ennobling and troubling aspects of Nas's public pedagogy.

Since the rise of political rap in the late 1980s and early 1990s, the Afrocentric paradigm has been highly influential in progressive rap discourse.[27] While more sophisticated forms of Afrocentricity attempt to counter European cultural imperialism by challenging its claims to universality, crude forms of Afrocentricity merely replace Eurocentric truth claims with equally dubious tales of a utopian African past.[28] This romantic sentiment is reflected in much of the "conscious" hip-hop corpus. For example, artists like Ras Kass, Public Enemy, Dead Prez, and Talib Kweli have all painted romantic, or at least uncritical, portraits of Africa in the body of their music.

It is this uncritical, historically suspect portrayal of Africa and its inhabitants that often emerges in Nas's more didactic songs like "I Can," in which he provides a highly questionable history lesson that paints Africa as a utopia. Like many of his peers—both conscious rappers and Afrocentric scholars—Nas frequently articulates narratives about pre- and postcolonial

African life that reflect a preoccupation with placing Africa on equal footing with Europe. While useful for self-esteem building, particularly in comparison to the current body of mainstream rap music, this approach forces the African into a perennially defensive posture, always measuring herself against the oppressive forces that the Afrocentric paradigm encourages her to discard.

In addition to his problematic depictions of Africa, Nas's public pedagogy reiterates the "bitch/queen binary" that has plagued "conscious" hip-hop discourse since its inception.[29] In this narrow-minded split, women are either abused rhetorically and physically as "bitches," "hos," "chickenheads," and "tip drills," or placed on pedestals as pure and virtuous objects of male protection and genuflection as "queens," "goddesses," and "earth mothers." The latter half of this binary (and in some ways the former) is also an inheritance of the black nationalist (such as the Black Panthers) and black Islamic (such as the Nation of Islam) traditions. The gender politics of these traditions have historically privileged male-centered political agendas, often under the misguided premise of restoring the purity of the black female.

It is this propensity toward female objectification that drives Nas's misogynistic commercial releases like "You Owe Me," as well as their "conscious" counterparts like "I Can," where he emphasizes the importance of young girls getting married and becoming the "queen" of their husbands. This failure to recognize the complexity and full humanity (and full range of sexual and social identities) of black women undermines the progressive inclinations of Nas and his conscious counterparts. While male artists like Jay-Z ("I'm Che Guevara with bling on") and Common ("Dealin' with alcoholism and Afrocentricity") are presented to the world as complicated beings, women are typically forced to be "either bitches or Queen Mama Zulu."[30]

Although these tendencies are highly problematic and demand intense critique, they do not undermine a claim about Nas's status as an intellectual. As scholars such as Hazel Carby have argued, the black intellectual tradition within and outside the academy has been permeated by well-meaning but nonetheless patriarchal projects that operate against the interests of black women.[31] With regard to Nas's romantic discussions of Africa, such allegations continue to serve as fodder for "culture war" debates about Afrocentricity, multiculturalism, and black studies. As such, Nas's examples of reactionary cultural and gender politics, however flawed, place him within the same intellectual vicinity as many recognized black intellectuals. More importantly, by placing these tensions within the public consciousness, Nas demonstrates an ethic of intellectual risk that is requisite for transformative public intellectual work.

It is worth noting that these issues neither exhaust nor dominate Nas's musical corpus. In contrast, "Halftime" reflects a more subtle and nuanced form of African-centered pedagogy that resists, or at least avoids, the aforementioned tendencies and is delivered through a brilliant deployment of the hip-hop vernacular tradition. Through "Halftime," Nas demonstrates his commitment to the hip-hop vernacular tradition by engaging in one of hip-hop's primary lyrical exercises: the battle. Unlike many battle songs (e.g., "Ether" or "The Takeover"), where a rapper stages a personal attack against another rapper, Nas uses "Halftime" to spar with an imaginary opponent by boasting about his lyrical prowess. While this type of battle is a common practice within hip-hop (although hip-hop's increased focus on personalized battles and physical violence has reduced its salience), Nas also uses it for a pedagogical purpose, as demonstrated in the opening verse of "Halftime":

You couldn't catch me in the streets without a ton of reefer

That's like Malcolm X, catchin' the Jungle Fever

> King poetic, too much flavor, I'm major
> Atlanta ain't braver, I'll pull a number like a pager

And in the final verse of the song:

> And in the darkness, I'm heartless like when the narcs hit
> Word to Marcus Garvey I hardly sparked it

In these six lines, Nas sustains our attention with skillful lyricism while simultaneously giving historical nods to key figures and sites of the black freedom struggle. Malcolm X, Martin Luther King, Marcus Garvey, Atlanta, Georgia, and Spike Lee's controversial 1991 race film, *Jungle Fever* (which may have also been mentioned as a way of subtly dissing its inferior counterpart, *Zebrahead*) are all cited in this battle rap.

Nas's references to Malcolm X, Martin Luther King, and Marcus Garvey also demonstrate his sustained commitment to political subject matter in spite of the culture's shift from overtly political music like Public Enemy and Sista Souljah to the gangster rap sounds of Ice-T, NWA, and Snoop Dogg that had begun to dominate both hip-hop and American popular music. At a historical moment when drugs, violence, and misogyny were becoming mainstream hip-hop's central themes and conscious hip-hop was again relegated to hip-hop's underground, "Halftime" and the rest of *Illmatic* represented a viable commercial alternative that appealed to fans of various orientations without mitigating its critical intensity.

The notion of Nas as a black public intellectual is not a mere theoretical indulgence but a sorely needed act of resistance during desperate and trying times. By reimagining the form, substance, and sources of black intellectual life, we are better equipped to challenge the forces that have denied the existence of fundamental intelligence and humanity among ordinary black people. Through this shift, we can find new sites of possibility for knowledge, struggle, and, most importantly, hope.

41ST SIDE SOUTH

"MEMORY LANE"

ON JAZZ, HIP-HOP, AND FATHERS

6

MARK ANTHONY NEAL

For much of my life I've watched my father from a distance. The distance was not so much physical—homie was definitely on his regular grind, but he was always *there*—as metaphorical. A product of the last stages of the Great Migration, my father hit the hardscrabble concrete of New York City—Harlem to be specific—in 1959, having spent the first twenty-four years of his life living just outside of Augusta, Georgia. Truth be told, my father never really left rural Georgia. He regularly summoned the spirits of the South into our apartment on Sunday mornings as he sat in the living room (a glass of whiskey not far away) listening to the sounds of the South on his hard-earned Fisher stereo. Gospel groups like Sam Cooke and the Soul Stirrers, the Mighty Clouds of Joy, and the Dixie Hummingbirds or the down-home (via Chicago and New York) blue notes of B.B. King, Bobby "Blue" Bland, the late Jimmie Smith, and Jimmy McGriff provided sustenance for a man, who, like the unnamed subject of Gladys Knight's "Midnight Train to Georgia," often wanted to return to the "world he left behind." My father said little about that world he left behind and even less about the challenges he faced in the "big city." Instead, he let the music speak for him. Eventually I began to *hear* my father's music—that of a migrant son trying to come to terms with an inadequate education, inequitable wages, and a tenuous relationship with the promise of America. When Sam Cooke and the Soul Stirrers sang "That's Heaven to Me," for my father, that was the hope that I would achieve all that he couldn't.

Like my father, Olu Dara was a migrant son. Born and raised in Natchez, Mississippi, twenty-three-year-old Charles Jones III was discharged from the navy in 1964 and landed in New York City. Charles Jones III was part of a generation of southern black men who could smell freedom just around the corner. Serving in the armed forces enabled those men to put a down payment on that freedom. In the armed services men like Jones and some of his contemporaries such as alto saxophonist Lou Donaldson or former James Brown sideman Fred Wesley Jr. traveled the world and passed time honing their skills as musicians. With the breezes of change blowing through black America, by the end of the 1960s Jones had dubbed himself Olu Dara and with his little cornet in hand, began to play the music that helped synthesize his deep Mississippi roots with the dramas of the built environment of New York City—a sound he would refer to as "gumbo." As Dara admitted in an interview, "I knew in the back of my mind that I always wanted to combine my experiences and not settle for one sound."[1] Art Blakely, Taj Mahal, Leon Thomas, Julius Hemphill, Oliver Lake, and Arthur Blythe—part of a New York–based avant-garde with roots in the black arts movement of the 1960s—were among the artists Dara performed with during his first decade in New York. Also during that first decade Dara met and later married Fannie Ann Jones, eventually settling in the Queensbridge projects in Queens, New York.

Dara's oldest son, Nasir bin Olu Dara Jones, was born in the place affectionately known as "the Bridge," not so ironically, at a time when the "gumbo" that Dara sought in his music was simmering throughout the five boroughs of New York City. The Queensbridge projects—which the elder Jones refers to as "Little Africa"—were part of a generation of federally subsidized public housing projects that offered a "moving on up" alternative to the dusty tenement housing that was part of the lore of the immigrant experience in New York City. As many of these projects were being erected, there was a critical influx of migrants from the South, as well as immigrants from South America and the Caribbean, creating the context for a rich exchange of culture—the literal sounds and smells in the hallways of twenty-story high-rises. This particular gumbo—the embryonic musings of the thing we now call hip-hop—was the product of the spaces and places shared by African Americans and a generation of immigrants from both the Spanish- and English-speaking Caribbean. Yes, spaces and places, like the Donald Byrd song "Places and Spaces," later sampled by Pete Rock and CL Smooth, that refers to the liminal experiences of immigrant and migrant communities, for which "here" and "there" are something beyond geographical. Literal places like the Queensbridge projects or the Bronx River houses of Afrika Bambaataa lore that helped provide a home for folk for whom movement was as much about what they dreamed as it was where they hoped to reside one day. Two generations after many of these projects were built, the economic opportunities that had brought so many to the big city in the first place disappeared and the projects themselves became a metaphor for dreams deferred.

I grew up a few miles away from Bronx River in the Throggs Neck Houses, and I have vivid memories of me and my boys beating on hallway windows, trying to re-create the rhythmic intensity we heard in the streets. Hundreds of other cats must have honed their skills in project hallways, trying to get down with the heat that was happening in the park. Our parents called it noise: "How come they won't let the whole record play and why they wearing out the needle like that?" The more enterprising shorties got to making pause-button tapes on first-generation boom boxes—looping the break beats of tracks like T-Connection's "Groove to Get Down" or Captain Sky's "Super Sporm" by hitting the pause button after the break and then recording again at the beginning of the break—and playing them in those same project hallways, common areas, and bedrooms. No one made much of these micromoments in hip-hop history at the time—I'm talking the mid-to-late 1970s—as even the grown cats doing it for real in the park ignored most of the stuff happening in project bedrooms. But the same cats who were too young to partake in the burgeoning scene, except by looking out "project windows," possessed skills that were well polished when they were old enough to be out in the street. Against all of the conventional thinking, the projects were not the place where our fathers' dreams simply died, but the place where their sons and daughters incubated a culture that has thrived for thirty-five years; the projects themselves were the metaphoric and literal woodshed for a sound that we simply call hip-hop.

Nasir Jones once sat in those "project windows." By the time he turned twenty-one, many referred to Olu Dara's son as the "'king of new york," one of the greatest hip-hop artists to emerge out of the New York metropolitan area. *Illmatic*, the poetic and cinematic debut recording from Nas, helped establish his credentials early on as the heir to a legacy that includes rhyming geniuses such as Melle Mel and Rakim. To his credit, Nasir Jones—Nas—is clear about the relationship between his music and his father's: "My music is the child of his music."[2] Though Olu Dara appears on "Life's a Bitch," the most striking use of jazz on his son's recording is the song "Memory Lane," produced by DJ Premier. "Memory Lane" samples the music of soul jazz organist Rueben Wilson from his recording "We're in Love" (from *Set Us Free*, 1971). As the title suggests, "Memory Lane" is a nostalgic narrative about Nas's childhood and teen years in the Queensbridge housing project. In many regards Nas shares the experience of many in his generation growing up in public housing during the age of deindustrialization, when high unemployment rates, black-on-black crime, and drug-related incarcerations were part of the normal terrain. Throughout, Nas is more observer than participant ("I hung around the older crews while they sling smack to dingbats"), though his ability to be at the center of the mix buttresses his position as a lyricist: "I rap divine Gods check the prognosis, is it real or showbiz?/My window faces shootouts, drug overdoses/Live amongst no roses, only the drama, for real." Noticeably missing is any mention of Nas's father, though his presence is so palpable in the music.

For so many black men and their fathers, their relationship is marked by distinct silences—each marking his own masculinity with the subtleties of respect, fear, anger, arrogance, disappointment, pride, and wonder that are rarely directed at each other, but always lurking unspoken. My father and I rarely broached any subject beyond casual banter about baseball, the weather, and as I got older, his fixation with my annual salary. I've always sensed a world of emotions and ideas that remained the undiscovered country of our relationship. The late filmmaker Marlon Riggs suggested much the same in his film *Black Is, Black Ain't.* On occasion it has been the music that has powerfully filled those silences between sons and fathers—the sharing of generational melodies, rhythms, cadences, harmonies, dissonances—and the grudging acknowledgment that perhaps there was a common grounding. For my father and me, it was the singing of Sam Cooke, Marvin Gaye, and Joe Ligon, lead singer of the Mighty Clouds of Joy. Such sharing moments might even be more profound when both father and son are musicians, as is the case with Dara and Nas. According to Nas, "When we get together, there's no words thrown away, no idle talk. . . . We'll sit down, play drums and just conversate musically."[3] And indeed Olu Dara and his son Nas have been fortunate to record some of their musical "conversations."[4]

When Nas and Olu Dara released the single "Bridging the Gap" (from Nas's double disc recording *Street's Disciple*) in late 2004, much was made of their collaboration, in part because the recording occasioned the kind of intergeneration conversation seemingly missing in the relations between the hip-hop generation and its elders. The theme of "Bridging the Gap" centers on lyrics made famous by Muddy Waters in his song "Mannish Boy" ("Now when I was a young boy/At the age of five/My mother said I'll be/The greatest man alive"). In "Bridging the Gap" Dara recounts, in a slurred southern drawl, "I named the boy Nasir . . . I told him as a youngster, he'll be the greatest man alive." Throughout the song, Nas's lyrics are buttressed by his father's invocation of the pride and integrity that he instilled in his son as a child. Nas uses his father's assertions as an opportunity to pay tribute to his father's music and to highlight the role of that music in their relationship ("Bridging the gap from the blues, to jazz, to rap/The history of music on this track/Born in the game, discovered my father's music/Like Prince searchin' through boxes [in] *Purple Rain*"). Nas refers to a scene in the film *Purple Rain*, where Prince's character "the Kid," discovers sheet music to songs that his father had written. Throughout the film, "the Kid" and his father are at odds—often violently—but "the Kid's" discovery provides another context for him to better understand his father as an artist and ultimately as man. No doubt for men like myself and Nas, having an intimate relationship with the music and culture that produced our fathers has given us deeper appreciation for the world that they navigated.

More specifically, "the Kid's" embrace of his father's music (he performs his father's composition "Purple Rain" at the end of the film) places his own iconoclasm into a broader framework. For the hip-hop generation, the aforementioned scene in *Purple Rain* is not unlike the experience of "digging in the crates." As Joe Schloss suggests in his book *Making Beats: The Art of Sample-Based Hip-Hop,* "digging in the crates," "the process of acquiring rare, usually out-of-print, vinyl records for sampling purposes" has become a highly developed skill."[5] While "digging in the crates" is often thought of exclusively in the context of pushing the boundaries of hip-hop production (Schloss argues that this is an integral component of sample-based hip-hop production), there are DJs, MCs, and producers who found useful hip-hop beats in the record collections of their parents. For some of these artists, sampling is as much an opportunity to recover and recontextualize the past, including their own relationship with their parents, as it is an act furthering the art, particularly when that musical past is connected to intimate relationships.

In his book, *Race Music,* scholar and musician Guthrie Ramsey Jr. argues that the kinds of intervention noted above are part of a larger phenomenon of cultural memory. According to Ramsey, music and other forms of cultural expression "function as reservoirs in which cultural memories reside. These memories allow social identities to be knowable, teachable, and learnable."[6] Ramsey refers to the site where cultural memory is performed as "community theater," where "communal rituals" and "everyday blackness . . . combine to form living photographs, rich pools of experiences, and a cultural

strumental version on his album *Hot Dog*. Twenty-five years later a sample from Donaldson's recording was the featured loop on Brand Nubian's "Punk Jump Up to Get Beat Down," stimulating interest in Donaldson's music and that of drummer Idris Muhammad, his frequent collaborator.

In this context, hip-hop is not only creating a new audience for aging jazz musicians but also making a claim on the critical importance of music in the lives of those on the political and economic margins of American life. In this context, hip-hop as a cultural practice was doing real archival and archeological work that recovered notions of community and pleasure that desegregation and deindustrialization had long placed in distress. For a postsoul artist like Nas, neighborhood jazz clubs and dance halls belong to the nostalgic memories of old men like his father. But a track like "Memory Lane" recovers the utility of those institutions for a generation that experiences the project bench, fenced basketball court, and other common areas as sites of communal leisure and community. Ironically, attacks on sampling—largely for a failure to properly credit the artists whose music is appropriated—have made it more difficult for the kind of intergenerational connections that a track like "Memory Lane" hastens. Given the history of recording companies exploiting their artists, much of the policing of sampling in hip-hop has little to do with the publishing claims of older musicians themselves, but rather with the corporate entities seeing the music as a product and not something that was living and vital to the lives of the audiences the music was largely intended for. Thus sampling has become a bit of an outlaw act, in which crafty producers deftly obscure the source material for their artistic expression. But since many of these sampling practices help create the context for intergenerational exchange, particularly among black fathers and sons, the policing of hip-hop sampling could have the added effect of undermining such opportunities. Perhaps understanding the stakes, Nas suggests that his collaboration with his father on a track like "Bridging the Gap" was a "powerful message—and a dangerous one, because a lot of people don't want to see a black man with his father."[8]

When Nas and his father first collaborated professionally on the track "Life's a Bitch," it was released at a time when hip-hop artists were mining the crates of hard bop and soul jazz recordings from the late 1950s and 1960s. DJ Premier and Guru of Gangstarr emerged at the forefront of the so-called hip-hop jazz movement on the strength of their relationship with saxophonist Branford Marsalis and filmmaker Spike Lee—Gangstarr's "Jazz Thing," a history of jazz set to hip-hop beats, was featured on the soundtrack to Lee's film *Mo Betta Blues* (1990). A year later, Dream Warriors helped further popularize hip-hop jazz hybrids with "My Definition of a Boombastic (Jazz Style)," which sampled liberally from Quincy Jones's 1962 classic "Soul Bossa Nova," a song that was also sampled later by Ludacris for "Number One Spot" (2004). Several prominent hip-hop producers became adept at using jazz-based samples, particularly Ali Shaheed Muhammad of a Tribe Called Quest and Pete Rock of Pete Rock and CL Smooth. By the time Digible Planets released their debut, *Reachin' (A New Refutation of Time and Space)*, which sampled music from Sonny Rollins and Art Blakey—the horn line from "Rebirth of Slick (Cool Like Dat)" is drawn from the latter's 1978 recording "Stretching"—there was a full-fledged hip-hop jazz movement in motion. This so-called movement encompassed hip-hop groups whose sound was indebted to jazz (The Pharcyde, US3) and high-profile collaborations between jazz and hip-hop artists, notably Donald Byrd's work with Guru on *Jazzamatazz, Volume One* (1993) and Easy Mo Be's production on Miles Davis's final studio recording, *Doo-Bop* (1992). In addition, several jazz artists recorded albums that incorporated hip-hop sensibilities, including M-Base saxophonists Steve Coleman (*A Tale of Three Cities*, 1995) and Greg Osby (3-*D Lifestyles*, 1993).

Hip-hop's affinity for jazz, particularly the subgenres of hard bop and soul jazz, is not surprising. Jazz critic David Rosenthal describes hard bop as "expressive . . . sometimes bleak, often tormented, but always cathartic."[9] Olu Dara's cornet solo on Nas's "Life's a Bitch" literally embodies Rosenthal's description. Just as hard bop was the basic idiom of black youth in the decades immediately after World War II, by the time *Illmatic* was released, hip-hop was generally accepted as the preferred idiom of black youth in the United States. Nas was at the forefront of a renaissance of East Coast hip-hop. After nearly half a decade of commercial dominance by West Coast artists such as Hammer, N.W.A., Ice Cube, and Dr. Dre—responding to the early hegemony of East Coast hip-hip—a distinct East Coast style of so-called gangsta rap appeared, led by the late Notorious B.I.G., the Wu-Tang, Kool G Rap, and Nas. Some of these recordings featured what I refer to as a "brooding introspection," which highlighted the existential realities that dictated an engagement with street-level criminality—tracks like Wu Tang's "C.R.E.A.M.," the Notorious B.I.G.'s "Everyday Struggles," and Nas's "Life's a Bitch" serving as prime examples.[10] In this artistic environment it was only natural that Nas would seek to integrate jazz into the sound of *Illmatic*, but of course Nas's interest in the music was more profound.

For a young man growing up in urban New York, the jazz landscape that proves so fertile to many of the ideas on *Illmatic*, particularly on the track "Memory Lane," was a love letter to the life that his parents imagined for themselves and their children as well as a deliberate attempt to reach out to his father and the men of his generation. Much has been made about the absence of black men in the lives of their sons (it has often been cited as a national crisis), but the presence of jazz in hip-hop music clearly shows that those men have always had a presence in the lives—and the music—of their sons.

"ONE LOVE," TWO BROTHERS, THREE VERSES

7

MICHAEL ERIC DYSON

["One Love"] just came from life, it's a song about letters to prison inmates, friends of mine, shout-outs to childhood friends and their uncles and people who were like family to me. I was, again, too young to be going through all of that. That's what I think about when I hear that album. I was too young to be going through all of that.
—Nas, *ROLLING STONE*, 2007

When I first heard Nas's "One Love," cast in the form of letters to friends locked in prison, I thought immediately of my brother Everett, who is serving a life sentence for a murder I believe he didn't commit. Sure, he sold drugs on the tough Detroit streets on which we both hustled and matured. But that doesn't justify his incarceration for a crime he's innocent of, even as he takes responsibility for his errors and manages to find the good in his bad circumstance. "I've not always made the best of choices," Everett says, "and therefore I must suffer the results thereof. I've learned that. However, I've come to learn also that going through this does not negate the fact that I can become what I choose to become."[1]

By the time Nas's song appeared in 1994, Everett had been in the "stone hotel" for five years. Now he's been locked down for twenty years, his plight captured in a nationally televised 2008 CNN special on black men hosted by Soledad O'Brien that ended by focusing on me and Everett.

Whenever the segment on me and Everett aired in a screening across the country, I invariably received an email, call, or comment from another black person, telling me that *our* story is *their* story. Not necessarily our particular truth—one brother an author and professor, the other a prisoner incarcerated with a life sentence. But so many black families are plagued by a similar mathematics of misery: prospering members are divided from loved ones behind steel bars, multiplying the cruel twists of fate. One may teach, as I did for years, at Penn. The other is locked away in the pen.

The temptation is to believe that the individual choice Everett spoke of accounts for such differences in destiny. Successful black family members did their work and played by the rules; suffering family members ran afoul of the law and were locked away, as they are in "One Love." There is a vicious prison system that hungers for young black and brown bodies. In America, the more young black and brown folk are thrown in jail, the more cells are built, and the more money is made. As a society we spend far more money on penitentiaries than university education for poor black and brown males. During the 1980s and 1990s, state spending for corrections grew at six times the rate of state spending on higher education.[2] Moreover, American incarceration has been globally exported. Torturous practices flare at the U.S.-operated military prison at Guantanamo Bay, the detention center at the U.S. Air Force Base at Bagram, and the American-run military prison at Abu-Ghraib in Iraq, all part of what cultural critic Judith Butler has termed the "new war prison."[3]

Even as 2 million Americans occupy prisons and jails, prison and jail have come to occupy the American imagination in everything from sobering foundation reports to fiery rap lyrics. According to a 2008 Pew Center report, there are 1,596,127 adults stowed in state or federal prisons, and another 723,131 locked in local jails. The total of 2,319,258 sums up an astonishing statistic: more than 1 in every 100 Americans is incarcerated in America. Predictably, the news is even worse for blacks and Latinos. For white men over 18, 1 in 106 are behind bars. For Latino men, the number is 1 in 36, and for black men, it's 1 in 15 locked up. Sadder still, for black men between 20 and 34, the number is a startling 1 in 9 behind bars. In light of these depressing numbers, it is no mystery why incarcerated young black males occupy so much space in hip-hop's lyrical universe.[4]

It makes demographic sense for rappers to seriously grapple with prison and jail, especially since hip-hop culture is largely created by the young males who are most vulnerable to incarceration. Just as they grapple with the plagues of poverty and police brutality, hip-hop artists contend with the prison bars that seal the fate of many of their peers, and in some visible cases, that of rappers too. Hip-hop's roots in working-class and poor black communities make its artists attuned to the hardscrabble conditions that either become fodder for rap careers or an expressway to incarceration. The lyrics of rap artists are flooded by references to prison, making up an informal "carceral canon,"[5] including songs as varied as Ice T's "The Tower," Public Enemy's "Black Steel in the Hour of Chaos," Akon and Styles P's "Locked Up," AZ's "Fan Mail," and Jay-Z's "Do You Wanna Ride."

In 1995 a distinct shift occurred: no longer rapping *about* prison, hip-hop's artists were increasingly rapping *from* prison, or at least releasing records while they were accumulating prison records. That year Tupac Shakur stalled in a prison cell on a sexual abuse conviction as his CD *Me Against the World* rocketed to the top of the pop charts in its first week of release. Nearly a decade later, rapper Shyne was in prison on a first-degree assault and reckless endangerment conviction as his CD *Godfather Buried Alive* debuted at number 3 on Billboard's album charts. He even recorded a remix of a single from his CD in his jail cell. In 2005 rapper Cassidy, incarcerated and facing first-degree murder charges (he was later cleared), released his CD *I'm a Hustla*, which debuted at number 5 on Billboard's album charts. Rapper Beanie Sigel's *B. Coming* CD debuted at number 3 on the music charts in 2005 while he was incarcerated on a federal weapons charge. And Lil' Kim released her CD *The Naked Truth*, which debuted at number 6 on the Billboard 200 charts, while she was imprisoned on a perjury conviction.[6]

The list of other rappers who have served time doesn't just include superstars like T.I., who went to jail on a weapons conviction at the height of his career, and men like John Forte, DMX, DJ Quik, and Prodigy. The roll call also includes female rappers like Foxy Brown, Da Brat, and Remy Ma. Beyond the realm of rap, doing time has become a tragic rite of passage for too many black youth, often harming their chances for sound employment and stable family life after getting snagged inside the machinery of the prison-industrial complex. Thus prison supplies a metaphorical and literal destination for black males. Partially in self-defense, they drape poetry around their imprisoned limbs or those of their jailed loved ones and offer a sometimes negative glory to the prison cell as an unavoidable stop on their journey to manhood.

Nas's sonic epistle "One Love" trades on many of the conventions established in hip-hop's carceral canon—remembering one's "homies" locked away, speaking about the harsh circumstances of their incarceration, decrying the social forces that left them little choice to pursue an illegal path that ended in prison. But it also occupies territory staked out by the Apostle Paul and Martin Luther King Jr.—and by figures as diverse as Mohandas Gandhi, Malcolm X, Dietrich Bonhoeffer, George Jackson, the Marquis de Sade, Mumia Abu-Jamal, Fidel Castro, Wei Jingsheng, Imam Jamil Al-Amin, Thomas More, Jean Genet, Birtukan Midekssa, and Antonio Gramsci. Their letters and other writings from prison offer wisdom, express political dissent, explore the criminal mind and lifestyle, proclaim their innocence, analyze social ills, trumpet religious conversion, tout spiritual awakening, uplift fellow believers, or spark civil disobedience and social protest.

But Nas also reverses the trend: instead of writing (better yet, speaking) the letters as an inmate, he writes to imprisoned comrades, offering them not a way out but at least a view outside the prison walls that confine them. If prison means obstructing the sights and sounds of the world beyond bars and limiting information about its happenings, Nas's narration casts a sharp eye and literate tongue on the streets from which his mates have been temporarily banned. "One Love" teems with gritty details of unfaithful lovers, menacing rivals, criminal apprentices, unseen offspring, mourning mothers, troubled siblings, and a neighborhood fraught with murder and other moral mayhem. It probes what Sohail Daulatzai terms "the carceral imagination" with lyrical elegance.[7]

"One Love" is both reportage and pep talk, a morality tale of lost innocence and lost life in degrees and proportions, a missive that smoothly melds empathy and caution. It captures poignant moments of black male intimacy and vulnerability forged in the crucible of urban desperation and poverty. In telling his friends' stories, Nas reflects on lives carved from suffering and struggle, interpreting their experience in a tale that marries vernacular and formal poetic devices.

From its opening sounds, "One Love" is located in classic black literary and musical territory. The voices of several black inmates can be heard in a prison yard during recreational activities as one prisoner excitedly speaks of "a letter I got from my man Nas." His boast not only establishes the song's epistolary conceit, linking its sonic fictional ambitions to works like Alice Walker's *The Color Purple*, but "One Love" harkens back to another black music classic: Marvin Gaye's "What's Going On." Gaye's 1970 song begins with the party banter of his friends Mel Farr and Lem Barney, who were then football stars for the Detroit Lions. In sweetly dramatic contrast to his pals' playful mood, Gaye denounces war and generational strife, and pleads for love in a heavenly tenor that weaves inside the jovial atmosphere.

Nas, however, amplifies the tone and theme of his intimates' yard exchange to comment on their plight and that of hundreds of thousands more black males. While Gaye laments the age bias of elders who distort youth culture through a moralistic lens ("who are they to judge us/simply 'cause our hair is long?" the crooner asked), Nas jumps back a generation to ride the beats of a soul jazz classic by the Heath Brothers, "Smiling Billy Suite, Part II." Rapper Q-Tip, who produced "One Love," cleverly selected a sample of the Heath Brothers track that underscores the dulcet tones of Stanely Cowell's Mbira thumb piano and a nimble Percy Heath double bass line that spreads across the melody. Q-Tip spices the sonic stew with a deftly disguised drum track borrowed from Parliament's "Come In Out of the Rain."

Nas's song-letter opens a window to the world his friends left behind, keeping them abreast of changes that directly bear on their personal lives and street hustling. In both instances, Nas's lyrics resonate with his hearers because they tap existential and epistemic roots: his knowledge of the world they inhabited is joined to his knowledge of the people and events that matter to them, making Nas a rhetorical hinge on which their insight and information swings. As their eyes and ears,

Nas spins poetry on the pavement of their existence, drawn from the textures of their stories and the threads of their ambitions and aspirations, which archives and distributes happenings in the hood and home.

The point of framing "One Love" as a letter is to root his reflections on prison in existential soil by accounting for the shifting allegiances, shattered affections, and sustaining alliances that sprout in the aftermath of incarceration. The point of telling us about Jerome's niece and Little Rob and Born's brother is to convey the menace that dogs the lives of even the youngest ghetto resident. The point of telling us about a faithless girlfriend and disappearing friends is to portray how hood relationships crumble under the pressures of survival and cutthroat competition. And the point of making things so personal is to make them universal. Beyond the chaos of urban violence and poverty, Nas expresses care for vulnerable children, hurting parents, wayward youth, and suffering friends, just as members of the broader society do. This may be the other America, but in the grammar of human aspiration and social desire, the noun is just as important as the adjective.

It is this other America that endures cruel blows to its personal and communal sense of intimacy. Not only does incarceration take a toll on prisoners, but it inflicts psychic pain and domestic distress on loved ones and communities left behind. It is this world of ruptured emotions and fractured psyches that Nas lyrically captures. "One Love" resonates so powerfully because it is a gesture of rhetorical intimacy in the form of a series of love letters—about the men who are his friends, about their families, about the members of the hood they all sprang from, and about the young men who will now be its beneficiaries or bullies. The creative force of love and intimacy weaves throughout Nas's sonic epistle and transcends the boundaries of mere reportage, ascending to elegy and exhortation.

In the opening verse of "One Love," Nas regrets that his unnamed letter recipient hadn't come to his house to escape the cops in his scrape with the law, but says that there's "no time for looking back it's done." Since many prisoners are poorly served by an obsession with how things might have turned out differently, Nas smartly chases away such thoughts with a focus on the present. Nas quickly communicates, or confirms, a number of facts to his friend: the birth of his son, the disdain his son's mother feels toward him since his imprisonment, the existence of a group of males who are his friend's bitter rivals, and the disloyalty of his son's mother who fails to write him yet fraternizes with his enemies.

Nas's knowledge of his confined comrade is similarly confined to particular quarters of his life—he hasn't yet seen his friend's son, though he knows of his existence. Nas's knowledge is instead targeted and functional, serving ethical priorities generated in an urban male culture where loyalty and bloodline are a big deal. Nas need not have seen his friend's newborn son to acknowledge his importance in a masculine stronghold where black males endure social suffering but nevertheless claim patriarchal privilege within their own clans and circles. To be a black male means to be a king and a pariah all at once. When Nas congratulates his friend for having a son, he acknowledges the pride a black male often takes in having a seed to carry his life further.

The miracle of birth is heightened when black male infants announce their existence in a cry that reverberates in moans and shrieks later in life. It is the wonder and brokenness of black male life in the ghetto that Nas implicitly grasps and shares as an unspoken bond with his jailed compatriot. Still, Nas's failure to see the son is an unavoidable metaphor for how many black males fail to witness the growth and maturity of their own sons and daughters, whether they are locked in jail or imprisoned in narrow visions of family and manhood. Having *a* son is sometimes more important than *my* son. In this sense, Nas's effort touches on the tortuous gender relations that grip the ghetto.

"One Love" configures and then complicates the poor relations between young black men and women, relations already pressured by poverty before they are further strained by an extended stay in prison. Women's harsh judgments are standard in hip-hop, making it difficult to separate the wheat of natural gender conflict from the chaff of misogyny. Nas avoids the sexist trap by framing his friend's loss of his lady with the facts of male prison life: lovers and wives often lose momentum or fall away under the unforgiving silences and distances incarceration brings. As his friend's rhetorical double and symbolic substitute, Nas speaks to, and for, his isolated brother in arms, scorning his woman's traitorous behavior while relieving him of the burden to say it himself.

Nas speaks for his friend's lady, too, as she indicts her lover for his rough behavior and his failure to heed her advice. In the "One Love" video, a female character mouths Nas's words as he spits them. In other contexts, such an act might appear as little more than patriarchal ventriloquism: a woman's mouth is moving but a man's views are spoken. Nas ties her complaint about her lover's hardheadedness into a nasty trick of subversion. The apparent concern for her man expressed in her diatribe is a deceitful prelude to stabbing him in the back by taking his rivals' side. The less his friend has to reckon with his lover joining forces with his enemies, the more time he has to adjust to a life of curbed desires and severe restrictions. His friend can claim vicarious victory without breaking a sweat or busting a gut, since Nas defeats her treachery by calling her out and naming her fatal flaw. Nas makes clear in such a gesture that the costs of incarceration are far more than the money it takes to keep prisoners locked away; they include the shredding of the bonds that tie men and women to networks of support and intimacy at home and in society.

Nas extends his charge of betrayal beyond the female realm in the second verse of "One Love," addressed to his homeboy Born, as he highlights another example of a friend joining a foe, in this case a former associate of Born's who gives Born's glock to a man he shot a year earlier. Instead of a baby in common, these men shared a "block" on which they hustled and committed crime as a crew. Nas satisfies Born's unspoken wish for justice and relieves his imprisoned friend's burdened heart by emphasizing the responsibility that comes with his liberty, pledging to Born that he would handle things for his imprisoned friend.

In this verse, and throughout the song, especially as he shouts out other friends locked away from society, Nas signifies on a lively and expansive conception of brotherhood: his "brothers" in prison, the brotherhood of males who struggle to escape the desperate circumstances of the projects, and the brotherhood of mankind implied in his complex vision of a just community that flows throughout *Illmatic*. By conceiving of his neighborhood as a brotherhood, Nas contests a strand of social criticism that views the hood as a zone of unrelieved terror that, ironically, could be supported by his lyrics that cite the lethal competition that undermines community. By acting as his brothers' keeper, their eyes and ears, their scribe and conscience, Nas generates a holistic vision of black brotherhood that reflects the goodness and potential of one man reflected in the eyes of the other, despite the prevalence of negative circumstances.

That vision of brotherhood rings in my brother Everett's words as he takes measure of the competing forces that shaped him and me as we came to maturity on the tough streets of Detroit. "Whenever I see Michael," Everett says, "it becomes testament to the fact that I could have done this, that, or the other. It becomes a testament to the fact that I can *still* do this, that, or the other." Everett also argues that despite the trauma of prison, it was perhaps the path he had to take to become his best self, just as my own path permitted my talents to shine.

> I've come to see that each man must work out his own path of life. The experiences that Michael has had, that have taken him to where he is right now, is a great and beautiful thing. Michael couldn't have been in the streets doing what I was doing, and become who he is. That's not the experiences he needed to unfold, spiritually, mentally, socially, physically. However, I couldn't have gone to Princeton, taught at Chicago Theological Seminary. I couldn't have been a critically acclaimed author and learnt the lessons that I needed to learn.

Everett also links his understanding of the familial and personal forces that shaped us to an analysis of the societal factors that shape the lives of poor black men. Everett understands, as Nas understands, too, that the bonds forged in the streets create a system of recognition and reward that is vital to all human beings. Beyond such benefits, the fundamental human cry for nurture, love, and association animates even the sometimes destructive actions of street hustlers. Nas taps into this intimate network throughout "One Love," but nowhere more poignantly than when he explores the emotional and existential bonds between struggling men.

Nas's pledge to Born, as well as his earlier defense of his unnamed chum, is a kind of lateral love, where hustling together in a crew creates bonds of masculine intimacy and loyalty. As omniscient street narrator, Nas is deliberately ambiguous about his role in the hustling he observes, though his knowledge of the details of their lives (his friend fleeing the cops, which in the video for "One Love" Nas views from his apartment window, and Born shooting a rival) suggests Nas's deep connection to his underground peers. Nas's understanding of what his imprisoned peers should know is one of the few acceptable displays of love and intimacy that even hardened men might show each other in the face of vulnerability.

In this guise, gestures of intimacy and an ethic of care for the lives of Nas's beloved "boys" bathe the lyrics of "One Love." Nas asks his unnamed pal about mutual friends and sends his greetings to others. Nas reminds his friend of the practical function of their intimate bond—men who forged connections on the street can sustain each other and try to make prison a scene of extended intimacy and care. In case there's any doubt about how Nas feels about his jailed partner, he proves that money—literal capital—can be made into the symbolic capital of emotional and spiritual intimacy when it is offered in fraternity and gratitude. "I left a half a hundred in your commissary/You was my nigga when push came to shove/One what? One love." Short of having their sentences reversed, there is nothing prisoners need more than cash and visits. Nas offers the former to his unnamed friend and the latter to Born.

The bond between Nas and Born, like all such courted and constructed intimacies, has collateral advantage and links Nas to Born's mother. After offering half a bar's progress report on Born's troubled sibling, Nas pivots from the cool grief of meditations on lost innocence, the loss of innocent life, wounded aspirations, arrested developments, and imprisoned hope to the hot grief evoked by a mourning mother. "I hate it when your moms cries/It kinda makes me wanna murder, for real-a/I even got a mask and gloves to bust slugs/But one love." The tears of Born's mother unleash in Nas a murderous empathy. Ironically, it leads him to the brink of a powerful emotional identification with her that threatens to overwhelm a reasoned refrain, both musically and morally, from the same crime that Born may have attempted. Nas escapes such a fate, at least lyrically, through a crucial conjunction: "But one love." Even in the projects, love is a superior force that brings order and encourages strategic restraint.

Nas's care shows up, too, in the events he chooses to reports on, especially the urban catastrophe that plagues young victims. "But yo, guess who got shot in the dome-piece?/Jerome's niece, on her way home from Jones Beach—it's bugged." The young lady who gets shot in the head isn't even involved in the criminal activity that gets Nas's friends sent up the river. Nas adds dramatic urgency to his reporting by naming the geographies that are the site of terror, which is all the more devastating because the locales are familiar to New York natives. It's local knowledge and inside code for the cognoscenti.

Nas extends the reach of his inside signifying and reinforces the repetitive trauma to young lives of the events he describes with internal rhyming, where rhymes impatiently repeat near the beginning and middle of sentences, and then at the end, as in "piece . . . niece . . . Beach," or in the line to Born that issues an abbreviated state of New York for the urban poor in the not-quite postcrack mid-'90s: "The crackheads stalking, loud-mouths is talking." Nas reports, too, on another young victim who got sucked into the drug game already crowded by adolescent peers: "Plus little Rob is selling drugs on the dime/Hangin' out with young thugs that all carry 9s." At the heart of Nas's description is a veiled lament of the illicit lifestyle that snares young lives, not a boast of the drug seller's gain or glory.

Hip-hop's artists have often defended themselves against the charge of adding glory to carnage by insisting that they are not making the news but reporting it. Of course, every act of reportage is also an act of interpretation, of selecting what events merit coverage and deciding how to state what happened and why, a valuable recognition for reporters as well as rappers. Nas's reportage, even at the tender age of nineteen, is long since done with the objectivity and neutrality that are ostensibly among the reporter's greatest goals. Nas is not merely transmitting but transforming knowledge. He is both reporting and editorializing; he spits facts and provides frameworks to interpret the facts he chooses to share. Nas's version of interested reporting—of reporting invested in the values, priorities, biases, and interests of the community from which he speaks—as well as his adoption of the epistolary form, gives him intellectual space to breathe in rhymes that "drop science" and share wisdom.

Nas's vision of knowledge grows from a Five Percenter view of the transformative function of self-knowledge and the appetite for "doing the knowledge" in quarters of hip-hop culture. Hip-hop often offers an alternative set of ideas to the official knowledge of society, whether from culturally conscious rappers like KRS-One, who began to unfold his compelling brand of cultural knowledge on his song "My Philosophy," to self-described "socialist guerrilla" hip-hop artist Immortal Technique, whose music draws on several of his political inspirations: Malcolm X, Che Guevara, César Chávez, Augusto César Sandino, Marcus Garvey, and Túpac Amaru II. In addition to generating a grassroots pedagogy of the oppressed, hip-hop amplifies the black cultural suspicion of, and exclusion from, sanctioned bodies of knowledge and the institutions they are tied to, including schools and churches. Ironically, prisons often became hothouses for the mental and spiritual growth of black inmates; Malcolm X is perhaps the most famous example of the personal redemption and intellectual transformation of black men behind bars. But the impulse to be critical of the religious and educational authority of dominant culture is shared more broadly in the informal but vital traditions of black male learning in prison.

In his sonic missive, Nas wars against religious and educational authority in a brilliantly condensed and breathtakingly acute four bars: "Sometimes I sit back with a Buddha sack/ Mind's in another world thinking about how we can exist through the facts/Written in school text books, bibles, et cetera/Fuck a school lecture, the lies get me vexed-er." Nas's wordplay is masterly and unmistakable. The Buddha sack that takes him to another world—another frame of mind, an alternate intellectual vision, a competing conceptual order, a rival paradigm of experience—is a variety of weed. He's mellow and his higher reasoning is freed from the constraints of conventional wisdom. But Buddhism, too, takes us to another religious world outside the hegemony of Western versions of Christianity. That tack is important. It references the Five Percenter theology Nas dabbles in and gives him the intellectual courage to link and then challenge canonical religious and educational texts. The separation of church and state might be given lip service, but Nas understands the collusion between schoolrooms and church sanctuaries in extolling narrow versions of shared truths, especially about the poor black communities Nas represents.

Nas's poetically ambiguous phrasing underscores the breadth of his dispute: when he starts "thinking how we can exist through the facts/Written in school text books, bibles, et cetera," his query is both cosmological and sociological. Nas is questioning the religious creation narratives that specify the origins of human existence. He is also interrogating the validity of history textbooks that underplay, isolate, or leave aside the existence of black culture and the "Afrocentric Asian" as Nas refers to black folk on his track "It Ain't Hard to Tell." Local knowledge trumps traditional knowledge. The knowledge of the streets, the common sense of communities whose character shines in wise sayings, sound moral habits, and skeptical inquiry is to be trusted more than institutional knowledge that denies the humanity of black folk.

Nas bravely enters the fray and draws an important distinction between schooling and education: "Fuck a school lecture, the lies get me vexed-er." The fact of Nas's inquiry—the existence of his intellectual curiosity—shows he's interested in learning and knowledge. His problem, like that of many black youth, is with the schools in which the transmission of knowledge is institutionally embedded, and too often in which cultural distortions and racial myths take on the force of fact. As he said in an interview:

> First month of ninth grade, that was my last month. School ain't shit, the teachers is full of shit, the whole system is bullshit, to me. I'm there riffin' with the teachers, dissin' the teachers. I mean, I wanted to finish school, I didn't want to drop out of school, I wanted to finish school and do something. I was drawin' and shit, I wanted to do that, or write a movie, some ill shit. I used to write all type of shit when I was young, I thought I was blessed. But they crushed that type of shit, they crushed that in my head. I dropped out of school, start to smoke weed, that's what that was all about.[8]

The lies vexed Nas so much that he dropped out of school but added a suffix to the end of the adjective, "vexed-er" in his vernacular rendering, to underscore his agitated state. Too often schools that train poor young blacks are sites of shortsightedness, or outright sightlessness, about the aims and ambitions of young learners. It is small wonder that Nas and millions more reach for the Buddha sack to weed out the lies, myths, and distortions that riddle their existence.

My brother Everett also grapples with the destructive consequences of the cultural ignorance that clouds many segments of poor black life. Everett has acknowledged the negative effect of such ignorance on his own life. He has also confessed how tragic it is that prison became for him, and for thousands more, a pedagogical opportunity to absorb critical knowledge of himself and the world.

> The law states, under the Fourteenth Amendment, that [blacks] aren't official persons. So when we go to our neighborhoods and we see death, destruction, when we see crime at a rampant pace, more so than elsewhere, when we see the mortality rate of our babies, higher than some third-world nations, then you ask the question, "Why?" And it boils down to this, simply: if we knew who we are, and had something to look to greater than the South for pride, then we would understand that we're the builders of civilizations. . . . Now isn't that sad, that I had to come to prison to learn this? Why couldn't I have been taught this in the streets? Why wasn't I taught this in our school system?

Everett apparently agrees with Nas that official religious and educational knowledge has not served poor black communities. Nas's vexation over the official knowledge of mainstream society is reflected in Everett's lamentation of black people's lack of self-knowledge. And just as Everett "had to [go] to prison" to learn his lessons, "One Love" implies that Born's prison predicament leaves him open to Nas's wisdom and the virtues of self-examination.

Nas's wisdom sings most memorably when he offers advice to Born and to a young thug to save him from his errant ways, serving as his street mentor and a teacher spreading wisdom and offering tips on survival. Nas cautioned his friend Born to "chill" after he'd used an "ox" (a blade or razor) to assault a fellow prisoner. Nas pleads with Born to "stay civilized, time flies/Though incarcerated your mind dies." Nas realizes the cruel psychic and mental effects of prison; incarceration doesn't just bind the body but kills the mind and deadens intellectual energy. (Tupac said as much when he revealed that, contrary to popular belief, he found little creative inspiration in prison.)

Nas still says that Born's prison sentence might pass more quickly were he to "stay civilized," arguably in the eyes of the prison authorities and in the interior space of his personal identity. Prison often fails to offer true penitence to prisoners, much less a civilizing or rehabilitative influence. Often those who are deemed savage and beyond correction before they get locked down find an internal moral compass to navigate through the perils of prison. That may be one meaning of the civilizing impulse Nas seeks to strengthen in his friend. It is just as likely that Nas is alluding to the Five Percenter view that imprisonment, as a tool of white supremacy, can make a "civilized" god "savage" again.

When Nas turns his attention to his young street-corner charge, his verbal mastery roars. Grabbing his weed and getting "ghost" for a couple of days respite from the projects, Nas leaves his phone and gun behind to recharge his batteries. The stress of the streets, he says, can lead to a choice between prison and the emergency or psych wards, and can "have a nigga up in Bellevue/Or HDM, hit with numbers from 8 to 10/A future in a maximum state pen is grim," he says in a dazzling display of synecdoche and metonymy. Upon his return, Nas is greeted by a youngster in a bulletproof vest rolling blunts and sporting a .32-caliber pistol for protection as he slings crack. Nas's description is novelistic, even cinematic; indeed, this verse inspired a scene in director Hype Williams's black crime film, *Belly*, starring Nas and fellow rapper DMX.

The video clip for "One Love" is equally dramatic. Directed by legendary graffiti artist and hip-hop aficionado Fab Five Freddy, "One Love" realizes Nas's lyrics through flashback scenes and weaves together visual threads of parallel events in prison and the free world. "One Love" also intercuts various shots of Nas in full color with drained black-and-white landscapes, largely in prison and in the hood, signifying the lifelessness that threatens to stifle the incarcerated and those stuck in the ghetto alike. The video portrays the precocious youngster whose illicit actions are rendered more ironic and painful by his baby-faced adolescence. As Nas's words race to catch up to the images of his young apprentice's destructive behavior, the scenes quickly shift from black-and-white to color to paint the conflicting, often confused moral energy that fuels criminal activity in the hood.

The video for "One Love" literally frames Nas as the adolescent's guide through the perilous urban terrain. Nas fills the void in the young man's life left by inadequate schooling and limited learning. Nas provides the youngster with the "unofficial" knowledge that derives from marginal sectors of society and offers invaluable insight for thriving in the hood. In the song "One Love," Nas's internal rhymes unfold furiously as he vividly portrays the life of the criminal prodigy whose ambitious corner agenda prods Nas to offer him brotherly advice from a mature hustler.

> I had to *school* him, told him don't let niggaz *fool* him
> Cause when the pistol blows the ones that's murdered be the *cool* one
> Tough luck when niggaz is *struck*, families *fucked* up
> Coulda caught
> your man, but didn't look when you *bucked* up

Mistakes happen, so take heed never bust up
At the crowd catch him solo, make the right man bleed

In a gesture of ethical triage, Nas starts with the given, that the young man, "Shorty," is committed to a life of crime that will have negative effects on his community. In offering advice based on his experience in the streets, Nas seeks to influence his young peer's thinking and minimize the devastation of his drug dealing. Nas's narrative poignantly captures the moral complications of the hustling lifestyle. It erodes the bonds of community even as it sometimes seeks to answer the social and racial inequalities that make hustling necessary and useful to so many poor men of color. The tender age of Nas's hardened student hustler is a crime in itself. It is an offense that Nas brilliantly underscores as he wrestles with the question of whether he was schooling the youngster or the youngster was schooling Nas. The elder is taken by the young man's surprisingly confident reaction to his advice.

Nas poetically acknowledges the jarring contrast between Shorty's youth and his exuberant worldliness, compelling Nas to conclude his impromptu lesson and his weed smoking. Nas understands, as St. Paul understood, that he planted the seeds, another man watered them, but only God, or destiny, or fate, could make them grow. Having done his part, Nas rises to depart, but not before releasing the inhaled smoke of a final hit of blunt, and not before acknowledging, in a beautiful metaphor, that he left "some jewels in the skull that he could sell if he chose," highlighting Nas's urban altruism. Shorty was free to treasure the precious knowledge Nas had deposited in his brain, or, like the crack he pumped, he could trade it later for cash or influence or power.

As Nas announces his final words of wisdom, it becomes clear that he is attempting to keep Shorty out of prison. As he cautions Shorty to watch out for Jake (slang for police), Nas brings "One Love" full circle and ends where he began: he couldn't prevent his unnamed friend from being caught by cops and sent to jail, but he could try to keep another young-ster free of their grasp and out of the pen. Proving useful as a secular benediction after the fact of incarceration, "one love" becomes a gesture of preventive maintenance, a cry of sur-vival uttered from a loving friend or brother.

One love. It is the phrase I often share with Everett before we hang up from a collect phone call or a prison visit. It pains me deeply—often to tears—to see him suffering so long for a crime that he didn't commit. I feel the hot grief that Nas felt when he confronted the tears of Born's mother. It hurts as well to know that prisons are being built to fit the failures and struggles of other young black and brown men just like him. In some states, future prison cells are projected to be built based on third-grade reading scores, making literacy and in-carceration indissolubly linked. Like Nas in "One Love," I feel an obligation to raise my voice in defense of millions of young black and brown men and women who may one day follow his path. I want to warn them away from the destructive personal habits that make them vulnerable to prison, much as Nas warned Shorty. But I must also cry out against a society that would punish them in such unforgiving fashion while extend-ing mercy to millions more who aren't poor or black. In my mind, it's inequality and racial injustice that are the real crimes.

Besides hearing from my brother, I get a lot of mail from many other prisoners. Recently one wrote me: "I have followed you for years. I actually grew interested in who you were when I heard a song by this rapper named Nas and he mentioned your name." I suppose I feel tied to Nas because of my brother Everett, and other prisoners may feel a tie to me because of Nas, and because of Everett. The three of us enjoy a brotherhood formed by our common experience of prison, either being incarcerated or loving those behind bars. And because our stories have reached millions more—Nas through "One Love," me and Everett because of our segment on CNN and my open letter to him published in 1996—we have formed a brotherhood, as well as a sisterhood of sorts, with thousands of other prisoners, and those who support them as they endure their plight. That feeling of intimacy and hurt, of love and grief, is what makes "One Love," like the Bob Marley song whose title it borrows, a rhetorical tour de force and a poetic blast of sonic consolation.

"ONE TIME 4 YOUR MIND"
EMBEDDING NAS AND HIP-HOP INTO A GENDERED STATE OF MIND

KYRA D. GAUNT

em•bed or im•bed v
1. fix something deeply in the mind or memory (*often passive tense*) **a.** fix (an object) firmly and deeply in a surrounding mass. ➜ verb (embeds, embedding, embedded) [with obj.] **b.** implant (an idea or feeling) so that it becomes ingrained within a particular context: the Victorian values embedded in Tennyson's poetry. **c.** [often as adj.] (embedded) design and build something as an integral part of a system or device.

While black women from the street to Spelman to Congress have launched various critiques of misogyny since the early 1990s invasion of gangsta rap, I can count the major critiques by black men in hip-hop on one hand. Most recently in 2006, Byron Hurt, a former football player, was masculine enough to launch an antisexist campaign with his PBS documentary film, *Beyond Beats and Rhymes*, focused on men in hip-hop rather than the video vixens objectified by it. Ironically, white broadcaster Don Imus triggered a hailstorm of misogynist criticism by men and women alike in April 2007 when he called black women "nappy headed hos" on air and then blamed his words on hip-hop. Even Oprah, who dislikes hip-hop, dedicated two back-to-back shows to the Imus controversy. But have we really learned about misogyny?

Years ago, I read a chapter by Eve Kosofsky Sedgwick, a queer studies scholar, that had me question the limits of my own available thinking about sexuality despite my expertise in the study of gender and the body (Sedgwick 1993).[1] Her writing left me, as a professor of hip-hop music, with a provocative thought: what would help students interested in hip-hop question the limits of their own thinking about misogyny and its impact on women *and* men? Hip-hop discourse rarely steps beyond clichéd conversations about misogyny, so I created a list of axioms—ideas or statements that people accept as self-evidently true—following Sedgwick's lead to disrupt the available thinking about Nas and black masculinity in hip-hop. The list includes ideas most know but don't seem to consider in their analysis of hip-hop:

1. Sometimes Nas spends a lot of time rapping about manhood and masculinity, other times not.

2. Some male and female hip-hop heads, of all races and all classes, experience Nas's portrayal of masculinity as deeply embedded in a matrix of gender meanings and differences. Others do not.

3. Many male and female heads have their richest mental/emotional/kinetic involvement with Nas's rhymes about acts they don't do, or even don't want to do ("Understandable smooth shit that murderers move with," from "The Thief's Theme" on *Street's Disciple*).

4. Sometimes Nas's performances are embedded in gendered contexts resonant with meaning, narrative, and connectedness to actual relationships in his life (e.g., brothers in hip-hop, his father, his wife,

his daughter, to children); sometimes it is important that they not be (murderers, Mafia bosses); at
other times, it may not occur to Nas, his audience,
or his critics that they might be.

Sometimes there is little willingness to go to the edge of
what's familiar and look beyond simply labeling songs and
videos as misogynist to discover what is driving not only individual misogyny but the institutional subordination of girls
and women relative to the key realms of social stratification:
wealth (economic power), power (political power), and prestige
(social status) (cf. Weber 1968). Instead, we often settle for
what is widely accepted as true. "Keepin' it real," which has
fast become a cliché in and of itself, is no longer expanding
knowledge but is limiting it. Elected officials have exerted little influence in the matter of misogyny, try as they might. On
September 25, 2007, the 110th U.S. Congress held hearings on
hip-hop music entitled "From Imus to Industry: The Business
of Stereotypes and Degrading Images" that seemed to have no
impact and received little media coverage. The focus on degrading images did nothing for the actual people degraded by
misogyny in hip-hop.

In his written testimony, Doug Morris, the CEO and
chairman of Universal Music Group stated, "Rap and hip-hop
may be the vehicle by which [rappers] escape lives of hopelessness, injustice, and poverty. Their words reflect their lives,
which, regrettably, is often an unpleasant picture" (Morris
2007). If corporate executives and fans are unable to distinguish rappers' words as a *view* of black life (rather than life itself), then hip-hop will become just another form of social
control, a leveling mechanism that operates to reduce diversity
and bring standouts in line with dominant stereotypes. Mi-
crophones literally and metaphorically amplify how an MC

represents life and are easily confused with generalizations of black life itself. That's part of the business of hip-hop, part of the game, unfortunately. Male (as well as female) MCs on some level count on the illusion of certainty that being a recording artist in hip-hop gives to their points of view about black life.

Nas, then, is a perfect candidate for exploring gender issues within hip-hop. He has performed different manifestations of black masculinity and patriarchal dominance (hard-core street rapper, Mafia don, thug narrator, the second coming of Rakim, a father and son, the last real nigga alive, and God—as in the Five Percenters' ideology).[2] He is also well versed in different styles and contexts of hip-hop music (underground hip-hop, R&B, crossover, mainstream, featured artist, freestyle, MC battle, video, etc.). Despite this diversity, he never loses his street credibility. Nas has been able to stay "true" to the game of black masculinity and Western patriarchal dominance without ever being forced to choose. If we take a walk down memory lane, we begin to see how Nasir Jones's various personas including God's son, Nas Escobar, Nasty Nas, and Nastradamas, were born out of a much larger context of gender stratification and patriarchy that is bigger than the 'hood—it encompasses hip-hop.

Instead of attributing Nas's constructions of black masculinity to his own individual invention as an MC, what if we looked at the key conversations that were already around in 1973 when he was born? I once told a colleague in African American studies that *keeping it real* is old. I want to keep it *hypothetical* for a minute. What other things might be possible to project about hip-hop by stepping outside the box? So, I decided to look at a few events surrounding September 14, 1973—the birth date of Nasir bin Olu Dara Jones—as well as the release year of *Illmatic* in 1994, Nas's rebirth as a public artist.

1973: The Birth of Nas

Nas was born to Fannie Ann Little from North Carolina and Charles Jones (Olu Dara) from Mississippi. 1973 was full of extreme political and social controversy in the U.S. The Watergate trial began bringing down the Nixon administration and led to his eventual resignation. *Roe v. Wade* legalized abortion and led some right-to-lifers to bomb clinics and commit murder. At the Oscar ceremonies, the Mafia classic *The Godfather* was awarded Best Picture, but Marlon Brando refused to accept his award for Best Actor in a dramatic and political fashion. At the ceremonies, the actor flipped the script from the imagined violence in Sicily to the real violence taking place during the Wounded Knee incident that year. His refusal to accept the Oscar was delivered by Native American Sacheen Littlefeather dressed in a squaw dress and headband to protest Hollywood's depiction of indigenous tribes. The media accused her of not being Indian. She was also an actress at the time, but she actually was of indigenous descent. Despite the fact that Brando's intentions were sincere, Littlefeather's credibility was further tested when she appeared in *Playboy* magazine later that year.

Hip-hop's use of women in videos might be viewed as analogous. The reality that an actor would use his award ceremony as a platform offscreen to critique his own industry was novel. The use of women as objects or tools in the process of raising political or professional consciousness in the film or the music video industry is another matter. Brando probably thought little of using a female Native American to make his point and seemed oblivious to the impact on her life just as many music video directors think their intentions have little impact on videos' vixens.

Political tricks by elected officials (Nixon and Watergate), battles over women's bodies (*Roe v. Wade*), and the public's fascination with the Mafia (*The Godfather*) but not with violence against minorities were just a few of the stories that cradled Nas's entrance in the world. Misogyny, homosexuality, and public decency became the "centerfold" of media attention in 1973 when PBS aired the first network nudity (*Steambath*) and Larry Flynt launched *Hustler* magazine leading the way for songs like "Hate Me Now" by Nas. Even PBS proved that sex sells; *Steambath* was nominated for two prime-time Emmys.

On the East Coast, 1973 saw the completion of the twin towers of the World Trade Center. On the West Coast, race and gender triumphed in the Compton election of Mayor Doris A. Davis, the first African American woman to govern a major metropolitan city. This seems important because so much of what I learned about the black power era was about the Huey Newtons and Elaine Browns, not the elected officials like Davis. The popular media still prefers the angry militant stories of black power and stereotypical views of hip-hop fit that narrative. Nas in many ways has defied a single narrative of black masculinity.

Before hip-hop enterpreneurship, men of color with power looked like Asian actor Bruce Lee, who established his social and economic prestige in Hollywood. Just a year earlier, he had achieved unprecedented power in the film industry, acquiring complete control over his productions as the writer, director, lead actor, and the choreographer of his fight scenes. Unfortunately, the most influential martial artist-actor who redefined hand-to-hand combat as well as what masculinity looked like on the big screen died in 1973 at the age of thirty-two. *Enter the Dragon*, released posthumously, was one of the year's highest grossing films. Hip-hop artists from Nas to Wu-Tang to Russell Simmons to Jay-Z would follow Lee's steps with their entrepreneurship. CEOs like Queen Latifah and Eve have also contributed their share.

A major milestone hit Broadway and the big screen with the portrayal of "God's son" by actors in 1973, which was considered as sacrilegious as putting the Prophet Muhammad in a cartoon. Broadway closed its production of the rock opera *Jesus Christ Superstar* after 711 performances, and the film adaptation opened in 1973 despite criticism from religious groups. The film was nominated for an Oscar and for two Golden Globes. The biblical and apocalyptic allusions that Nas represents throughout his career might be said to have had their seeds in these popular and controversial events.

So far, we can see that both Nas and hip-hop culture were born into a context of race, gender, and issues of representation that went beyond what we have learned about hip-hop and the South Bronx (see Jeff Chang's book *Can't Stop, Won't Stop*). Understanding the context of gender surrounding hip-hop requires that we look at more than black folks' past for historical explanations.

1994: The Rebirth of Nas

> *Peace God—now the shit is explained.*
> —"MEMORY LANE" (1994)

Almost twenty years later in 1994, *Illmatic* dropped. Apartheid had ended and the first multiracial elections in South Africa took place. Mandela became the first black president after spending twenty-seven years in solitary confinement. (Maybe Mumia Abu-Jamal will become president of the United States.) There were battles of age and might that year. Forty-five-year-old George Foreman, known today for his entrepreneurial enterprises, became the world's oldest heavyweight boxing champion. He hadn't been champ since 1973, when he defeated Joe Frazier. On the silver screen, it was also the year of one of the most memorable bad-ass performances of all time by Samuel Jackson starring in Quentin Tarantino's *Pulp Fiction*. The film also let us see white men openly dating black women and featured the controversial use of "nigger" by whites. (That's probably where Imus got it.)

Back in New York City, Rudy Giuliani inaugurated his crackdown on crack as the new mayor in the name of unity. Crack-ravaged black neighborhoods made the news as did carjackings, while some of the most controversial criminal scandals of 1994 involved white women. American ice skater Tonya Harding clubbed her competitor Nancy Kerrigan at the Winter Olympics; Susan Smith drowned her two children after her boyfriend rejected her, initially blaming a phantom black carjacker for the tragedy; and Lorena Bobbitt exacted the ultimate crime of passion by dismembering her husband's penis. Check out Ursula Rucker's "The Unlocking" on The Roots' first CD, *Do You Want More?* from that same year. Unlike Bobbitt, Rucker chose to rhyme her challenge to masculine dominance while reimagining an alternative universe where women flip the script with the ultimate sexual gangsta rap. "Now tell me [click-click (the sound of a gun being cocked)] what's my name?" (Rucker 1994). White women pay attention: write a rhyme, you'll do less time.

Internationally, 1994 was a devastating year of invasion and genocide in the African diaspora. The United States invaded Haiti (again) and ignored the Rwandan massacres, which were at their peak. On the domestic front Americans distracted themselves from Rwanda with the O.J. Simpson trial, and a Los Angeles jury awarded $3.8 million in damages to Rodney King. Finally, in the most curious irony of all, Ralph Ellison, the author of *The Invisible Man*, quietly passed away; the legacy of his classic text was itself a "eulogy" to the nightmares of black manhood, to the loss of liberty experienced by black men in America. At twenty-one, Nas was living in a world that knew a little something about difference and power, about black masculinity and femininity, and about gender stratification and misogyny in ways that go beyond the confines of any ghetto.

Paradoxically, it would be a woman, a Korean journalist from Chicago, who made sure a new audience didn't sleep on Nas's new release. MC Serch, formerly of the white rap group 3rd Bass and better known as the MC of VH-1's *The (White) Rapper Show* in 2006, also helped put Nas on. *Illmatic* received five mics in *Source* magazine from Minya Oh, then known as Shortie, now known as radio personality Miss Info. "I gave [Nas] the first ever five-mic rating. It was pretty controversial back then and set the tone for his being heralded as the second coming of Rakim" (email communication to author, April 19, 2005). Shorty's rating was controversial because the *Source* editorial staff maintained a strict "no 5 rule" (Dennis 2005).[3] Also, *Source* fans of Dr. Dre's *The Chronic* felt dissed because it had received only four mics earlier that year. The fact that the messenger was a "shorty" rather than a dude probably added fuel to the fire. The battle over albums by Dre and Nas probably fueled the rising East Coast/West Coast battle that culminated with the murders of Tupac and Biggie in 1996.

Take what you will from this constructed historical array. It reveals that a context of racial and gender stratification mapped onto violence, corruption, nudity, all the things that make great news and popular culture. All of this was already prevalent in the 1970s and in the 1990s beyond the emergence of gangsta rap. From this trip down memory lane, I assert there is more to discover about the context of the performance of race and gender than we could discover from limiting our view to hip-hop or black history alone. Now that a broad historical context has been opened up, I want to explore how we define misogyny concerning hip-hop.

Nas: The Man and His Music

> *A man must know how to defy opinion;*
> *a woman how to submit to it.*
> —GERMAINE DE STAEL (1766–1817)

When you consider the increasing percentages of African Americans who have never married with the second-highest rates of divorce and the increasing femininization of poverty experienced in urban communities—female-headed households account for 50 percent of American poor—what is predictable (not inevitable) is that more and more children from households that are less likely to be well educated will rely more and more on mass media as their primary means of enculturation, the social process by which culture is learned and transmitted across generations. In fact, they already do.

According to Karen Dill's testimony at congressional hearings on hip-hop in September 2007, the average American child devotes forty-five hours per week to media consumption, more time than is spent in school; two-thirds of his or her waking hours (Dill 2007). Consequently, Nas and other black male artists are surrogate fathers to the black broadcast family. Black men are employed by record labels and big media execs instead of by the post office. When the issues of degradation come up, the integrity of the black family is rarely addressed. Who would have imagined that black music making would be the very mechanism through which the black family would turn around and assault itself with arguably one of the most liberating cultural expressions of our time—hip-hop.

Some women will question celebrating an MC who portrays himself as "God's son" in one breath and raps about "The Makings of the Perfect Bitch" in another.[4] Generalizing about artists gets us nowhere. As Mark Twain once said, "The world will not stop and think—it never does, it is not its way;

its way is to generalize from a single sample." Whether we celebrate or dethrone Nas, his relevance as a hip-hop artist cannot be denied. Every one of his albums has gone platinum or better and he maintains fierce street credibility even among female MCs like Toni Blackman, a hip-hop cultural ambassador to the State Department. "Look, I can go by the water front, sit with my rhyme book and listen to 'One Mic' on repeat for at least thirty minutes before it gets on my nerves. So it's hard to spend energy criticizing Nas for his shortcomings. He has inspired me in so many different ways" (Blackman 2005).

Some male and female hip-hop heads, of all races and all classes, experience Nas's portrayal of masculinity as deeply embedded in a matrix of gender meanings and differences. Others do not. We women might take a harder stance on misogyny if we opened up our definition gender, as I will explain below. We tend to be either for or against men when our relationships can be complex—they can be loving, demanding respect and honor, and carefree in expressing the impact on us and them.

Male fans laud Nas in ways similar to Toni and Jigsaw, the CEO and cofounder of allhiphop.com. He praises *Illmatic* as a classic with its return to a "roots" style of early male rap involving hard (read: masculine) beats harkening back to the heyday of Big Daddy Kane, Rakim, and Kool G Rap. For Jigsaw, *Illmatic* represented being on foot in an urban space with its rugged use of language. "It was the cracks in the concrete, the subway, the projects, the potholes, the dirt and the streets. It was so visual that people from other areas could see exactly where Nas was coming from at that time in his life." The CEO viewed the album as the best of hip-hop: "rebellious, creative, uncompromising, [and] lyrical" (Jigsaw 2005).

When asked about "One Time 4 Your Mind," Jigsaw's passion simmered. It was a mediocre album cut to him. He preferred "N.Y. State of Mind," "The World Is Yours," and "Life's a Bitch." Unlike Jigsaw, I loved the track because of the way Nas crafts a rhyme out of the story of Cinderella. Perhaps this alone makes the song too feminine for rugged listeners like him. Nas slips in a rhyme about responsible condom use ("spend the night for sexin'/cheap lubrication/lifestyle protection") and exhibits a playfulness through his use of alliteration and his reference to a classic fairy tale ("I try to stay mellow, rock/Well a cappella rhymes'll make you richer than a slipper made Cinderella fella"). The music analyst in me loves the way he flips and connects vowel sounds ("try," "rock," and the first syllable of "a cappella"), the way he creates internal rhyme schemes (well, a cappella, Cinderella, fella) that anticipate and delay creating a sense of syncopation through phonic manipulation and interplay. Nas combines "liquid" consonants and alliteration in terse, powerful phrases packed with detail. One anthropologist asserts that women are more verbal than men, so maybe that's why I like it (Fisher 2006). But since hip-hop is highly verbal, that would mean it's highly feminine, right?

The point I am making is that gender roles and constructions are fluid rather than static. Interpretative rather than real. Since the early 1990s, misogyny has been loosely applied to any kind of female bashing or any kind of criticism regarding male dominance in rap and hip-hop.[5] In binary conceptions of gender, being *masculine* stereotypically gets its life blood from being completely different from the *feminine*, and vice versa (Scott 1988).

Misogyny is not simply angry words about women in a rap song or objectified sexual images captured in a video, as the 1993 congressional hearings led by the late C. DeLores Tucker once had the public believe. It can be fostered by all manner of culturally learned "activities, postures, speech patterns, attitudes, affects, acquisitions, and styles by virtue of which a woman becomes feminine (a man 'effeminate') and a man masculine (a woman 'mannish')" (Hyde 1983, 103). While misogyny can be connected to actual sexuality, according to scholar Lewis Hyde, it may also support and affirm a culturally defined creation myth, perpetuate the exploitation of men by subordinate women, organize MC battles and freestyles, and ensure the distribution of prestige from crew to crew. "It may, in other words, serve any number of ends unrelated to actual sexuality" (Hyde 1983, 103). Misogyny can even occur within the practices of women in hip-hop in ways totally unrelated to sexuality and other video games.

In my book, *The Games Black Girls Play: Learning the Ropes from Double-Dutch to Hip-Hop* (2006), I trace a musical dialogue that has been taking place between young girls and male recording artists for decades. "Oochie Wally" by Nas and the Bravehearts (2003) is a perfect example of it. As a producer, Nasty Nas appropriated the folklore of a girl's game-song for the hook of this popular and explicit single. Nelly did the same in 2000 with the release of "Country Grammar" (2000) and won a Grammy. "Oochie Wally" brought together an all-male crew of Nas's homeboys from Queensbridge to rap rude rhymes in between a chorus based on a Caribbean girl's playground chant. Using adult women's voices on the hook transformed a girl's game-song (oochie wally wally, ootchie bang bang) into a hoochie mama chant (hoochie mama mama, who'd she bang bang?). The men's rhymes on the verse traffic in words that objectify women, parading their sexual domination over women while also luring black female consumers into the song with their own girlish sounds but for a very different outcome (oochie bang bang). The chorus of any song draws listeners in to sing along. In this case, "Oochie Wally" teaches the subordination of women by allowing them to indoctrinate themselves into submission.

By contrast, since at least the mid to late twentieth century, black girls have been "sampling" melodic hooks and lyrics from commercial songs by male artists in their handclapping games, cheers, double-dutch, and the chants and rhymes they compose to accompany themselves. Girls "remix" musical ideas from the opposite sex, ideas that circulate in the black public sphere via local broadcasting networks including boom boxes, house parties, radio, TV, and now iPods. The music these female composers transmit through *kinetic orality* (passed on by word of mouth and body) are marked by lyrical references to the performance of gender, ethnicity, musical blackness, and social dancing such as in Michael Jackson's "Rockin' Robin" (1971), Afrika Bambaataa's "Planet Rock" (1983), or Boogie Down Productions' "Criminal-Minded" (1987). While Nelly's "Country Grammar" (2000) and Nas and the Bravehearts' "Oochie Wally" (2001) had commercial success, there were no royalties for the song makers of double-dutch. Instead, girls and young women get paid for playing the role of the video hos in hip-hop except in those rare cases where girls and women have the courage to rhyme or freestyle, calling themselves poets and singers more often than not.

This ongoing exchange between girls and men is a winning formula for the male artists. Their producers can make "new" songs sound familiar in a "black" sense by drawing on gendered acquisitions that signify masculinity and patriarchal dominance while subordinating and relegating the feminine context of girls' games to an unrecognized source. These games are an insignificant source unworthy of receiving copyright protection as it is currently understood. This domestic-public dichotomy, the contrast between the role of black girls on the playground back in the hood and the role of black men in the studio making tracks in the mass production of music, contributes to the devaluation of girls' and women's roles and the stratification that leads to the experience of male dominance or patriarchy in public or commercial music making. Hip-hop maintains the ideal of patriarchal dominance not only through the sexual objectification of women's bodies in videos but also in its acquisition of material and lack of attributing coauthorship to black girls in this compositional process.

Before I am accused of playa hatin' or man hating, let me also note that women may play into this struggle for gender dominance when we give up our interest in our own musical games and pursue boys. The natural socialization process gets the best of us but we still could own that choice to leave our musical talents behind. Boys don't give up their games. Female MCs and DJs seem to forget all about these games as a resource for sampling beats, lyrics, or hooks. For male artists and producers, however, everything is open to the game. Women's subordination limits not just their choices but their thinking. The masculine social world of hip-hop dictates that women avoid the feminine, just as men do, except in the case of booty poppin', but the implications for women are more severe. Therefore, adult female artists rarely even think about sampling from their former world of music—girls' handclapping games, cheers, and double-dutch beats or rhymes—even though sampling is the order of the day.

I am left with an interpretation that gender is the hegemonic social force shaping the decisions and practices of women who have recorded major records who all have avoided sampling from girls' games (Missy Elliot's "Gossip Folks" from 2003 samples Frankie Smith's "Double Dutch Bus" from 1981, which my research indicates is not based on a girl's game). The idea of female hip-hop artists sampling from girls' games may be viewed negatively by men as too easy, and here the power of gender as a social construct that naturally and silently shapes our thoughts and actions rears its ugly head. Ultimately, gender shapes women's (as well as men's) choices. The context of masculinity, the expected performance of black masculinity in hip-hop, chooses what "activities, postures, speech patterns, attitudes, effects, acquisitions, and styles" makes a man a man and a woman a woman; a man a bitch or a woman a ho (whether real or imagined).

The acquisition of material in the process of sampling presents another case for examining gender. In "One Time 4 Your Mind" the subjection of women to men takes place in a nongendered way through musicianship or musical composition. DJs, producers, and MCs have been embedding ideas into the world with their sociomusical practices, and as a result, hip-hop sampling has become its own quintessential form of nongendered storytelling about masculine dominance and patrimony.

Combining a traditional African American approach to music making with new technologies, DJs and producers artfully assemble unfamiliar break beats from musical textures, timbres, hooks, lyrical phrases, political moments, and collective memories from the past for their usefulness in the present (Glassie 1995, 395). Consequently, sample-based hip-hop has redefined musical theory and history as "songs, albums, groups and genres receded into the background as units of musical significance . . . theme and variation rather than progressive development became the order of the day" (Schloss 2004, 32–33). This allowed hip-hop's innovative composers to reign supreme while they sustained codes of gender stratification.

In the opening moments of "One Time 4 Your Mind," producer Large Professor creates a striking dissonance through the sampling of a metallic event featuring a dissonant tritone (an interval of an augmented fourth/diminished fifth) played on the vibraphones.[6] This event is accompanied by a slick, low-end bass line that slithers and creeps chromatically up the vertebrae of a major scale. Through musical sequencing Large Professor weds the striking metallic dissonance to a kick drum sample and triggers them simultaneously like five chimes designed to command your attention at the very top of the track—*bling, bling, bling, bling, bling*.

Acknowledged in the album credits, the sample is from the track "Walter L" found on an obscure jazz LP titled *Tennessee Firebird* made in 1966 by jazz virtuoso Gary Burton. According to one source, the LP represents Burton's experimentation with a fusion of jazz, rock, and country years before the jazz-rock fusions of the 1970s became popular (Burton 2005; Rose 2005; Wynn 2005). Large Professor brackets less than a second of the original—the moment when the vibraphonist uses soft mallets to dampen the metallic, ringing sounds of the dissonant tritones, causing the ringing to stop with a sudden thud—to create one of the defining elements of the four-beat loop featured throughout "One Time 4 Your Mind." Large Professor, like other hip-hop composers, creates a new sonic event that did not exist as a musical unit in the original context, which marks the downbeat of every measure, beginning each funky four-beat loop throughout the entire song. Once the groove is established, the next sonic feature that grasps our attention is Nas's entrance: "Yeah . . . It's *Illmatic!*"

Words cannot do justice to the feel of the groove the way dancing can. Women (as well as men) know how to embody hip-hop grooves despite the usual misogynist narratives featured in rap videos like Nelly's "Tip Drill" ("It must be ass cuz' it ain't your face/I need a tip drill, I need a tip drill"). After all the hype, there is little room left for studying and appreciating the power of an embodied groove that gets up under your pelvis and makes you wanna move. The communication from DJ to dancer requires little translation, though black dancing is definitely a gendered act. The rapper's words add a linguistic dimension that sometimes interferes with and obstructs the exchange. Misogynistic claims tend to limit the study of these relationships. "Given the ongoing struggle to have black music perceived *as* music, black culture recognized *as* culture, black people respected *as* people . . . the body [becomes] a stumbling block in the way of [a] full appreciation of black artistic achievement" (McClary and Walser 1994, 77–78). Most stories about gender—the kinetic orality of black expressivity—are not found *in* the musical performance or composition in and of itself. They exist and are experienced *between* the DJ/producer and the dancer(s); they come alive in the relationships *between* people. This is complicated in video editing by directors whose male eye is on the prize of what will be sexy for broadcasting. To explain, let me turn to an analysis of the video "I Can" to highlight the complex contradictions of race, gender, and the body when visually broadcast as hip-hop.

Misogyny: When Fathers Grow Up ("I Know I Can")

Stylized dancing for pleasure is common among children as young as age four or five throughout the African diaspora. By the age of seven, most children of both sexes have mastered eroticized social dancing and practice it long into adulthood. Participation in sexual or erotic activity is not the aim, but as girls mature sexually, their fathers especially have growing concerns about policing their bodies and their behavior. These concerns are heightened when images of young girls are broadcast to mixed audiences with varying class and religious values about the body, sexuality, and dance. The legacy of racial and class stereotyping in the United States tends to assign intellect and high esteem to formally trained European styles of dance while emotional impulse and physicality, as assigned to African-influenced styles of social dance, are considered low-class, "vulgar," and unschooled. Thus at a very young age most black and Latino boys and girls are disciplined in sophisticated forms of embodied intelligence including the eroticized art of social dance, but they are chastised for it in more mainstream educational and social contexts.

The video of the single "I Can" (2003) is a visual and sonic anthem for raising children to avoid the wrong influences, many of them generated through hip-hop culture. The concept for the song was developed from Nas's own concern for his ten-year-old daughter, Destiny. A girl standing on the threshold of puberty, given her growing breasts and training bras, and facing the threat of sexual subordination to men, would trigger her father's concerns.

Being a father to a daughter changes hip-hop's masculine game: "I got a daughter, so I'm like dag! My daughter, she's of age now. She's starting to listen to more of the radio, starting to know what's going on with more of the music." Nas dances around the threat, never naming it. He continues, but he generalizes the threat to the locality of children's musical tastes: "There's millions of kids like her that love rap music. But they ain't no records like when I was a kid coming up lovin' rap music." Then Dad justifies his shift from hard-core masculinity to parental guardian and fatherly role model inspiring young kids. "So, I owed that to the kids [and] I'm very happy I did that record. It became a song a lot of people [were] singing in their graduations" (*Nas Video Anthology*, 2004).

I appreciate Nas's intention to cater to children's listening and developmental needs. What concerns me about the video directed by Chris Robinson accompanying the single is the paradox of the broader context of hip-hop. The rest of the game of misogyny and sexism in hip-hop ain't changed by "I Can." In fact, the sexist camera work pays special attraction to young girls, ranging in age from about seven to thirteen, gyrating and stimulating the viewer's gaze.[7] What makes the video excessively sexual is its aesthetic use of slow-motion editing that heightens the male *and* female view of the girls' "dirty dancing." In the meantime, a chorus of children sings "I know I can/Be what I wanna be/If I work hard at it/I'll be where I wanna be."

Videos rely on the fact that 70 percent of human perception is visual. Popular culture, as Stuart Hall has distinguished, always uses the experiences and pleasures of everyday people, as well as sexual, "African," and carnivalesque practices that are often viewed suspiciously by those with dominant middle-class values (Hall 1992, 25–26). The video editing in "I Can" is consistent with what makes black popular music popular to the masses. But the sexual objectification of girls "workin' it" remains as the dominant narrative despite Nas's lyrical narrative contradictorily asking "grown-looking girls who are only ten" to stop doing what they see on TV and in this very video. He also warns girls to be careful of rapists and older men with HIV. Curb your style of dress, don't act too grown. But the slow-motion editing guarantees that the nonverbal lesson may be the real message. Nas is but the messenger inviting them to be Oprah instead of a ho. Beethoven's "Für Elise," played on acoustic piano throughout the track, does another kind of cultural work needed to signify respectability, high culture, and intellect for kids. Advertisers and popular artists like Alicia Keys capitalize on performing and sampling Western classical music to signify high art and middle-class values.

Three significant and highly eroticized shots, contrasted by one "respectable" shot signifying on Oprah, serve to contradict the behaviors Nas seems to be chastising in his rap. In the end, it is the girls who use their ordinary gestures to do the dirty work of misogyny as well as cultural work of popular pleasure within the video's frame of hip-hop masculinity and the director's male gaze.

Slow-Mo Shot 1 "This is for grown lookin' girls who's only ten" (Nas 2004; Track 14, 1:43–1:45). The director's gaze fixes on a fair-skinned Latina who actually looks fifteen in snug jeans and a low-cut, sleeveless top that bares her midriff. She appears in makeup, unlike the younger girls. Slow motion captures her auburn tresses tossed in midair and we see the intimate articulations of her rocking pelvis seductively thrust back and forth in the center of a ring in two quick, seamless shots. The scene is brief, less than two seconds, nearly subliminal, but sexually compelling. Boys' movements are never captured in slow motion in such sexual suggestions of embodiment.

Slow-Mo Shot 2 "Careful, 'fore you meet a man with HIV" (Track 14, 1:50–1:51). Another slow-mo shot less than a second (26 frames to be exact) featuring a light brown-skinned Latina teenager, hair slicked in a bun, her back slightly to the camera, arms raised high in the air. She pumps her pelvis in her red pants, and the slow-motion edit and camera view focuses our gaze directly on her behind.

Contrasting Shot ("Respectable girls") "Like Oprah Winfrey" (Track 14, 1:52–1:54). This shot features a dark-skinned girl of seven or eight in a frilly red tank top with short cornrows laced with white and black beads at the ends. She stands smiling holding a mic in her hand. The shot cuts away smiling looking off to the upper left next to a little white girl who looks directly into the camera, but in the dominant context of kids of color, she is practically invisible, a prop at best. She represents America's top host.

Slow-Mo Shot 3 "Don't pretend to be older than you are" (Track 14, 1:58–2:00). An eight-year-old chocolate African American girl in a cute plaid sleeveless top and jeans shorts is captured with her "backfield" in motion crouching above the pavement shifting her weight from one hand on the asphalt to the other as her long braids anchored by white butterfly-like barrettes fly life taffy through the air. Two seconds of slow-motion shots of girls and the misogyny subtly returns to capture both male and female attention.

The camera also captures the entranced facial expression worn by those who perform hot (meaning highly skilled) dancing in the center of a ring and on the dance floor of communities of color. This facial expression is not limited to girls and women. But here, with her young mouth held open and her eyes slightly shut and gazing off to the side, the eight-year-old's performance is open to, perhaps even slanted toward, the interpretation of being sexual. Her facial gesture could be saying, "I can't look because this is so deep." Her expression could also be read as spiritual, but that is not likely within the sexist and misogynist context of a mass-mediated hip-hop video. The sexual take is reinforced when another female onlooker in the shot feigns embarrassment, inviting viewers to direct their misogynist distaste at the female dancer rather than the male director whose slow-motion editing created these "dirty" little shots.

Popular male MCs, as well as male video directors, can't seem to hear concerns about misogyny and sexism unless they begin to see them through the eyes of their daughters (and sometimes their sons) as they reach puberty. Only then does the issue become real for many artists in hip-hop. But by the time they have this revelation, their "do what I say, not what I do" method of teaching doesn't work no matter how much authority and promotion they put behind a single or a video. Despite Nas's best intentions, this video may promote self-esteem among children only to tear it down when authorities perceive their socially learned dancing as too sexual.

In the final verse in the last moments of the video, the words "and hos" are completely muted. No bleep or other sound effect signals the absence. Since Nas is out of our view in this shot, young viewers are protected from viewing him lip-sync the original content of his rhyme. The uncensored version is, "Nobody says you have to be gangstas *and hos*/Read more, learn more, change the globe." The need to protect girls but not boys is curious. You can hear the word "bitch" all day on TV and radio but back in 2003 BET decided it would censor "hos." The logic escapes me.

The competing narratives of the video and the song make "I Can" a perfect text for analyzing the complicated and contradictory ways adolescents and teenagers learn the stratification of gender and the subordination of women through visual perhaps more than through lyrical content. Some might thank the producers for omitting "hos" from the final BET cut, but all this video promotes is a highly scripted stereotype about female subordination that is ironically consistent with the reality that black women will be seen as less and less likely to marry these days.

Artists like Nas galvanize heads around notions of a forgotten golden era of hip-hop when women dissed rap and men had hip-hop to themselves. Speaking about 1988 in his *Video Anthology, Vol. 1*, Nas broadcasts a generalization that women don't like *true* hip-hop. He says, "the rap music that I used to love was the type of music that my mom *hated*. It was the type of music that a lot of *women* didn't like. Not cause it degraded women at all. It just had an energy that was so . . . for the fellas, you know. It was just *our* thing, you know" (*Video Anthology*, 2004). Who should determine whether it is degrading to women? A male hip-hop artist or the women who listen to hip-hop? Such generalizations deny female artists participating in hip-hop who have DJ'd or MC'd for longer than a lot of brothers—white and black.

To build on the axioms started above:

1. Some sisters love R&B and hip-hop equally. Some men too. Some hetero-, homo-, and bisexual sisters, not to mention gay men, listen exclusively to hip-hop's hardest styles and male artists although they have concerns about its impact. Some don't.

The lack of diversity about women in hip-hop is a leveling mechanism that engrains gender stratification in the cultural practice of hip-hop. MCs talking about what's real in hip-hop is also about keeping girls and women in their rightful place outside notions of becoming MCs, DJs, and producers. Just keep working hard to embody those beats in videos.

It never occurs to Nas that sisters throughout the history of the genre ditched and dissed hip-hop, then and now, because they were always left out of the club, left out of the narrated and shared sociomusical history told by MCs. Women had to be integral to early hip-hop in the South Bronx and other boroughs because there ain't no party with all men. That was called a "set." (For more on this, see Gaunt 2006.) In Nas's partial vision of reality, the old school and the underground occupy special places for the fellas who give special attention to women and girls only when it's convenient.

Despite all this, Nas does his part to expand the gender narrative in hip-hop by recording songs about getting married and including his father on record. Nas, like his dad, is a wordsmith, a signifying man; they just work in different genres and reflect different times. His father, trumpeter and composer Olu Dara, is a significant recording artist in his own right who emerged in New York City during the avant-garde loft scenes of jazz. I have known Olu Dara for about ten years. We met at a Charlottesville, Virginia, show featuring his phenomenal band in 1997. Olu is a mack daddy, a playa *PLA-YA* playa, and a southern gentlemen. "Girl, you must be from down South with gams [big legs] like that!" He's got an irresistible charm about him, he's fun on- and off-stage, and he wrote the book on the art of black male flirting better known as rap in the old days. "Yeah, of course, I remember you. . . . Wha's ya name?" Olu Dara is a travelin' bluesman, a ladies' man, and a sage trickster steeped in the sounds of the diaspora. He embodies the aesthetics of black verbal and musical improvisation and the politics of being a black man moving the crowds through the blues, bebop, or verbal social play.

Father and son have recorded three times, first, "Life's A Bitch" on *Illmatic*; second, on a "jazzy African beat" track on Olu's recording *In the World* (Atlantic Records, 2001); and in 2004, on *Street's Disciple* with a Muddy Waters blues beat to create a powerful mix of old school meets new in a track called "Bridging the Gap." The response to their "father-and-son" thing has been interesting, according to Olu. "It's been very effective in Africa," but in America people thought Olu was an actor. They would ask him if he was Nas's *real* father. I asked if Olu thought that reaction had anything to do with the fact that in the media we rarely see black men with their daddies, especially in hip-hop. The black family cliché includes female-headed households and dead-beat dads. Olu responded, "I got a lot of comments when they were little. I always had [my children] with me. People would say, 'It's so nice to see you with those kids.' [pause] That took me aback! What am I *supposed* to do? They're my kids. . . . That's what my father did."

Rather than limiting our conversation to misogyny, the subordination of women to men, or the discrimination against black men and black fathers, hip-hop and musical blackness will greatly benefit from embedding discussions about masculinity and femininity into a larger framework about gender as well as race. A more complex context that focuses our attention on the learned, rather than given, activities, effects, acquisitions, and styles of language, thoughts and beliefs "by virtue of which a woman becomes feminine (a man 'effeminate') and a man masculine (a woman 'mannish')."

Conclusion

The story about gender, unlike perceptions of Nas as an artist, is not rebellious, creative, and uncompromising. Although the system of gender identification always appears coherent and fixed, especially in mainstream hip-hop, it is in fact highly unstable and is only made stable through generalizations about gender roles. One feminist scholar argues that we must embed our critical attention in "the persistent associations of masculinity with power, [to resist] the higher value placed on manhood rather than on womanhood, [to understand] the way children seem to learn these associations and evaluations even when they live outside nuclear households" (Scott 1988, 38).

When we question or alter any aspect of the binary opposition of gender that signifies subordination, we always seem to end up threatening the entire system of power and thereby masculinity itself (Scott 1988, 38). Social constructs like race and gender persist because they seem natural, as if they have always been the way they are now. Black masculinity has changed over time, as has black femininity, and in nonlinear patterns (from enslaved to liberated; from conservative to liberal). Men rarely wore earrings in one ear twenty years ago and women did not play basketball professionally. The performance of gender has been constantly shifting, even within hip-hop, over the past thirty years. Thus interpretations of misogyny and gender stratification will also shift. We cannot escape misogyny altogether. In fact, misogyny is a useful sign for checking on the tensions between the sexes.

Some rappers may never rap about the feminization of poverty or the fact that 70 percent of black women are unmarried. But as we are beginning to see, being hard, keepin' it real, and big pimpin' are bankrupt concepts. They divide the sexes and limit the possibility of powerful and peaceful unions between young black men and women from dating to marriage. The costs to the black family—parents and kids—are taking their toll. We are winning the game we are playing in hip-hop concerning gender. But at what cost? Nas said in one of his video commentaries, "It's the microphone that gives us the opportunity to speak to the world about whatever we want to do. . . . All you need is one mic" (transcribed from *Nas Video Anthology, Vol. 1*, 2004). If Nas is right, when will brothers begin to use the mic to transform misogyny? Transformations can happen in a second. When you move your tassel from right to left at graduation, you are no longer a student but a college graduate. When you say "I do," you become husband and wife. With the stroke of a pen, other declarations and social contracts create businesses, corporations, and nations. Though the power of broadcasting is in the hands of more black men than ever, as a result of hip-hop, their ability to transform reality, not just keep it real, is an altogether different game.

Male rappers have the power but they are not using it to transform reality. Nas, for instance, has the mic, but he hasn't said anything transformative about gender roles. Maybe it's not his place to do that. But it is mine.

Bibliography

Blackman, Toni. 2005. Email interview, May 22, 2005.

Dara, Olu. 2005. Telephone interview, July 20, 2005.

Dennis, Reginald C. 2005. "Jon Shecter, Miss Info, and *Illmatic*'s 5 Mic Rating." www.hip-hop-blogs.com/hiphop/2005/04/jon_shecter_mis.html.

Gaunt, Kyra D. 2006. *The Games Black Girls Play: Learning the Ropes from Double-Dutch to Hip-Hop*. New York: New York University Press.

Glassie, Henry. 1995. "Tradition." *Journal of American Folklore*, Autumn, pp. 395–412. Special issue: Common Ground: Keywords for the Study of Expressive Culture.

Grove Music Online. 2005. "Burton, Gary." www.grovemusic.com.

_____. 2005. "Rose, Wally (Walter L)." www.grovemusic.com.

Fisher, Helen. 2006. "The Science of Love, and the Future of Women." www.ted.com/index.php/talks/view/id/16.

Hall, Stuart. 1992. "What Is the 'Black' in Black Popular Culture?" In *Black Popular Culture.* Edited by Gina Dent, pp. 21–33. Seattle: Bay.

Hyde, Lewis. 1983. *The Gift: Imagination and the Erotic Life of Property.* New York: Vintage.

Jigsaw [Chuck Creekmur]. 2005. Email interview, April 21, 2005.

McClary, Susan, and Robert Walser. 1994. "Theorizing the Body in African-American Music." *Black Music Research Journal*, Spring, pp. 75–84.

Miss Info [Minya Oh]. 2005. Email communication with author, April 19, 2005.

Nas. 2004. *Nas Video Anthology, Vol. 1.* New York: Sony Music/Columbia Music Video.

_____. 2004. *Street's Disciple.* Sony BMG Music Entertainment.

Rucker, Ursula. 1994. "The Unlocking." On *Do You Want More?!!!??!* by The Roots. Geffen Records.

Scott, Joan Wallach. 1988. "Gender: A Useful Category of Historical Analysis." In *Gender and the Politics of History.* New York: Columbia University Press.

Schloss, Joseph G. 2004. *Making Beats: The Art of Sample-Based Hip-Hop.* Middletown, CT: Wesleyan University Press.

Sedgwick, Eve Kosofsky. 1993. "Axiomatic." In *The Cultural Studies Reader*, edited by Simon During, pp. 243–268. London: Routledge.

Weber, Max. [1922] 1968. *Economy and Society.* Translated by E. Frischoff et al. New York: Bedminster.

Wynn, Ron. 2005. "Tennessee Firebird." *All Music Guide.* http://allmusic.com.

9

"REPRESENT," QUEENSBRIDGE, AND THE ART OF LIVING

EDDIE S. GLAUDE JR.

O n May 8, 1993, at about 5:45 A.M., residents on the sixth floor of the Queensbridge housing project in Long Island City awoke to the screams and pleadings of Stephanie Pagan as she was brutally attacked by Ronald Woodson. He stabbed her to death, together with her two children—an eight-month-old daughter and a seven-year-old daughter—and seriously injured Ronicia Rodriquez, Pagan's roommate. The *New York Times* reported that the children's grandmother, after seeing the crime scene, fell to her knees and shouted, "I can't deal with it. Take me away from this." As residents of Queensbridge gathered in front of the apartment building, the *Times* reported, many seemed dazed. An unidentified man was quoted as saying, "We're not all like this here. This is the projects, but there are some good people here."

In spite of such pleas, New York, especially certain communities, was indeed a dangerous place to live. A *New York Times* headline read, "New York City Is No Dodge City. It's Deadlier."[1] Much of the terrible violence that plagued New

York City during the 1980s now seems a distant memory. Since 1991, the city has experienced a declining crime index. Homicides have fallen to levels not seen since the 1960s. Of course we need to ask ourselves at what cost: the booming business of prisons. Black men and women, once traded on the slave-auction block, are now traded on Wall Street in the form of prison blocks, and the consistent violation of the rights of minority communities has left many neighborhoods feeling besieged. But the homicide data for 1991 should not be misread or misunderstood, for it only reflects a slight decrease from the extraordinary number of murders in 1990—with well over 2,000 murders occurring in that year alone.

Residents of Queensbridge experienced this violence intensely. The largest low-income housing development in the city, with 3,142 apartments, had been overrun by the drug trade. Residents complained of random shootings and worried about their safety. Given the widely shared belief that the state had abandoned them to rogue forces, residents even asked the New York Housing Authority in 1992 to hire the Fruit of Islam to patrol the project. The agency refused, citing that of the 324 public housing projects, Queensbridge ranked forty-third in the rate of crime; it was not the worst place in New York after all. But the violence and overall environment of crime remained palpable.

Beginning in the 1980s and solidified by the early 1990s, Queensbridge and much of public housing in New York City experienced an intensive demographic shift. The New York City Housing Authority, prior to this period, had made a point of admitting working families, but in the 1980s the Housing Authority began admitting the very poor and homeless.[2] The result was a hyperconcentration of poverty and, according to some, a rapid deterioration in the quality of life for the residents of public housing. These peak years of violent crime in

New York and the reality of daily life in Queensbridge shaped the lyrical imagination of Nas and his hip-hop classic *Illmatic.*

Nas's *Illmatic* stands as an extraordinary example of the artistic power of hip-hop and its ability to describe with stark and vivid imagery aspects of African American life. Bereft of the more annoying features of much of contemporary hip-hop—sleek marketing, caricatured personas, and relatively uninteresting rhymes—*Illmatic* takes the listener into the depths of Nas's world and discloses not only his individual artistic genius but also the striking and often brutal challenges to self-fashioning in our nation's housing projects. As he says near the conclusion of "Represent," "This goes out to everybody in New York living the real fucking life and every project all over."

Illmatic generally stands as a great example of lyrical ethnography, which involves a rich description of one's life and circumstances that produced specific meanings about life, death, survival, and success. The classic track by Grandmaster Flash and the Furious Five, "The Message," is a straightforward example of the technique. MC Melle Mel draws a vivid picture of his surroundings and their immediate challenges. That picture, from its opening line of "broken glass everywhere" to its closing message, "you lived so fast and died so young," generates meanings about a group's or an individual's lived experience and frames how they see others and confront problems.

These ethnographic descriptions acquire a lyrical quality in the hands of the hip-hop artist, who renders the stock of meanings that make up the common sense of what it takes to live under certain conditions and do so in such a way that we, the listeners, find those meanings beautiful and suitable to dance to. Raekwon's powerful track "Incarcerated Scarfaces," from his 1995 album, *Only Built 4 Cuban Linx*, comes to mind.

With stunning virtuosity, Raekwon describes a particular way of life that marks the journey of the "Black Stallion, Wildin' on Shaolin." His lyrical play releases the track from a simple representation of his experiences in Staten Island. Instead, he fully displays his lyrical skills while offering a compelling and chilling account of those who reside "on the crack spots."

Lyrical ethnography calls attention to the multiple levels of representation used throughout *Illmatic* and specifically on the track "Represent," produced by DJ Premier. The word "representation," of course, can refer to a number of things.[3] It is most readily associated with the sense of the accurate reproduction of something. A photograph of a tenement in Queens, for example, stands as a reproduction of the actual building. It stands in for the real thing and takes on the quality of the real. But representation also carries with it the remnant of an older meaning, one tied to the word "represent": a sense of the word that is associated with making oneself present or standing for something that is not present.[4] This sense of the word points us to a dimension of representation, at least within the culture of hip-hop, that is all about self-fashioning and its representativeness of a particular way of life. One can embrace a sense of one's own uniqueness and declare that individuality as exemplary of "keeping it real" or being authentic. The difficulty, of course, lies in keeping the claims of accurate reproduction from overwhelming the more daunting task of self-fashioning.

Nas's track "Represent" points up all these levels of representation. First, we see representation of the sociological realities of Queensbridge. Indeed the theme of Queensbridge provides one of the coherent threads throughout the ten tracks. Second, Nas represents a certain rap pedigree. He refers to the Boogie Down Production (BDP) battles with the Juice Crew, a battle over the purported origins of hip-hop, situating

Queensbridge and himself within the formative history of hip-hop culture. Last, the track alludes to a particular form of self-fashioning. "Represent" is a kind of lyrical reflection on the processes of self-creation that involves the importance of friendships (or associational bonds), ideas of excellence (wrongly or rightly conceived), and notions of authentic (i.e., real) and inauthentic (i.e., fake) existence figured in the challenging world of Queensbridge.

Queensbridge, 1994

The album insert offers a photographic glimpse of the "home" that informs Nas's phenomenal lyrics. On the front cover, the streets of Queensbridge overlay the loss of innocence captured in the narrowed eyes and slight frown of the young Nas. The typical joy of a child has been stolen. This loss of innocence is juxtaposed with the loss of life. The three head shots of deceased friends placed against the all-black background remind us of the deadliness of "the Bridge" and the truth of AZ's manic cry that "Life's a bitch, then you die." Indeed, Nas's facial expressions capture the pressure of life in Queensbridge (a place defined, in part, by the menacing presence of the police, the prospect of prison, and the dire poverty depicted by a man enjoying a meal garnered from a nearby garbage can). A "New York state of mind" involves, then, the nearly impossible task of living a reality that can best be described as absurd.

Ironically, the album dropped during the economic boom of the 1990s, revealing that the enormous wealth generated during this decade did not make its way to the poor and working poor. Instead, many found access to wealth by way of the underground economy. The profitable crack business and subsequently prisons became central themes in the imaginations of many young African American men and women in New York

City. Nas had ready-at-hand metaphors for writing rhymes and making music based in the unseemly enterprise of trafficking drugs and its attendant violence.

When Nas opens "Represent" with the verse: "Straight up shit is real and any day could be your last in the jungle. Get murdered on the humble, guns'll blast, niggaz tumble. The corners is the hot spot, full of mad criminals who don't care," he engages not in mere reportage but rather in the *creative* (re)presentation of the "hum and buzz" of Queensbridge. Indeed, throughout *Illmatic* Nas's references to Queensbridge function not only to authenticate the supposed rough edges of his artistic persona but also to display a set of living conditions that reflect the night side of American life. AZ's opening verse to "Life's a Bitch'" describes the significance of living in Queensbridge (or any housing project for that matter) as his dreams for a better life are couched in crass American consumerism and limited by a sense of imminent or at least inevitable death amid constant struggle.

In spite of such stark images, life in public housing does not constitute a constant nightmare. People live, love, and laugh there, as they do anywhere else. In its description of Queensbridge, *Illmatic* gives voice, despite the hardships, to the buoyancy of love and life in the 'hood that makes survival possible and human flourishing imaginable. To be sure, "Represent" paints a dramatic picture of drugs, violence, and money that simultaneously takes up the fantastical image of fictive gangsters *and* portrays an experience of actual living that becomes the raw stuff of art.

The album is also full of the sounds of friends that sustain and maintain one another in the Bridge. Indeed, the images and sounds of Nas's crew belie the conclusion that the disease at the heart of Queensbridge inevitably destroys those who live there. We see a gathering of young men and boys posing defiantly (with smiles, frowns, and gestures) as the high-rise apartment buildings behind them fuse into a seemingly impenetrable wall. We know that the creative sounds and the lyrical genius of generations of hip-hop artists from Queensbridge enable some, figuratively, to leap tall buildings in a single bound.

Illmatic is the quintessential example of this success, taking the "facts" of experience and arranging them in such a way that for a brief moment (just ten tracks) "reality" comes into sharp and significant focus. The album must be celebrated for its extraordinary artistry and its imaginative representation of the difficulties of living in urban ghettos. And not necessarily for an overriding political purpose; in some places Nas actually sides with the villain. For example, he rhymes in "New York state of mind": "Be havin' dreams that I'm a gangster—drinking Moets, holdin' Tecs, makin' sure the cash came correct then I stepped." Under the challenging conditions of project living, then, traditional examples of virtuous character and excellence come from the most unlikely, and perhaps unseemly, places.

The rich tapestry of Nas's environment, with its joys and sorrows, constitutes the backdrop of "Represent." The track does homage to those in New York City and elsewhere who live and attempt to create themselves in the face of the debilitating circumstances of their living. Much of hip-hop is too often held to be a simple representation of the actual day-to-day doings and sufferings of communities in urban ghettos. Too often, in the name of "keeping it real," a one-to-one correspondence is believed to exist between the lyrics of rap music and the lives of those who dwell in so-called "concrete jungles." Indeed street credibility serves as the litmus test of authenticity. However, we should resist such simplistic claims. Not simply because the results can be deadly (witness the loss of Tupac and Biggie) but also because it can often obscure the artistic dimensions of the music. When we listen to hip-hop as only a sociological or politically driven account of misery in the ghetto, we often miss the beautifully constructed word portraits, lyrical wonderment, and rhythmic timing that define the genre at its best.

Many of us who are hip-hop heads feel the need to defend the obvious contradictions in the music by appealing to its "realistic" portrayal of social and political misery. This hip-hop realism, as Imani Perry describes it, fails to capture the extraordinary work MCs do in making choices to present reality in one way or another (choices for which they can be held accountable).[5] The view seems to presume, wrongly I believe, that the MC simply lists the facts as he or she knows or experiences. And perhaps more importantly, it reveals a narrow view of black life defined only by hardship. This constrained view of the artistry of MCs and of black urban spaces has difficulty accounting for the creative power of hip-hop. We find ourselves too often concerned about its descriptions of reality and not mindful that the form itself represents an extraordinary example of creative power. In short, we emphasize one sense of the meaning of representation while turning a blind eye to the sense of the word that is about self-fashioning or making oneself present.

We also, unwittingly perhaps, deny the discipline of such artistry. Descriptions of hip-hop as mere reportage deny the hard work invested in becoming a towering figure in the genre. Jay-Z, for example, has mastered his craft and consequently he can, if he chooses, rhyme about whatever strikes him as worthy of a pen and a beat. Nas's *Illmatic* is an album-length illustration of this very point. The tortured dimensions of Queensbridge and the daily grind of escaping its deadly effects saturate the music and the rhymes of this classic album. But Queensbridge never overwhelms Nas's imagination. His artistic genius, on full display in every track, literally "represents" the limiting conditions of the Bridge. He actively transforms the realities of his living conditions, and that very act signals his mastery of the MC's craft. It is in this sense, *as an artist*, that Nas makes himself present—or, better still, "represents."

Too often those who reside on the underside of American life are seen as pawns moved about by circumstances. Yet beauty can be created by those whose lives are principally defined by the nastiness of the world. African Americans, historically, have been seen in this way. Our lives are often reduced to sociology—the fact of the plantation, the reality of sharecropping, the difficulties of the city, the devastation of the drug economy, and so on. Every gesture, artistic or otherwise, becomes a window to that reality, and we become flat, one-dimensional characters in a sordid tale about social misery. What gets lost in all of this is the creative role *we* play in living our lives and in creating art that makes our lives, if just for a moment, enjoyable. Instead, we are reduced to a ghastly environment represented by our very presence in the world. This view, especially of hip-hop music, blinds us to the brilliance of the artist.

This perspective is reminiscent of criticism that James Baldwin and Ralph Ellison leveled at the social realism of Richard Wright's *Native Son*. Both worried that Wright's descriptions of African Americans not only flattened the complexity of black life but also compromised the art of the novel by reducing it to social and political commentary. As an artist, Nas reflects what he knows and lives. His music, however, is not reducible to these realities; his extraordinary imagination shapes them into art. But resistance to simplistic realist claims about hip-hop should not be understood as a denial of the music's effort to represent poor urban communities. Too many critics lose sight of the extent to which art provides insight into particular conditions of living. However, the varied representations within

hip-hop do not necessarily have to be viewed as good or as politically progressive.[6] They simply offer a perspective on life, perhaps highly stylized or maybe gruesomely direct. In the end, we
can take the artistic descriptions of urban ghettos in hip-hop as
seriously as we might the descriptions of the slums of London
in a Charles Dickens novel.

A review of perspectives on the American novel helps explain the way I understand the artistic power of *Illmatic*. For
Ralph Ellison, "every serious novel is, beyond its thematic pre-
occupations, a discussion of craft, a conquest of the form, a
conflict with its difficulties and a pursuit of its felicities and
beauty."[7] Understood as such, the novel should never be limited to reflect the actual goings-on of our world. The novelist,
and I believe the rap artist as well, understands herself as engaged in an artistic endeavor involving the use of certain conventions that confine, limit, and enable the communication of
a vision of experience. Indeed, the novelist hopes to communicate this vision in such a way that the reader finds it compelling, what Ellison refers to as the magic moment when the
writer and reader are in communion.

The possibility of communion, however, presupposes a
body of shared assumptions about life, about what it means to
get up and go to work every day and to struggle to make ends
meet, along with a body of feelings in relation to that struggle; it presupposes a set of shared assumptions about necessity, possibility, and freedom, which arise from the particular
circumstances of similar conditions of living.[8] Something
then connects the novelist and the reader, the MC and the listener. By playing on our shared assumptions and appealing to
our sense of experience, both reveal to us that which lies beyond our sense of the familiar, revealing what Ellison calls the
unfamiliar within the familiar. Ellison believes "that the primary social function of the novel [and I would include hip-

hop here] is that of seizing from the flux and flow of our daily lives those abiding patterns of experience which . . . help to form our sense of reality, and from which emerge our sense of humanity and our conception of human value."[9] The success of both forms, then, relies in part on their ability to communicate and help forge our sense of the world around us. I use the phrase "lyrical ethnography" to capture this point, and to my mind hip-hop at its best aspires to the same.

Hip-hop is a craft that involves innovation against and within prevalent forms as well as a pursuit of a certain style of expression and beauty. It also relies for its success on an intimate relationship with those of us who listen to the music (those necessary collaborators who must participate in the culture in order to bring the music to life). The shared assumptions and sense of experience constitute the stuff of which the rhymes are formed and the music is made. Even MCs who rhyme with no sense of social purpose depend on this shared sense for their success. When the artist is successful, however, the music rides the rhythm of our daily living, having the "hum and buzz of implication," and reveals for us, lyrically, the unfamiliar within the familiar as we dance the night away.

Illmatic beautifully captures each of these characteristics. Nas acknowledges his indebtedness to those who went before and seeks to innovate musically to advance the genre. In the process, he produces music that captures the poignancy of the moment in which he finds himself. The lyrics reflect, then, a world teetering on the edge of the abyss, even as those who live in it love, laugh, and die. As such, the music rides the rhythm of daily living. In this sense *Illmatic*, and especially the track "Represent," captures both senses of representation: it takes on the quality of the real—that sense of the Bridge with its immediate dangers—and, in *representing* with masterful skill, Nas makes himself present.

Queensbridge, Hip-Hop, and the Art of Living

Nas opens the third verse of "Represent" with an explicit reference to the rap pedigree of Queensbridge and how it frames the persona presented throughout the track in particular and *Illmatic* in general. The battles between BDP and MC Shan and between Shante and the Real Roxanne merge seamlessly into the fabric of life in Queensbridge. Nas simultaneously situates himself in this rap lineage and with the streets that formed the stage on which these artistic battles took place.

MC Shan and DJ Marley Marl's "The Bridge" solidified the presence of Queensbridge housing projects in the history of hip-hop. A host of successful artists have come out of Queensbridge, from Marley Marl to Nas to Capone-N-Noreaga to Mobb Deep. But "The Bridge" established Queensbridge as an important artistic landmark in the imagination of many of these artists. What began as music for the intermission of the Queensbridge Talent Showcase has now become an important historical representation of the quality of talent and powerful personalities that inhabit what some take to be (with a note of irony) a very special place. MC Shan opens "The Bridge" by giving voice to the lore of this particular place:

> You love to hear the story again and again
> of how it all got started way back when.
> The monument is right in your face.
> Sit and listen for a while to the name of the place.

Like the hook to "The Bridge," Nas's refrain of "Represent" is punctuated by members of his crew shouting Queensbridge. Nas and his fellows represent a place and a history that demand from them a degree of excellence and acknowledgment of its centrality to their lyrical imagination. They put "the monument" squarely in our face through descriptions of the drugs and violence that make up so much of the thematic content of *Illmatic*.[10] (I suppose it's impossible to sentimentalize a housing project.)

Nas also invokes Queensbridge's rap lineage as a way of marking time and remembering the past. He tells, in effect, a story of his childhood. Instead of beginning with "once upon a time," however, he situates the listener in time by reference to classic rap battles. What follows are accounts of juvenile crime and the formation of a crude materialist ethic based in immediate gratification pursued at all costs.

> If it wasn't hangin' out in front of cocaine spots,
> we was at the candy factory, breakin' the locks.
> Nowadays, I need the green in a flash like the next man.
> Fuck a yard God, let me see a hundred grand.
> Could use a gun son, but fuck being the wanted man,
> but if I hit rock bottom then I'ma be the Son of Sam.

Queensbridge doubles, then, as marking the power of a rap tradition and the struggles of particular conditions of living.

DJ Marley Marl echoes this point. The legendary producer said of Queensbridge, "The Bridge is struggle. I was just a kid out here in Long Island City; the best thing I could think about doing was trying to rob factories. . . . If it wasn't for the entertainers, I wouldn't have had nothing to look up to, and possibly, I wouldn't have had a dream."[11] Here DJ Marley Marl figures hip-hop as his saving grace and articulates a sentiment about "dead dreams, bought and sold" voiced by MC Shan in "The Bridge." But MC Shan doesn't end the verse with a fatalistic cry. Instead, he directs us to the extraordinary act of self-creation that takes place amid the rubble and ruin of our nation's housing projects:

Stop walking through life as if you are blind.
You should reach for your goal cause I'm reaching for mine.
And I'm from the Bridge.

"And I'm from the Bridge" is an unexpected twist that shocks the listener, for such words are not supposed to come from someone living in Queensbridge. But the art of hip-hop makes possible a kind of magic moment where the realities of living in Queensbridge are overcome (for the moment) by a vision of experience made possible by the MC's imagination. To be sure, Nas's lyrical invocation of his rap pedigree places his artistic intervention in a tradition of such interventions, where the Queensbridge housing project is transformed into a passageway of broader possibility by the exhibition of excellence in writing rhymes and making tremendous music. He literally transforms the words of the man outside of Stephanie Pagan's murder scene: "We're not all like this here. This is the projects, but there are some good people here." We have been listening to his music ever since.

This classic work demonstrates a level of excellence indicative of the potential power of hip-hop, but it also evokes excellence in a different sense. Nas's lyrical ethnography represents the art of living, a process of self-fashioning or the forging of a unique and powerful personality—of making oneself present through the medium of music. With the lyrical descriptions of the chaos of Queensbridge—the loss of loved ones, the reality of prison, drugs, and violence, the inevitability and imminence of death—Nas indeed rhymes himself into existence. The art of rap music here becomes, in some ways, an act of self-creation, and notions of excellence are embodied in that very activity.

In the context of *Illmatic*, this act of self-fashioning is not solely an individual activity; it involves a set of associational bonds (friendships and family members) that constitute the conditions for its possibility. Nas's crew matters a great deal. Their voices fill out *Illmatic* and frame much of Nas's lyrical genius. The refrain of "Represent," for example, consists of the excited shouts of a crew of friends. And the last verse of the track, by way of an analogy to the crack game, demonstrates the importance of these bonds to not only surviving Queensbridge but to the making and success of the art that is *Illmatic*. Nas rhymes:

> Then call the crew to get live too
> with Swoop, Hakim, my brother Jungle, Big Boo, cooks up the blow,
> Mike'll chop it, Mayo, you count the profit.
> My shit is on the streets.

The track ends with a series of shout-outs to particular personalities, crews, blocks, and the like that constitute the backdrop to the production of the music. It used to annoy me when I experienced and watched hip-hop performances. There would be seemingly random people jumping around and periodically shouting in the mic, creating a cacophony of sound. But these performances capture, however awkwardly, the importance of the bonds I have been talking about. Their presence literally conjures up the context of the art's creation.

Ideas of self-creation and activities of excellence often presume a set of conditions that make them possible. We tend to think of the pursuit of excellence, for example, under conditions that allow us to achieve it. Ideas of artistic self-fashioning assume that one is able to do so. But how do we imagine, say, excellence under adverse conditions? Conditions that militate against its pursuit or radically alter or invert our standard conceptions of what the activity of excellence involves?

Certainly life in our nation's housing projects is not conducive to the pursuit of excellence. Yet models of virtue exist there. Examples of individuals who escaped the projects abound, and decency does not require, though it wouldn't hurt, a certain standard of living. While the projects may not be the most optimal place for the pursuit of excellence, *Illmatic* demonstrates that excellence abounds in Queensbridge (and in projects all over this nation, for that matter). *Illmatic* was and continues to be a sign of hope, a lily in a concrete valley, which reveals the fact that individuals, with the help of cherished friends, do in fact forge selves that are unique, powerful, and unforgettable. This is what Talib Kweli calls the "beautiful struggle." The stuff of art.

"IT AIN'T HARD TO TELL"

A STORY OF LYRICAL TRANSCENDENCE

10

IMANI PERRY

"I

t ain't hard to tell." In homage to Nas, this line is repeated and referenced in dozens of hip-hop tracks by many artists, including Tupac, Mack 10, Noreaga, Bone Thugs n Harmony, Eve, MC Lyte, Snoop Dogg, Mystikal, Will Smith, Common, and more. This kind of tribute happens with the most brilliant lines in hip-hop. Remarkably, this song has two such oft-cited lines, the title refrain, as well as the second half of "Nas is like the Afrocentric Asian half man, half amazin'." The half-man, half-amazing self-definition from Nas comes from the kind of talk popular in young populist black religions of the twentieth century, and specifically from the Five Percenters he references when he calls himself "Afrocentric Asian." Being half man, half amazing is a statement of the divinity in the flesh-and-blood person, a radical concept when embodied by a black man, the member of a group often demonized, stereotyped, and abused by society. Nas therefore adopts a political self-concept that is part of an African diasporic religious nationalism. The ways he references Five

Percenter theology and the heavens in this song is in some ways an early version of the way he mentions black power, African American intellectuals, and the history of black music and art in his later songs. Nas always wants to give you something to think about that is bigger than you. He appreciates symbolism and his connections to a larger community: spiritual, racial, and political. At the same time, he's also committed to a kind of political realism. He never disses or departs from the life of the street; instead, he makes it plain and puts it into economic, historical, and social context.

To understand this, we must consider Nas as a poet. One way to see his poetry is to use a metaphor from literature. Michael Thelwell's novel, *The Harder They Come*, is useful because it captures the kind of Caribbean influences that become prevalent in hip-hop, and also because it tells the story of a young, musical street disciple, Rhygin. When Rhygin is coming to the big city, Kingston, to make it as a musician (and outlaw), he looks out the window of the bus and sees countless people riding bicycles. They fall into two categories. "One approach was Spartan. Slender, swift, mean-looking, no-nonsense machines. . . . The first operated on the principle of elimination, of unending reduction, the pursuit of pure function; the second was an expression of accretion of endless accumulation. Their frames were hardly discernable under a profusion of knick-knacks, baubles, talismen, medallions, ornaments of metal, glass and even fur, ingeniously attached."[1]

These two types of bicycles are both beautiful, one simple and clean, the other ornate and complex. One way to think of poetry is as a balance between the two sorts of bikes. The abundance of ideas, beautiful words, and concepts that poets wish to share must be pruned, undressed, and made clean and neat, in order to make the writing good and effective. You can also think of street or hip-hop celebrity life as the same kind of balance between extremes, bling, shine, cars, women, on the

one hand; poverty, hood, rawness, efficiency, and even loneli-
ness on the other. Nas as a poet, and as an MC, strikes the balance between extremes.

Nas satisfies our imagination with a plethora of "things."
He makes careful use of a rich world of ideas and experience,
yet he crafts elegant rhymes into something whole, straightforward, and piercing.

The track is full of images from the ordinary lives of hood-
dwelling, hustling young men. He references Rikers Island,
wearing an army jacket, glocks, tech 9s (and makes a pun about
their tendency to jam), and drugs (heroin, weed in its various
forms, ibuprofen). The references to everyday things are employed, however, to indicate his lyrical gifts. The rhymes hit
you like heroin, and they freeze listeners like the crystals in
the nostril of the user. Nas can release stress like the commercials proclaimed Motrin would. Hell, he's even nice enough to
smuggle an Uzi onto Rikers. (And by nice, I mean it in the vernacular sense of slick, cool, hot.)

Integrating a panoply of features of urban life into songs
is quite common in hip-hop to ensure credibility. And the use
of unexpected metaphors to profess artistic talent is ever-
present as well. It is unusual, however, to use the features of
urban life to create such unexpected metaphors as Nas does
in this song. He could say, "I tote tech 9s and rhyme wit' correct techniques" but instead he says, "Jam like a tech with correct
techniques" and you get the double entendre of jam (which
comes from the knowledge of how to use one: you have to be
careful the gun doesn't jam) as well as the power of the gun,
both expressing his lyrical gifts. He could say, "Wisdom be
leakin', I be creepin' in my grapefruit troop," but instead he
says, "Wisdom be leakin' out my grapefruit troop" and we get
this visual image of a gush coming out of his brightly colored
troop jacket. He's stylish and geared up like thousands of
other young men, but even leather isn't strong enough to hold

his power. Nas uses the symbols and features of hood life to make a statement about his skill. Consequently the song is at once a celebration of regular life and also an indication that he transcends the mundane. It bends to his will or, better yet, his gift.

Illmatic was released during a hip-hop renaissance. Wu-Tang Clan, Snoop Dogg, Black Moon, Outkast, and of course Biggie heralded the diversification of hip-hop. The arsenal of voices showed the divergence between that which would go platinum and that which would remain underground, and yet it also revealed the growing complexity of hip-hop, even that which would be consumed largely by white audiences attuned to pop sounds. In this flourishing time, many artists distinguished themselves by focusing on one theme in their music, be it violence, sexuality, conspicuous consumption, heavy symbolism, regionalism, or what have you.

Illmatic avoids such narrowness and instead presents itself as an *ars poetica*, a definitive statement of the art of hip-hop poetry, for which "It Ain't Hard to Tell" is the anchor. It has been said that this ambitious debut album embodies the entire story of hip-hop, bearing all of its features and gifts. Nas has the raw lyrics of old schoolers, the expert deejaying and artful lyricism of the 1980s, the slice of hood life, and the mythic. He narrates, exhorts, warns, and engages in prophylactic battles with prospective competitors. He talks about Queens and we remember the Juice Crew All Stars and how they put their borough on the map. The history of hip-hop up to 1994 is embodied in *Illmatic*. And the same can be said of this one song.

Biggie's *Ready to Die* album came out several months after *Illmatic*, and as Biggie was crowned king of New York in the popular culture of hip-hop heads, *Ready to Die* unfairly overshadowed *Illmatic*, which is truly a classic album. Though they were quite distinct artists, they innovated in analogous ways.

Biggie merged language that was high and low, vernacular and vocabulary words, in a way that sounded natural. He did this with a sophisticated understanding of the patterns of black language. When a different or unusual word or phrase could be introduced while still maintaining the aesthetics of black language, he inserted it.

Nas, in contrast, merged concepts that were high and low, vernacular and metaphysical, in a manner that was whole rather than pieced together, thus presenting a complex unity that is unusual in any music outside of jazz. What Biggie started to do with language in 1994, Nas had already begun to do with ideas on *Illmatic*. He carries us through the "righteous steps" of the cosmic, oceanic, and literal dimensions of his person. He transcends.

The jazz inflections in this song, and Nas's work in general, are likely a result of having a father, Olu Dara, who was an accomplished jazz artist and a member of the New York jazz loft scene. Moreover, Olu Dara's diverse artistic influences, the Caribbean, Africa, Mississippi, and Louisiana, have been filtered to his son, whose first album has both classic soul and reggae riffs abounding. In 1985 Olu Dara performed on an album called *Conjure*, which was music set to the text of Ishmael Reed poems.[2] Anyone familiar with the black arts movement will understand the influence poetry albums had on the development of hip-hop. I remember sitting on the floor as a child listening to the Last Poets, Gil Scott Heron, and Nikki Giovanni, knowing that speech could be as powerful as notes, and more powerful with notes. It is hard to imagine that *Conjure*, a more developed version of the black arts poetry album genre, didn't have a significant influence on Nas, who would become a poet-musician.

One review of *Conjure* stated, "One of the year's ten best records (1985), *Conjure* creates an exquisite tension between

word and sound, accentuates the rhythms of both and intensi-
fies the perceptions contained in each. It's immediately enjoyable, yet rich and challenging . . . funky jazz, blues, R&B
stewpot that bubbles, gurgles and steams."[3] The same review
would apply to the remarkable blending of word and sound
on *Illmatic.* Another review of *Conjure* stated, "Music to conjure with. . . . This is poetry that sings, music that makes you
think. . . . Reed says that the universe is 'a spiraling big band in
a polka-dotted speakeasy/effusively generating new light
every one-night stand.' Hanrahan and his friends embody that
last line perfectly."[4] And that review, referencing Reed's dance
between the universal and the simple act of human frailty, the
one-night stand, shows that the kind of transcendence Nas engages in comes to him honestly, through his personal music
history.

It is not hard to imagine Nas listening, as a young adolescent, to *Conjure.* Both Biggie and Nas had childhood images
of themselves on their album covers, suggesting that the
artist is not only a participant in hip-hop but a child of it.
Moreover, it indicates that the artist's creative power emerges
from being reared in the hood. Buildings can be seen behind
Nasir Jones's childhood face, which is partly transparent. He's
one with the city from the beginning. There is also an other-
worldly quality to the cover, and so it is a visual reminder of
his lyrical transcendence.

Transcendence refers to an existence beyond the limits of
material experience. African American spiritual traditions have
embraced transcendence as a means of maintaining faith in
the face of a white supremacist world. The encounter with
God, religious ecstasy or "getting happy," the vision of the
spirit in campground or over Jordan, have all been celebra-
tions of the self that is beyond the material world. When Nas
describes himself as transcending the physical world, he is par-

ticipating in a long-standing theological tradition. It is philosophical as well, since he argues for a self-interpretation that
both celebrates the material self (young, black, hood), and yet
understands a universality of personhood that is much larger
than those signifiers. Nas's statement goes beyond "I am more
than just a young black man." Instead, he says "as a young
black man I have a vast universe inside me."

The nineteenth-century transcendentalists rejected religious orthodoxy and celebrated the soul. They also sought liberation, spiritual and otherwise, as antislavery thinkers. Nas,
like earlier literary transcendentalists, uses spiritual tradition
without adhering to religious orthodoxy. Although Nas sees
beauty in God's world, that doesn't mean trees (actually it
does, but trees in the hip-hop sense—weed) but the physical
world of humans that is both ugly and beautiful. But Nas does
something distinct from the transcendentalists because when
Nas rejects mainstream social conventions, he doesn't use
moral superiority to justify it. He makes no case that he is better, although he does see that he is fundamentally good.

On the other hand, Nas is no Bigger Thomas, Richard
Wright's infamous character whose spirit is destroyed by racism
and classism, leading to the development of monstrous behavior. Rather, he is fully human and surviving in the hood. And
he's unapologetic for the dope slanging and gun toting. Why?
Because he's hip-hop, and hip-hop has an ethos of refusing to
adhere to the African American civil rights generation practice
of acting as the moral conscience of the nation. He isn't playing what is perceived as a futile game of appeal. But on the
other hand he isn't trying to scare white people into justice as
the figure of Bigger Thomas was supposed to do, as if to say,
"Look at this monster you have created." Nas is too embodied,
too much himself, to use his person as a point of political ar-
gumentation. He makes arguments instead. "It Ain't Hard to

Tell" is a song of survival. And his method of survival (beyond the practical matter of making money by hustling) is to transcend, to engage the full spectrum of his being.

The song has elements of the sort of black consciousness characteristic of early 1990s hip-hop. The Afro-Asiatic black man, the powers of weed, the black proletarian, no, scratch that, underclass, subjectivity. We can see a landscape of nascent dreadlocks and Ls, thick weed-packed cigars, street corners, rooms burning with hot-to-the-touch radiators in the projects. The lyrical revolutionary consciousness we hear in the song comes from its hood-centrism and rhetoric of positive racial identity. In 1994 Nas was doing something different with his work that marked him as definitely not old school. And he's retained it and carved a special place for himself in the history of the music. This is abundantly clear in "It Ain't Hard to Tell" and the narrative, or story, it tells.

The narrative form is a classic in hip-hop. From the beginning stories were told in hip-hop, either as entire songs or as subsections of songs. They tell of romantic or rival encounters, they are warning narratives, they are comedic indulgences. Sometimes they are even fantastical. In the twenty-first century the narrative form has fallen from popularity, but it always returns, if for no other reason because of the human need for storytelling.

In contrast, what has retained great popularity is the song that is an exhortation of the artist's skill or personal greatness. In "It Ain't Hard to Tell" Nas blends the forms and constructs a new kind of narrative by using exhortations as the vehicle moving us through the story. First, he announces himself and then he contacts the mic, sounding almost like he's just landed on the planet. He inhales with the silence of a sniper and exhales with the weed smoke blowing out of his airways. He takes steps, and we feel like they're underground. Then he's at Rikers, doing the bold and unbelievable.

We're brought back to the point of contact with the earth, "hit the earth like a comet invasion." And again, using Motrin as a metaphor, he goes in and then out, and then down to the depths, drinking Moet with Medusa in hell. The motion of explosive encounter, traveling in and out, then down, is repeated in various forms throughout the song. Perhaps that's why he tells us, "I dominate break loops, givin' mics men-e-strual cycles" because he creates a cycle that has a double entendre, sounding at once like menstrual, ministerial. He chooses an inanimate object, the mic, to give these cycles to. He becomes a powerful force because he breathes life into the mics. He's deific as he controls the forces of nature, and he's holy as the preacher. Of course, the motion and the references to the female body and the preacher are erotic as well.

The music loop is appreciated by this lyricist, as Nas tells us stories, going around and around, each time a variation, like the final line of a blues stanza, or the improvisation in a jazz standard, that relies on the beats for coherence. Large Professor's compositional brilliance makes the case even stronger for the song. The sample from Michael Jackson's "Human Nature" doesn't sound like the original's sensual ode to human passion, but instead like a celestial rhythm, that meta (physical). Its reuse for different purposes is the musical corollary to Nas's lyrical transcendence, human and yet more. The unity between the lyrics, the production, and the delivery is extraordinary on this album. He works seamlessly with AZ, Premier, Large Professor, and others, and in the end it is Nas's show and journey. As in Michael Jackson's "Human Nature," New York City has a living, breathing human presence that sets the rhythm for the song and album.

Hip-hop is New World music with roots in West Africa. When studying West African dance one of the first things you learn is to always listen to the drums. It is not dance, like ballet, where you count in your head, but rather you respond to the music and go where it takes you. Nas takes us on a journey with this song, unexpected in places, and we're coaxed into its rhythms and cycles, a meditation that prepares us to go with him each time the track is played. The journey the song takes prevents it from getting old. It appeals because it is repetition, taking us through again and again, to know it more and understand it better.

Although this song is "Nasty Nas" from early in his career, it suggests what is to come. There are elements of the wise braggart that we see in *I Am* and the humble servant of *God's Son*. The latter is present not in proclamation, but in the way he turns himself into elements of nature, things that are both mundane and yet powerful. In this song, you see the kind of metaphysical lyricism that characterizes a few special songs in his later career, such as "Nas Is Like" or even "Stillmatic." Although "Stillmatic" tells a story, it captures the mythic quality of his anchor track on the first album, and his transcendence as a poet who has the "blood of a slave, heart of a king."

This song also demonstrates the kind of courage that would distinguish Nas throughout his career. Critics have always compared his subsequent albums to the masterpiece *Illmatic*. But Nas, unlike so many MCs, refused to be formulaic with his future projects. He always tried something new, whether it was different production styles or the personification of new characters, collaborating with R&B singers or rockers, giving a history or politics lesson, or a lesson in street life. He has refused to be put into an artistic box. In "It Ain't Hard to Tell," we can see that Nas will be his own man and MC in two ways. One, he adopts a lyrical style that had been attempted by few people and done successfully by even fewer. Perhaps only Rakim before him had crafted such compelling metaphysical, symbolic, and transcendent lyrics. There was a risk with this song. And it departs from the kind of storytelling he does elsewhere on the album. It's a totally different kind of track and yet it works to bring the album full circle. Even as a newly signed artist, Nas had plans to experiment.

The reason, perhaps, that *Illmatic* came out as that perfect ten-song album is that it was so early in his career. He was already a brilliant MC, but perhaps there weren't yet all the ideas, experiences, books, stories, bursting forth in his head, that would appear as a vast and varied body of lyrics on future albums. On albums criticized for having too many tracks or being uneven in quality, those challenges are due to his experimentation with everything from commercial sounds to prayer songs. "It Ain't Hard to Tell" indicates that he plans to take journeys during his career as an artist, and yet in the midst of that remain connected and committed to the streets where he grew up.

Nas is such a brilliant lyricist because he always says just the right thing. The critics agree on that point, even if they think he sometimes has too many tracks or should have chosen different producers. His lyrics are always universally appreciated. Part of that is because he edits so beautifully, and we can see the beginnings of that skill on this track.

While Nas is a writer whose work is nuanced, complex, and rich with symbolism, he keeps his sentences clean. He drops out unnecessary words, so we get lines like, "not stories by Aesop," rather than "these ain't stories by Aesop," or "Speak with criminal slang, begin like a violin," rather than, "This brother speaks with criminal slang," or "I begin like a violin." He also resists setting up his allegories and metaphors where it is unnecessary. So, "place your loot up, parties I shoot up," is full of meaning yet only nine syllables.

Second, the phrasing is varied, so while the lines, "So analyze me, surprise me" are intensive and hard-hitting, the phrasing that follows, "I leave em froze like her-on in your nose," has first three, and then two, then three down beats before an accented syllable, making this phrase much mellower than the previous one. He is not excessive with intense "coming at you" words. Instead, he frequently pulls back and gives the ear time to rest, which of course creates emphasis when your ear is called to listen hard again. You can see the development of this skill in his later song "One Mic," which has an R&B ballad backdrop yet slowly heats up to a hard-hitting old-school gritty pace, only to get quiet again at the end.

Finally, Nas simplifies his lyrics by reusing the same words and metaphors multiple times. This adds to the unity of the piece, and also the sense that the song is "making it plain." More than once he describes audiences as frozen. He repeatedly tells us how he inhales and exhales. The gun comes in at least four times as a metaphor or a synecdoche of his hustler flow, and he's deep, deep, deep. Many gifted MCs resist this kind of reuse because they want the audience to know they can think of countless different words and metaphors for self-description. But Nas, a superior lyricist, understands the poetic effect of the repetition. The piece then can be about something, can be unified around several concepts and images, not just a string of brilliant phrases. The whole album is only forty minutes long. Not a word is wasted or excessive.

In spite of such brilliance, "It Ain't Hard to Tell" was never a number 1 single. It hit 91 on Billboard's Hot 100, 57 on Hot Hip-Hop/R&B Tracks, and 13 on Hot Rap Singles. But you'd be hard-pressed to find any listener of hip-hop in the early to mid-1990s who doesn't remember the song, and the majority will be able to cite at least three phrases from it. This is partly because the song gives you an adrenaline rush and yet doesn't have an iota of sentimentality. It is raw, authentic, even ugly at times, and at the same time, there is this exuberant hopefulness about it. On later albums Nas, still savvy and confident, comes across as a person with more wisdom, hurt, and scar tissue.

On "It Ain't Hard to Tell" Nas believes he can do any-thing, and he doesn't say that to buck himself up or keep him-self strong. He simply believes he can do anything. The song is mythic in a fresh and open way. Remember, this is before Nas has experienced the drama of leading a public life, before the loss of his mother, before the questions about ability to reach the musical heights of his youth. This is Nas looking forward to his career. And without hesitation he tells you it is going to be ridiculously hot.

Not just the hubris of youth, this is really faith and a cele-bration of human divinity in the midst of chaos and destruc-tion. It's also a celebration of human frailty. Nas doesn't shrink from calling himself a hustler, but he's a comprehensive, com-plex hustler, not a caricature. And so it is a song that builds and grows; it creates energy and ideas. So it doesn't matter that it wasn't number 1, because neither was Eric B's "My Melody," and every hip-hop head knows the universal impact of that song. This song not only inspired the undistinguished mass of listeners but accomplished artists as well.

The MC's who reference Nas by saying "It Ain't Hard to Tell," his lyrical descendants, have each taken a piece of his en-ergy to craft their own narratives. For example, Mack 10 cap-tures the nose thumbing to propriety and respectability that's part of unapologetically singing the hustler's song. Bone Thugs N Harmony's lyrics have the kind of hope and sense of personal power rather than despair at being dealt difficult cards that Nas offers in the original. Noreaga brings the infec-tiousness of the MC and his lyrics. He makes you want to buy them and he uses "busting heads" as a metaphor for the power of his words, like Nas. And Tupac makes plain that which Nas never says explicitly, but which he rhymes against, within, and through. The material realities of ghetto living are crushing, and the spiritual struggles to make sense of it all are demanding.

Nas doesn't reveal the struggle until later in his career, when he makes it look easy. And in that way, he says, it's a struggle you can survive and even flourish in.

This message is directed to those who live in the hoods. They "already know" about the struggle. He offers them strategies, armor. As his mind and spirit go high and deep in his lyrics, he can escape the surveillance of the police state that pervades the lives of black men in the hood. And then there are the final lines, "Nas's raps should be locked in a cell, it ain't hard to tell."

He tells us early on that he has the audaciousness to set himself up to break out of Rikers. But at the end he tells us that his lyrics, a symbol of his self, and himself should be locked up because they're so good. And so he flips the way prison and black men are depicted in our society. This is significant because the early 1990s were at the heart of the growth of the prison-industrial complex. Between 1980 and 2002, the number of people imprisoned in the United States quadrupled, and now the United States has the largest prison system on the globe. Close to 2 million people are incarcerated, and they are heavily and disproportionately people of color. Prisons are exploitive institutions that remove millions of citizens from regular view and social participation, under the guise of being "tough on crime" and "protecting the streets." Nas, like many hip-hop artists, refuses to identify prison as a place of shame. They remember those who are locked up (as in the song "One Love" on *Illmatic*) because they have hood consciousness. It is the poor who are in jail, and it is the poor who remember those who are locked up, who send them mail, who visit, who get their phones turned off because of exorbitant bills from the corporate price gouging for telephone lines behind prison walls.

To say, "I'm so nice, my rhymes should be locked up," is to not only flip it but embrace the Bad N**ga in our history. The one who violated social norms and dangerously flouted white authority. The trouble with hip-hop, according to many of its black critics, is the celebration of this character. Nas, however, hasn't been subject to as much criticism for using that image because his depiction is so complex and nuanced, and because it comes along with a social critique. The cell is not for those who are less than. The cell is for that which is too great, too much, for the world to handle. He slips in the reality of being caged by race and poverty, but quickly and confidently destroys its power. These are the last words on the album, and this choice speaks volumes. Nas has "heart" enough to say, "bring on the cell, it can't hold me." I don't mean heart in the sentimental sense, but in the New York black English sense, of courage, depth, and wisdom. He's telling us to get our heart on, too, and the song, the whole album, is a gift, both aesthetic and spiritual. In some ways it is more political than the explicit preaching of Public Enemy or Arrested Development, groups that preceded him. He refuses to take the high ground; instead, he brings his complex self into this critique. He's more like the gang members from the Blackstone Rangers who turned into Black Panther Party members, than the scholar revolutionaries; more Fred Hampton than Kwame Toure. He refuses to be a "good Negro" in any way. And he also refuses to make it easy to digest him. Importantly, this song lacks the pathos of a poem like Paul Laurence Dunbar's "Sympathy," which makes the reader feel the suffering of the caged bird singing. No, the way this song convinces the listener is through the argument and skill he brings, not sympathy. The author, from the projects in Queens, uses his character and vast personal mapping to convince us of what he has to say, and so for those of us listening, "It Ain't Hard to Tell."

REMIXES

THE SECOND COMING

JON SHECTER

(FROM *THE SOURCE*, ISSUE #55 APRIL 1994, PP. 45)

In hip-hop, as in life, perfection is hard to come by. When a rapper makes a full-length album, he bares his mind, his soul, and his skills for the world to digest. Usually we hip-hop fans can find parts of that whole that speak to us—a thumping track here, an ill verse there, this or that sequence of cuts. But every so often—and it has become more and more fair as this music develops—unique talent and a powerful creative vision combine to create utter potency.

The term "hip-hop classic" is not one we at *The Source* take lightly, but Nas is no lightweight. A product of the infamous Queensbridge Housing Projects, this is an MC injecting intelligence, creativity, and soul back into hip-hop. Nas captures poetic images so intense they force you to take heed, then once you're in his grasp he takes your mind deep into the essence of surviving, maintaining, and dealing with life in a vicious society. His debut album, *Illmatic*, brings together the cream of the crop in hip-hop production—Large Professor, DJ Premier,

Pete Rock, and Q-Tip—for an all-star excursion that lends new meaning to the phrase "looking for the perfect beat."

Nas got his rep with an ill voice and shocking religious imagery: "When I was 12, I went to hell for snuffing Jesus," "I'm waving automatic guns at nuns." The original idea for his album cover was to depict Nas holding Christ in a headlock. But his talent lies much deeper than mere shock value. Like the legendary Rakim, Nas is a true poet and a true MC. The lyrics themselves are technical masterpieces, full of layered rhythms and meanings, and his delivery is deft, changing cadence and flow like a musical instrument. He has the attention to detail of Slick Rick, the urban realness of Kool G Rap, and the vocal presence of Big Daddy Kane. But don't get me wrong, Nas (real name: Nasir, or "helper and protector") is a complete original. With a mere twenty years on this Earth, Nas has already raised the stakes in the hip-hop game, putting New York back on the cutting edge where it belongs. This is the story of the building of a hip-hop classic.—Jon Shecter

NAS: The first time I heard rap was in my projects. In the park, outside, summertime thing, when I was crazy young. They had them old disco records and shit, cuttin' that shit up. I witnessed all that shit, the beginning, you kno'm sayin'? Mad niggas, Private Stocks, blunts, fights, music. The first time I grabbed the mic was at my man Will's house—bless the dead. He lived right upstairs from me on the sixth floor, I was on the fifth. So I used to go up his crib and shit, in the morning, when his moms go to work. He used to hook his shit up, speakers and shit. We used to rhyme on "White Lines" and that old shit. Then later on, he bought equipment, like turntables, fader, we was makin' tapes like that.

First month of ninth grade, that was my last month. School ain't shit, the teachers is full of shit, the whole system is bullshit to me. I'm in there riffin' with the teachers, dissin' the teachers. I mean, I wanted to finish school, I didn't want to drop out of school, I wanted to finish school and do something. I was drawin' and shit, I wanted to do that, or write a movie, some ill shit. I used to write all type of shit when I was young, I thought I was blessed. But they crushed that type of shit, they crushed that in my head. I dropped out of school, start to smoke weed, that's what that was all about. I seen the other life, you kno'm sayin'? That's when we used to be runnin' around on the trains, beatin' people up, robbin' niggas and shit, on Queens Plaza, catchin' foreigners, Hindus, take their money. Young shit, wilin', drinkin' Old'Gold, you know? Me, Will, a whole bunch a niggas from my projects. That's when I did all that dumb shit, all them years.

I was just writin' on the down low. I ain't never tell niggas too much about it, 'cause for what? If I wanna rhyme one day, then they'll hear me. I just told my mans, 'cause we had a crew back in like '86, the Devastatin' Seven. They knew I could rhyme, but after them days, when the crew died out, I was just writin' on the dolo tip.

I met Large Professor in '89. And he was doin' shit for Eric B and them niggas, Rakim, G Rap and them. I met him 'cause I wanted to do a demo and shit with my own money. I was like, let me do a demo for myself, not even to shop. I ain't know what shopping was, I just wanted to do a tape for me. My man Melquan hooked me up with Large, and he had managed to get me in Power Play during the time he was workin' down there, in '89.

LARGE PROFESSOR: All along since even before "Live at the BBQ," I was trying be on Nas's side in this game. You know, I was tryin' to tell him, "Yo, if you want the ill shit, go to these certain people." I was hooking him up with these people so it wouldn't be some formal shit where the record company sets it up.

NAS: That nigga Akinyele was callin' my crib, "Yo, Nas, man, what you doin', man? Let's go, you gotta get your shit on." And me and him used to meet up, and we was goin' all over shoppin' my shit. That's the weakest part, shoppin' your shit, tryin' to find niggas who trust you, believe in you and like your shit. I knew niggas couldn't fuck with me in certain ways, I knew I had the potential to do my thing. But shit wasn't happenin' for me. I was like, kinda givin' up.

We went down there to Serch, when he was in the studio, and he was like, "Get on this joint!" So I kicked a rhyme I had right there, and "Back to the Grill" put a nigga on, gave a nigga a little leeway again. Right there, Serch like, "Who you signed wit'?" I'm like, "Ain't nobody fuckin' wit me, man." So he was like, "Let's do this!"

MC SERCH, EXECUTIVE PRODUCER: Nas was in a position where his demo had been sittin' around, "Live at the Barbeque" was already a classic, and he was just tryin' to find a decent deal. And I think Nas didn't know who to trust, and it seemed that no one was teaching him the ropes. So when he gave me his demo, I shopped it around. I took it to Russell first, Russell said it sounded like G Rap, he wasn't wit' it. So I took it to Faith. Faith loved it, she said she'd been looking for Nas for a year and a half. They wouldn't let me leave the office without a deal on the table.

DJ PREMIER: Everybody that really know hip-hop will always remember that record "Live at the Barbeque." Just hearing how his flow was on that record let me know that he was destined to be out here to last for a while. When I heard "Halftime," that was some next shit to me. That's just as classic to me as "Eric B for President" and "The Bridge." It just had that type of effect. As simple as it is, all of the elements are there. So from that point, after Serch approached me about doing some cuts, it was automatic. You'd be stupid to pass that up even if it wasn't payin' no money.

When it comes to beats, Nas is super picky. It's many times when I gave him tracks, and he'd call the next day and say, "Yo, I can't get with that." But it don't bother me 'cause I told him, "I want you to be happy, it's your record." There was many times when he liked a track, and then he was like, "Naa, I want to change it." I'd go back in there and change it, which is what happened to "Represent."

MC SERCH: Nas was very picky—no lie, we went through at least sixty-five, seventy beats on this album to find the ten that made the album. The most enjoyable sessions for me were the Primo sessions. I mean, Primo and Nas, they could have been separated at birth. It wasn't a situation where his beats fit their rhymes, they fit each other.

NAS: Then Large introduced me to Q-Tip, and he played some exotic shit. I was like yeah, he understand where I'm comin' from. I mean, everybody could make a rhyme about bein' a ill nigga with a ill, rough, rugged beat. But I like to take a nigga to another part of this shit, you kno'm sayin'? Get away from all that mass hysteria goin' around in the projects. That's how my music was, that's how the vibe was. When you chillin', not buggin' out like a little wild adolescent. I mean, when you mature over all of this, when you got a little common sense in the game—I try to make songs like that.

Q-TIP: Large Professor told me that Nas had wanted to work with me, so one night he brought Nas and Akinyele by my crib. I played him a couple beats, and he just said, "That's it right there." Later that night, he called and told me the concept for "One Love."

NAS: My man Will was up north—bless the dead. He used to write me, call my crib collect, or I write him. All my peeps got locked up, my brother too. I never got locked up. I was in jail one time, in a cell, a little ass cell, 'cause a dumb ass, stupid punk cop wanna tell me I can't smoke weed in my own projects! My whole projects is on probation, man. And that's all they talk about, is who they seen in there, who they left in there, who they was chillin' with, who they had beef with, who was makin' noise and how they tryin' to survive now that they home.

The Bridge is the biggest projects in the whole country—and that's a fact, you can look it up. Stars is born out there. We got some NBA players from out there and the whole shit. Queensbridge added a lot to hip-hop—we just put more science into the whole chemistry. Marley Marl was on some ill shit back then. MC Shan, "The Bridge," that's the anthem right there.

So when I was a kid, I just stayed in the projects; that shit is like a city. I ain't never go nowhere. Everybody's mentality revolves around the projects, just trying to survive. Everybody gotta eat, you know what I mean? It's just the attitude out there, it's just life. You can't be no sucker.

L.E.S.: I live in Queensbridge—been around for a long time—used to run with Shan and Marley back in the days. I knew it was just a matter of time before a brother would look out. Being that he had all these big-name producers on his album, I felt kinda good that Nas picked me to do something. I was never really presenting shit to Nas though, and he ain't really come to me for a beat. We was just in the crib chillin', playin' shit, you know, going through shit, and he was like, "Yo, that's it." What we was really doing was trying to put something together for an interlude, but Nas was just feeling it. The kid AZ, who's on, was there at the time, so he felt it when Nas felt it, and it was all right on time.

NAS: Large took me down to Pete Rock's basement years ago, back when Pete was DJing on Marley Marl's show. When we went to the studio, he laid the beat down to "The World Is Yours," but he had to break out. And me and my man stayed. I laid one verse down, my man made up the chorus, sung it. Then the next session we had to finish it, Pete Rock came, he checked it out, he was like, he felt that he could sing it better.

DJ PREMIER: After I heard brothers like Q-Tip and Pete Rock's joints, I was like, "Oh shit, I gotta go back to the lab." Them niggas represented with they shit. When we did "Memory Lane" towards the very end, he said he wanted something that was way different from the other stuff they did. Q-Tip's track kinda set a new tone for the album, along with "The World Is Yours" and "Memory Lane." Not anybody could rhyme to that. Most MCs would probably reminisce about situations like he did, but the way he did it is the way the niggas like to hear it, and we the hardest ones to please.

NAS: I knew that I could take this shit right here and put it in niggas' heads and have them listening to me. This is my hustle right now, this rap shit. When I'm bored, stressed out, no money, no bitch, no fuckin' nothing, no friends, I'm by myself, I'm like, damn. Or I might be fucked up in the game—my man get killed, or my man get robbed. Now we gotta go over here and do what we gotta do with them. Shit like that gets stressful, and you can blow your whole fuckin' melon thinkin' the shit, buggin' out. You could just go outside and just bust somebody— you know, that's how a lot of shit happens, stressful shit. When I was young, I was writin' rhymes like three songs a day like it wasn't shit. Now I don't hardly write no fuckin' rhymes; shit is different now. When I'm bored, and I'm thinkin' about all the shit that's going on, I get back to my old hobby. I just start writin' things down in a poetic form, you kno'm sayin'?

My little talent on the side. My whole thing is this: me gettin' established in this game, and then get my moms right, so then my brother could be all right. I'ma be all right regardless. My pops? That nigga broke out when I was like six. But we always stayed in touch, he a cool nigga. He played the horn on "Life's a Bitch," at the end of that shit he played the trumpet. He played jazz and shit.

FAITH NEWMAN, EXECUTIVE PRODUCER: Nas has an old soul. You kinda get the feeling he's been around before in the way he observes life. His mind is always kind of operating at a very mystical level. The people who are the most respected producers in hip-hop have a certain sense of awe when it comes to him. I have never, in all the fifteen years that I've been listening to rap, ever heard anybody express something so vividly and perfectly as Nas. He doesn't have to shout to be heard. It's so effortless. You listen to his music, you get this mental picture of where he's coming from. It's not gratuitously violent or sexist, it's just real. It's touching too.

NAS: This was '92, in May, May 23. Outside on my block, on Vernon and shit. We was throwin' a party the next day, and everybody had to give up money to contribute to a party for us. We was gonna bring the speakers out, have a cookout and everything. This dumb bitch was runnin' her mouth and shit, and Will was drunk, so he did whatever. I think he snuffed her or something. And then she wanted to call some niggas on the down low out here and gas them up. Corny niggas, they came out here. Came to my projects and just started wettin'. They seen Will, they was like, "What's up?" They wet Will up, shot him in the back, then they shot my brother in the leg. He layin' down there, dumb-ass police lookin' at him, ain't doin' shit. And then we see an ambulance come, cool, we jump in a cab. We get to the hospital, Astoria General. We get in there and we chillin' like, "Yeah, I hope he all right." Then fifteen minutes later they just gettin' him in there! So now we dissin' 'em. Then like an hour later they come and tell us he ain't make it. And then them bitch-ass niggas got locked up the next day, snitched on each other, scared like bitches. Still, it ain't over until it's over.

Q-TIP: Nas ain't got no gimmick to his style; you gotta sit and decipher what he says. He got a little old school in him too, but his shit is just raw. Aside from the shit that he writes, his voice is what's so ill about him. His voice is just butter.

NAS: I used to read lessons, actual facts, solar facts. I read books on African history. I used to read books on Egyptian times and shit, how they had shit locked down back in the days. And motherfuckers from all over the world was comin' to Egypt to learn; that was college for the world. Back in the break dancin', Zulu Nation, ballbreakin' days, there was this kid, this god, that was enlightenin' all of us that we was god. So we took heed to him, and then I took it upon myself to seek more knowledge, and that's how I started leamin' lessons and shit like that.

My moms used to make me and my brother go to church when we was little kids. I used to look at them like jokes, screaming around like fuckin' clowns. I'm like, if you wanna get technical, Mr. Preacher Man, let's go all the way back to the origin of all of that. You gonna sit here and talk about Jesus Christ and do this. We wasn't even up on it until black people came to America.

MC SERCH: If you trace hip-hop, every three or four years there's a group that breaks the mold. Nas is the new heart of what hard-core hip-hop is going to be about. Besides being the most prolific artist I've ever heard in my life, he is pound for pound, note for note, word for word the best MC I ever heard in my life.

NAS: This feels like a big project that's gonna affect the world, that's what it feels like we're working on. We in here on the down low, confidential, FBI-type shit, doing something for the world. That's how it feels, that's what it is. For all the ones that think it's all about some ruff shit, talkin' about guns all the time, but no science behind it, we gonna bring it to them like this. We got some rap for that ass.

Illmatic
Columbia
Production: DJ Premier, Large Professor,
Pete Rock, Q-Tip, L.E.S.

5 MIC REVIEW

MATT LIFE

While the media was hyping Snoop's album as the most anticipated debut of all time, many of us in the hip-hop core had our
eyes on another prize—*Illmatic,* the debut "reality storybook"
from Queensbridge's Nas (formerly known as Nasty Nas). After peeping his skill on "Live at the BBQ," "Back to the Grill,"
and the official bomb, "Halftime," street dwellers and industry
folks alike were predicting Nas's first album to be monumental.

Now, I'm not one to sweat the next man, but . . . I must
maintain that this is one of the best hip-hop albums I have
ever heard. Word. Let me speak on it.

Musically, when Nas hooked up with four of hip-hop's
purest producers, it seems like all of the parties involved took
their game to a higher level of expression. Whether listening
to the dark piano cords of Pete Rock's meaner side on "The
World is Yours," or Primo's sinister bounce on "Represent," or
Large Professor's old-soul sound on "Memory Lane," or Q-
Tip's jazzy marimba melody on "One Love"—it all motivates.
Your mind races to keep up with Nas's lyricism, while your
body dips to the beat.

Lyrically, the whole shit is on point. No clichéd metaphors, no gimmicks. Never too abstract, never superficial. Even the skit-intros are meaningful, and the album's only guest rapper, AZ, is dangerous in his own right. (And he's unsigned too? Not for long, son.) Nas is just the epitome of that "New York State of Mind" in terms of style and delivery. But even outside of the "Rotten Apple"—"Listeners, bluntheads, fly ladies, and prisoners, Hennessy-holders, and Old School niggas" from all over will be able to relate to Nas's many techniques. Nas creates fantasy: "I drink Moet with Medusa/Give her shotguns in hell/From the spliff that I lift and inhale." He philosophizes: "I switched my motto/Instead of saying 'Fuck tomorrow'/That buck that bought a bottle/Coulda struck the Lotto." He flows: "One for the money/Two for pussy and foreign cars/Three for Alize, niggas deceased or behind bars/I rap divine god/Check the prognosis, is it real as showbiz/My window faces shootouts/Drug overdoses/Live amongst no roses, only the drama/For real, a nickel-plate is my fate/My medicine is the ganja." And on, and on . . .

Nas's images remind me a lot of personal memories and people, both passed and present, so the impact goes beyond the entertainment aspect. All this may sound like melodrama, but it's not just me. I've been hearing similar responses all over. While "Memory Lane" is my shit, my homies claim "The World Is Yours," and if you've got peoples doing time, then "One Love" may hit you the hardest. There's nothing wack though, just different intensities for different people to relate to. The bottom line is this: even if the album doesn't speak to you on that personal level, the music itself is still well worth the money. If you can't at least appreciate the value of Nas's poetical realism, then you best get yourself up out of hip-hop. Keep it real, baby.

—SHORTIE

STREETS DISCIPLE

REPRESENTING QUEENSBRIDGE, NEW YORK, AND THE FUTURE OF HIP-HOP, NAS IS IN HIS OWN STATE OF MIND

BOBBITO THE BARBER
(FROM *RAPPAGES*, MAY 1994)

Queensbridge's own Nas represents more than meets the eye. No doubt, Nas represents New York. His deeply etched rhymes live and breathe the tough East Coast city streets, injecting images of hyped-up corner ciphers on cold NYC nights. And Nas definitely represents the gifted select few born to wreck mics with absolute ease. Since being featured on Main Source's "Live at the BBQ," Serch's "Back to the Grill Again," and then releasing the single "Halftime" off the Zebrahead soundtrack, Nas has followed no other MC's lead but his own. Nas's rhyme style, flow, phrases, concepts, reflections, and voice are all distinctly his. The only artist that he parallels is Rakim; they both have that air of mystery about them.

I have to admit that Nas's mysterious demeanor made me apprehensive about interviewing him. You hardly ever see him out at parties or functions, and when I have, I've noticed his mode of operation. He is not unfriendly, but he is definitely far from outgoing. He is the epitome of someone on the low, always to himself, which makes people around him wonder what the phukk he is thinking or feeling. Listening to his album almost clues you in. His perceived passivism is a paradox, because his attitude is really one of true active observation. Couple his acute observational skills with his command of the English language, and you end up with brilliant lyrics. Mix that up with a powerful delivery that does justice to beats by Pete Rock, Premier, Large Professor, Q-Tip, and L.E.S., and you end up with a classic debut album.

But more importantly, Nas represents hip-hop. He has the potential to push this music to another level, just as Rakim has done in his career. This young street disciple was raised on break dancing, graffiti writing, park jams, DJ mix shows, beat-boxing—the whole nine. Nurtured by a culture of heartfelt expression and blessed with a mastery of words, Nas's vivid music embodies hip-hop's positive energy. The massive buzz on Nas's debut album, *Illmatic*, among those with their ear to the street reflects on both local and universal levels. It's a true testament to the kinship of hip-hop when someone like Nas makes it. You can feel that desire to make it from both the megatalented artist from around the way and the peeps around him. Inevitably the game's about going for self, but at the same time never forgetting to give props where props are due—to the family (blood or otherwise) and neighborhood (especially the projects) that raised you. That's not just some "New York shit," because living the real life is universal.

RapPages: You're no longer called Nasty Nas, just Nas. What's the scientifics behind that?

NAS: I had crazy names. I've been MC Nas, Rapper Nas, Nasty Nas—all type of shit, so I'll just leave it as Nas. Straight to the pidoint.

RP: The first time I heard you was in early '91 on "Live at the BBQ," then "Halftime" in '92. Now it's almost three years later and the public is still awaiting your album. What's been the holdup?

NAS: You know how that is. I didn't even think I was gonna make [an album]; I was gonna give up. I was trying to make them shits back in the days, phukking with Large Professor when Eric B was paying for studio time. It goes back to when we was in the lab doing shit when I was fifteen. That was '88 to '89. In '89 I was sixteen, and we had some raw shit. I was gonna come out through Eric B and them. I was young and wasn't on top of my shit, so I kinda faded away from everybody. I missed out and lost contact. So later on I got back in touch with Large, and me and him started working hard. I had some demos for a year that I was trying to shop and I was phukking with mad niggas, trying to get signed. Then Large got a chance to put out his album. I didn't put mine out. He said, "Phukk it, just be on my shit," and that was on "Live at the BBQ." Boom. After that I was just chillin', cuz I thought I had caught enough wreck. I just wanted to have my clientele on the street. I met Serch one year later, and he thought I had a deal. And I'm like, "I don't give a phukk. Just get me on wax and all respect due and good looking out." He pulled a couple of strings and got a nigga on. Boom, then [came the] "Back to the Grill" joint. Then I got signed to Columbia. I came to see you when you were A&R at Def Jam and you fronted on me and 'n' shit. But you still my man.

RP: I remember that. It's funny, cuz seeing you develop from "Live" to "Back" to "Halftime" to where you are now, you've definitely grown as an MC and as a personality too. In '91, when Akinyele, Kool G Rap, and you came by my office, it seemed like on paper and on wax you were this quiet—not shy, but to yourself—almost mysterious character. I knew you would develop, but you weren't there yet. At that point, I knew Russell [Simmons] wouldn't be interested. I was more looking out for you. I didn't want to waste your time.

NAS: Like you said, I had to progress into me, into Nas. I was crazy young. I'm still the same person, but now I got a little more knowledge, so I can handle my business.

RP: I've noticed you uphold a lot of mystery in your character. It seems like you're on the mad DL—you really don't say much to people. You leave a lot to people's imaginations to figure you out. Is there a reason for that?

NAS: That's just me.

RP: You've never been the outgoing type?

NAS: Never. Only time I was outgoing was when I was whylin' in high school. Running around the train hitting people in the face with a bunch of niggas. Like we couldn't be stopped. That's the wildest I ever got—that's part of growing up. But even back then I was to myself.

RP: Your pops was an accomplished jazz musician. What's his name?

NAS: Olu Dara. My whole name is Nasir Bin Olu Dara Jones. Nasir is Arabic. It means "helper and protector." Bin means "son of." Jones is the slave part. Niggas weren't trying to say my name back in the days. When we used to tag up on trains and high places, we'd climb up—I didn't want to write Nasir, you couldn't even say it—I'd just write Nas or Kid Wave. I wanted to write riddles and rhymes and make it mean something, but niggas would say we didn't have time for that. But, yeah, [my pops] got a little busy. He bust my head. Miles Davis wrote something about him in his book. My pops used to bring me up to the studio. This is when they had no belief in rap. They didn't even understand it. Just like when we was break dancing, they didn't understand. But it's gonna stay in effect.

RP: You used to break-dance yourself?

NAS: I used to pop. I was Kid Wave. I was down with Breakin' In Action. We had the shirts, white gloves, and hats that said B.I.A. My man Will used to do the windmills.

RP: It seems like on your LP, conceptually, Nas represents a lot of different stories. You have entire songs that are thematically metaphorical. Before, you just did metaphors in one verse on your posse cuts, but now there's an outgrowth.

NAS: I knew what I had to do if I was gonna rhyme on a "Symphony" jam. The only way to catch somebody's attention is to say the right shit. That's how you gotta get off on posse cuts. But when you get a chance to put a whole album together with a format, a nigga isn't gonna want to sit down and listen to some ill shit all day. He wants to get some type of mental gain. Like reading a book, he wants to put the tape in and feel it. Before, I knew I had to come off real quick on the mic. But now it's more like letting my shit flow. Now people are ready to focus in on me. But I wouldn't have had a chance to do that if I didn't come off before.

RP: What is your process of writing?

NAS: I used to tape off the radio. Play it the next day, all day, then for the whole month straight. After the month was up, I'd feel it and write a whole bunch of songs. Then I taped again and [I would do] the same cycle. I tape other people's songs—Dr. Jekyll and Mr. Hyde, Shan, Shante, Kool Moe Dee, LL, Run-DMC—and I build off them.

RP: Is that where you draw most of your inspiration?

NAS: I listen to their style. I'm not trying to sound like anybody, but I'm hearing while they're teaching—everybody's teaching each other. There are mad different flows, and then you get your own. You see how everyone rides the beat, and then you see how you ride it. You put your whole heart into it.

RP: Who would you say are your favorite or most influential MCs?

NAS: First, I think New Edition made me want to come out. I seen them and I was like, "Phukk them niggas—I want to get on and be a star." I heard Dr. Jeckyl and Mr. Hyde talking about "Magic Potion" and said, "that shit is clever." Run-DMC was ill. Shan. Marley Marl used to do jams in the park. And Biz performed; Shante too. We didn't know who the phukk Biz was, and he came out doing the beat box. It was fat. Marley on the tables, right there. You didn't pay nothing. At the end of it somebody's ass was out. But that's how it was. It was butter, cuz we all had shows. If you was a little muthaphukka who didn't know shit about rap, but they said there was a show in the park, you were there, so now you gonna know something. The foundation was right there.

RP: Who out there now would you give stats to for being progressive?

NAS: I like just about all of them right now.

RP: Any MCs that you don't like?

NAS: Nah. [he winks at me] I just won't even listen to them. Or my peoples won't even play them, so they may as well not even exist to me if they're crazy whack.

RP: You came up to the Stretch Armstrong show that I host on WKCR and rhymed off the top of your head. You surprised me.

NAS: What I did with y'all was good for me. I haven't done that in a while, but your show is for real. I put mad niggas in my projects up on the show.

RP: It seems like there are a lot of meaningful things that you write about. What is your motivation?

NAS: I write the shit that I'm going through and what I see niggas go through. Just what's in me. It's rap. When you look at back in the days when niggas was rhyming, what made them grab the mic and start talking ill shit? Check *Wild Style* the movie—that's the Bible. They just expressing themselves. Young Africans and Latinos trapped in a cell of hell, screaming, telling somebody, "We still surviving out here and I'm doing my thing and nobody's stopping me, but I'm gonna tell you what's in my way." If I'm writing a letter to my man in jail and he's writing me back, and the shit is stressing me cuz he's doing hard time and he's mad at the world, and I'm like, "Damn, I wish he was home so we could be chilling," I'm thinking about that, so I might as well put it in a song. Everybody rhymes about smoking weed 24/7, so I'll try not to even phukk with that. But it's in my lyrics cuz it's a part of my life, but it's not the focus though. The focus is universal. There are so many things to rhyme about. There's not one particular thing, like it's gotta be guns and shooting niggas and smoking weed. I just rap.

RP: You haven't confined yourself to a gimmick or one theme. Nas is like a whole . . .

NAS: Life. It's life and death.

RP: Some of your close friends have passed. How do you perceive death and the afterlife?

NAS: X. Unknown. X equals Unknown. I can't even build on that; that shit is deep. A nigga been with you all your life, since you was young. I grew up in my man Will's crib. He used to have a big speaker. He'd play records like "White Lines." That bass line, he'd slow it up and we'd rhyme. He'd cut it up. We used to listen to Awesome Two, Chuck Chillout on 98.7, Mr. Magic on BLS, all the old-school shit. As we heard rappers come out and progress, in our own little world we was making tapes for only us to listen to. As the years went by, we had like little albums, so we was progressing right along with them. Will was my DJ, but he used to rhyme. He used to do everyone's style that you hear now. He used to just bug and rhyme like B-Real, start whylin' like Onyx, then slow it up like Rakim. He had crazy styles off the top of his head. I was the one who would sit down and write, so it took me longer to come up with shit, but we were making tapes. You grow up, we slinging, making a little bit of cash, just the average shit. He got locked up, then he came home, and then we was blowing up again. Then, boom, the nigga's gone. I had these pictures of how shit would be when he grew up. How shit would fall into place. The cipher is incomplete now, cuz my man is gone. Even though he's under, I'm still standing—that's understanding. Now I go to his crib and his moms is there, and I just feel him. Something that he left there. I look at his clothes, his equipment, his turntables, and I can feel him. So it's still there. I'm gonna represent and keep it real.

RP: Do you subscribe to any religion?

NAS: Nah. It's good to do research and study what the ancient Muslims or the ancient Christians were about and how the religion came about. Even if you're not a Five Percenter, it's good to look at the lessons and see how they tried to educate each other. I studied lessons. I have knowledge of self. I don't have no religion, but I studied my Black African history. I read up on Asian and Oriental spiritual rituals. They all similar. Right here in America, it's all about living and doing the right thing. Do the right thing, and that's righteous right there.

RP: What motivated you to do all that reading? Were you in school, or did someone guide you?

NAS: My man Jah Eddie was crazy smart. Everyone knew him in the projects as being a baby genius. He was doing crazy good in school and he hung out and drank beer and smoked weed. He always had a book on him, had a bag of fruits to give us. Always came around giving us lectures, and niggas would be like, "Go ahead with that bullshit, Jah." But he was a cool nigga and he understood and we used to laugh. He used to catch me on the solo tip and just drop it on me. Show me a book if I didn't believe his accuracy. He put me onto a few books. At one time, I was getting real Afro-centric, real into self. At that time, I dropped out of school. I wasn't doing shit.

I didn't want to be dumb, so [I was like], I'm gonna learn something while these other niggas is whylin'. If I'm not in school, I'm gonna be DL reading shit. Helping out my dome.

RP: You make a lot of references to religious figures. Do you have animosity toward them, or what's your motivation behind that?

NAS: Me and my man Bo—he's locked up right now, one love, kid, if you read this magazine—we used to read books on mysticism, real eerie type of shit. We used to play jokes on niggas when we were little, like put an egg on top of a refrigerator and tell 'em if the egg moves he got to get out the house as soon as possible. Reading up on ill witchcraft shit—it was bugged. We used to scare niggas and tell them fake stories. In junior high school, kids would bang on the lunchroom table and rhyme. When it was our turn, we used to say shit like, "Jesus came/he asked my name/I pulled out some roach spray and lighter and burst a flame in his face/then I chopped him in the face . . ." and niggas used to say, "what's wrong with y'all?" We'd tell them we the devils, take our middle fingers and chase them. Me and Bo used to write that deep shit, taking it one step further, but not dwelling on it too hard. I didn't feel there was that much wrong with it. I know his name wasn't Jesus Christ. There's more science to it than what we see in the Bible. You gotta do mad research to be accurate, cuz there are lies in books. If you are really praising, you'd find out who he really was and then praise him for what he did. You can't just accept what you hear readily. Before somebody tells me not to talk about Jesus, they should find out who he really was. I know that as times went on, people added little pieces, omitted others to the Bible, so it's not completely accurate. I could say, "I went to hell for snuffing Jesus." Phukk that, what has he done for me? I'm out here in Queensbridge. Jesus ain't coming to Queensbridge. If he is, he's not Jesus Christ, he's something more powerful and much deeper than that. That's all.

RP: Where do you see your future going? Do you want to produce, bring other people out?

NAS: I want to be the first black president. The president of the world. Somebody's gonna have to take me out. I'm not gonna reveal my secrets. I'ma just rhyme—be the rapping president. Be up on a chair telling mad poems all day till I get old. Even if I don't have a record deal and they stop putting records out, and they don't put nothing on the radio and said "Phukk rap" and dropped me, I'll still be rhyming. I'll just bring it back to the essence in the parks, where the real niggas survive, and clown that shit where niggas want to be different and talk bullshit when they wouldn't go to the park cuz they scared. I'll be there, twenty-nine years old.

AN ELEGY FOR *ILLMATIC*

GREGORY TATE

Like Balzac or Marquez, Nas doesn't just give you a story but an exotic world in words, a place you can imagine actual doomed but undaunted people living, sweating, hustling, drinking, drugging, shooting, and dying. Like Borges, Calvino, or Chuck Jones, Nas remains startled enough about this marvel of constructing fictive universes to be self-reflexive and comically knowledgeable about the act and art of speculative writing as a base form of quixotic reality. And as much as any Brian Eno ambient music project (like *Music for Airports*), Nas's work exudes the ephemeral, fugitive resonance of trace memory—conjuring hardened lozenges of a ritual-habitual space time and chaos already vanished into thin air. An already forgotten never was, still feverish and furtive, one that retains substantial mythopoeic presence

I was not surprised to learn a few years back that Nas once had aspirations to become a film director because his best lyrics—especially all those on *Illmatic*—scan more like a cinematic, panoramic array of shots, cuts, and ellipses than the poetic potpourri of personal statements that defined the styles of his lyric peers—those of both your resolutely allusive and your more in-your-face types. What distinguishes Nas is the logical, world-ordering point of view in his rhymes. It simulates the didactic yet dreamy surrealism of the motion picture camera—not just documenting what he has seen but framing the fractured actions of the world for us in ways that make us believe we too are behind a hidden roving lens directing the actions and interiority of endangered humans and their fraught habitats.

If the Notorious Biggie verbally takes us inside his body and thuggish muggish mind, letting us feel what it is like to move around in a world as big, brutal, jocular and intimidating as himself, Nas takes us inside his line of vision, his POV on the hood scene. In this way he provides us with a striking continuity of extreme long shots and close-ups, always giving us the best seat in the house while he conjures the carnival of lost souls that made camp in his 1990s Queensbridge neighborhood. Arguably, some of the most memorably dark, depressive but flowing lyrics in hip-hop history were written by Nas, Biggie, and members of the Wu-Tang Clan on the death knell of the crack trade. Lyrics full to bursting with desperate criminal intent and murderous deeds, raw panic, paranoia, random, indiscriminate violence, and a bunker mentality. The words and music composed by Nas and others in that time invented a truly black noir narrative form—a brilliantly scored urban counterpoint to Raymond Chandler, one bent on exposing an American underside where the nation's swarthiest Others define normality. Here is an apocalyptic and damned America where the moral codes echo those found in Depression-era gangster movies—codes that treat betrayal of your criminal brother as a sin greater than mass murder and glorify bestial ways of life that could only offer imminent extinction or incarceration as things to be cherished far more than civilized notions of evolution, progression, permanence, or stability.

On his lyrical masterpiece, *Illmatic's* "N.Y. State of Mind," Nas presents us with a peripatetic, spectral, metaphysical antihero outracing temptation, poverty, and evisceration in a razor-edged hall of mirrors, an antihero with enough fatalism and self-consciousness to know he's already a ghost, a figment of ghettos past, landscapes already dissipated and dispirited, a dead man walking and talking himself into an even more vicious and more bland next century that will have no place for his kind: self-starting lone wolves of a vanishing American urban wilderness. Men utterly romantic, profane, and self-mythologizing about their tall-in-the-saddle inner-city cowboy swagger and survival skills. Men who define an era that was already receding into nostalgia while it happened, men who opened wide those grimy, dark, subterranean tunnels where the most valiant and downtrodden of America's dreamers were plying an ill-icit, il-legal, illmatic inner-city trade. Borderlands whose only logic and sense showed up in hip-hop, where living to stylishly tell the ugly, gully-gothic tale offered a way out of that tale's most stereotypical and pathetic denouements. In the dramatic modes of the African American bush, a jungle we know to be as rife with celebration and contemplation as with concrete, Nas, upon the release of *Illmatic*, was revealed to be a tragician and tactician of the highest order.

BORN ALONE,
DIE ALONE

DREAM HAMPTON

As with all things modern hip-hop, my Nas story is about Tupac—he of the suspiciously cocked bandana, the eternally unconquerable spirit, and mediocre rhyme skill. Of the first and last, it seems, we argued endlessly. "You'd be cute if you did your hair," he'd opine about my tangled, perfectly-accept-able-in-New York freedom mop. "Why don't you take that goofy-ass bandana off the side of your bean head?" (Biggie had described said head as Q-Bert-ish, but I sat on that one; best to have an arsenal.) And so it went. Back and forth. White owls and nonlethal insults traded between us for the six months it took for me to cover for *The Source* the three trials in which he found himself defendant.

A FedEx-delivered advance of Nas's *Illmatic* arrived at my sun-soaked room at the Mondrian one early morning before court. Sounds a little archaic, I know. Advance CDs. Delivered to hotel rooms. Legally? This was the twentieth century, an ancient era, when rappers regularly scuffled with Senegalese bootleggers in midtown Manhattan and record labels directed Feds to warehouses, not teenaged boys' hard drives. I'd definitely held an *Illmatic* bootleg, seem to remember passing dubs back and forth to my neighbor Biggie. *Illmatic* was one of the most anticipated albums of the 1990s and Nas was considered nothing less than an heir to Rakim, the bearer of the new testament.

Two years before, in *The Source* office, Nas's verse on Main Source's "Live at the BBQ" was constantly on rewind. We knew then, with that one Nietzsche-inspired, Five Percent–informed lyric about snuffing Jesus, that we were witnessing the birth of a great. Same way Bird must have felt the first time Miles sat in with him. It doesn't take a decade's worth of work to signal greatness; sometimes a few bars herald a second coming. As LES, his longtime producer, blessed us with preview tracks and marathon freestyles, it became clear that Nas was the truth; a hyperliterate high school dropout, a near-nihilist who leaned toward optimism, a writer who lived in the details but could paint the big picture. There had been false prophets (Kurupt was once considered the next Rakim), but in Nas we'd found a true pilgrim. With the pen, he was indeed extreme.

Pac may have been born in New York and raised in a few other cities, but by the time *The Chronic* swallowed whole the early 1990s hip-hop scene, he was throwing up West Side. Fine. I got Snoop. Understood how perfectly matched his pimped-out character was to Dre's throwback cinema. But Nas—he was Harvard to their state college, Toni Morrison to their Terry McMillian. I sat through the day's court proceedings. Pac was itching for his opportunity to testify that, yes, he'd taken on the Hughes brothers, that he was guilty as charged (of instigating a fistfight), but was hardly the "menace" the prosecutor hoped to lock up for months. This wasn't that day. This was one of those taxpayer-sponsored days that just went on and on with pointless witness testimony and minuscule evidence being entered and logged. When we finally broke for lunch, Pac and I headed to an Italian spot on Melrose. I was holding an Alamo-issued Lexus (though *The Source* had reserved a Cavalier), but more importantly, I had *Illmatic*, the whole joint. Pac had yet to make his first important album, *Me Against the World*, and he was nothing if not a lyricist lover, so he hopped in my Lex and pushed repeat on "N.Y. State of Mind" four times before we made it to Melrose.

Illmatic was a dirty bomb thrown at the orchestral sonic soundtrack that was *The Chronic*. The snippets of New York life, the sound of an elevated train, the random gems niggas utter as you pass them on foot, they were the shrapnel. This wasn't a backyard bikini barbeque where the Ohio Players and DJ Quick are mashed up; this was a three-month bid on Rikers, a dirty dice game, blunts of brown Brooklyn sparked in the park after dark. And Nas was more than a conductor. He was the quiet genius, pen and pad unpacking multisyllables and complex stanzas the way tougher guys from his projects drew semiautomatics. Pac was an instant convert. I dubbed the CD onto a cassette for him. He got his manager to upgrade his rental to a Lexus (he traded some midsize rental from the Cavalier family). The next day he pulled into the courthouse parking lot, his interior cloudy. He pulled his dub from the whip, threw it in his headphones, and arrived in his assigned courtroom blasting *Illmatic* so loudly that the bailiff yelled at him to turn it off before the judge took his seat on the bench. That day during lunch break Pac got into a scrap with one of the Hughes brothers. The Fruit of Islam broke it up, but not before he tossed me said headphones for safekeeping during the scrap. "Life's a Bitch," Nas promised through the small padded speakers, "and then you die. So get high, cause you never know, when you're gonna go."

ALL THE WORDS
PAST THE MARGINS
ADAM MANSBACH AND KEVIN COVAL
TALK UNDERSTANDABLE SMOOTH SHIT

ADAM MANSBACH AND KEVIN COVAL

Adam Mansbach: I think we agree that "One Love" is a good place to start this conversation. In many ways, it's the center-piece of the album, the most conceptually coherent and complex song. It defines the two poles of Nas's universe: the Queens-bridge projects and prison. These locales are so encompassing that they erase all others. When Nas leaves Queensbridge for "a two-day stay" to preserve his sanity, he doesn't even bother to tells us where he goes. He takes his "pen and pad for the weekend," but wherever he takes them is off the map; the song restarts when he returns to the "haunted castle" of home.

Kevin Coval: Nas's cinematic-poetic is an aerial view of Queensbridge, and the metapronouncement of the record is *one love*—for the blocks he walks on and views from his apart-ment building, a stacked block of its own. Nas "holds [his] cell down single-handed," which speaks to the duality of feel-ing isolated and self-reliant despite living in such a densely populated community. The distinction between city block and cell block is intentionally blurred, manifest in the fluidity of reporting to his people on lock about Queens residents who are themselves locked down in a psychologically and physically oppressive housing project, and also about the illegal activities dictated by a rapidly growing and privatizing prison-industrial complex.

AM: One of *Illmatic*'s themes is the relationship between actual and virtual incarceration: "even my brain's in handcuffs." The stress of a constrained life threatens to boil over into some kind of criminality that will result in actual imprisonment. That tension frequently gets translated into and relieved by hyperbole, and those hyperbolic one-liners, "When I was twelve, I went to hell for snuffin' Jesus," "whenever frustrated I'ma hijack Delta," are what a lot of cats initially loved (and bit), as far back as "Live at the BBQ."

But when Nas addresses incarceration head-on in "One Love," he does it with the opposite of hyperbole. The realism, the practicality, of that last verse is striking. Nas came up during the age of overtly political rap and later aligned himself with the legacies of X-Clan and Boogie Down Productions, but there is an implicit critique of their approach in the conversation he has with the twelve-year-old sitting on the bench pumping crack. Keep in mind the physical setting: benches like this sit in the middle of a huge vertical project, "snipers could be bustin' off the roof," creating the equivalent of a Greek amphitheater. We've moved from epistolaries to stage drama. And Nas plays the teacher.

His pedagogy is subdued, realistic almost to the point of nihilism, but it's effective because he meets his student on that student's terms. He knows better than to tell this kid to get back in school or go march against police brutality. Their relationship is predicated on shared geography and mutual respect, and thus Nas owes him honesty. So the "words of wisdom from Nas" are to make sure you shoot the right dude instead of the wrong dude, and keep an eye out for the cops.

And before he dispenses that advice, he takes "the L when he passed it/this little bastard." There's a brilliant instant of tension: Nas has to decide whether to smoke with this old-before-his-time shorty, this kid whose lack of innocence marks him as a member of a different generation even though they're only a few years apart in age. What this kid represents is intimidating. He's too caught up in the hustle to mark time through hip-hop as Nas does ("before the BDP conflict with MC Shan/around the time Shante dissed the Real Roxanne"), too young to remember the things Nas is jubilant and nostalgic about. Even worse, he has the audacity to tell Nas he "likes his style."

If Nas takes the blunt, he levels the playing field between them considerably, but if he doesn't, he loses access. So he decides to become the kid's peer for a minute, and that allows him to leave "jewels in his skull." To a teacher, this is a totally familiar dilemma. At some point, your students want to be treated like adults, and you realize that you can't always be preaching at them. You've gotta ease up and take the L when they pass it.

KC: Nas's representing is not the bended corporate double-speak of "keeping it real" (a term reduced to irony by studio gangsterism and faux-reality rappers), but the confirmation of his participation in the poetic legacy of urban realism, from Walt Whitman, Carl Sandburg, and Gwendolyn Brooks to the New York School's Frank O'Hara to the Black Arts Movement's Amiri Baraka, Haki Madhubuti, Sonia Sanchez, and Nikki Giovanni. The hip-hop poet-reporter is rooted in the intimate specificity of locale. By naming streets, people, crews, infamous drug dealer celebrities, utilizing indigenous borough slang, and vividly sketching the corners and boulevards of Queensbridge, Nas is scripting the world as he sees it: writing portraits and vignettes of a community under fire.

Nas's world and worldview are criminal and criminalized. Hence he uses metaphoric violence as a central trope of his poetic: "musician, inflictin' composition/of pain, I'm like Scarface, sniffin' cocaine /holdin' an M-16, see with the pen I'm extreme." Nas articulates "the thief's theme," not necessarily as the criminal breaking the law himself, but as the counternarrative historian of the war on drugs, on young black men's bodies, and on the communities they inhabit.

Nas is the "young city bandit" because he humanizes and gives a voice to the most feared community in America, the housing project, simultaneously challenging and reinforcing the white supremacist hegemonic imagination by scribing and re-(in)scribing its fear. This makes sense when the writing and reading of a people have been made illegal. Black folks by law are supposed to have access to literacy, but in practice creating a counternarrative makes you an outlaw.

By "writing in [his] book of rhymes/all the words past the margins," Nas brings the fringes and the forgotten to the center of public discourse. The margins of society are made visual and visceral. All the words, faces, and bodies of an abandoned postindustrial, urban dystopia are framed in Nas's tightly packed stanzas. These portraits of his brain and community in handcuffs are beautiful, brutal, and complex, and they lend themselves to the brilliantly compounded rhyme schemes he employs.

Form and function are synonymous here. Fluid, multisyllabic compounded rhymes, internal half rhymes, masterful assonance, and ear-bending enjambment elevate the structure of dense sound to song. Part of the reason there are no real hooks on the record, I imagine, is due to Nas's fresh-out-the-rhyme-book type of presentation. *Illmatic* to me is one epic poem, with stanzas pieced together to match the sonics constructed by his all-star cast of East Coast underground beat makers. It's as if Nas, the poet-reporter, brings his notebook into the studio, hears the beat, and weaves his portraits on top with ill precision.

AM: I've been thinking about some of the less obvious reasons this album is considered a classic, and you just touched on one. In the late eighties and early nineties, albums were usually dominated by one embedded producer or production team—think Wu-Tang, Jeru, The Pharcyde, all the Native Tongues groups, Dr. Dre's whole camp, Cypress Hill, Gangstarr, Main Source, Special Ed, Stetsasonic, Public Enemy, Poor Righteous Teachers, Brand Nubian, Ultramagnetic MCs, EPMD, X-Clan, all the Juice Crew artists. The psychological impact on the listener of having all these elite producers—some of whom, like Q-Tip, really weren't known yet for doing outside production work at all—coming together to lace the debut of this kid from Queensbridge was tremendous. And so was the way their contributions came together so seamlessly. It was this sublime moment in which an aesthetic coagulated. And in the next couple of years, recruiting a stable of hot producers became the template for the high-impact debuts of artists like Biggie and Jay-Z.

I am also struck by Nas's absence on the choruses. He barely contributes. It's just music, it's AZ, it's Q-Tip, it's Sadat X on the "One Love" remix, it's Large Professor on "One Time 4 Your Mind," it's a scratched-in sample, it's a posse chant. It's as if Nas can't be bothered; his job is done when the verse ends, and there's a purist's sensibility to that. I mean, shit, even jazz horn players come back in on the chorus. Similarly, the standard three-verse format often gives way here to two long verses, whose length is determined by whim and content rather than structural concerns. And it's notable that the two oldest songs, "Halftime" and "It Ain't Hard to Tell," are the most conformist.

All this points to one of the most profound things about the record: Nas leads with his art. Sounds simple, but in the hip-hop landscape, it's actually a very bold move. Although I agree that it's deeply political to represent your community, I also think that Nas resists the kind of polemics, and even the battle-centrism, that dominate other albums. The ritual slaying of The Sucker MC is not happening here. Other cats were much more preoccupied with defending their rights to claim artistry. And to claim it is not to lead with it.

Think about a song like BDP's "Poetry," the opening salvo from another classic ten-cut debut album. It's KRS-One demanding that he be recognized as a poet, since he presumes a resistance to that notion. Look at the opening track on his next album: KRS demanding you understand that he's a philosopher. Nas bypasses this kind of declaration and takes for granted that both you and he know he's an artist. As the son of a musician, and also somebody whose poetic ambitions were validated from a very young age, he's able to take much more for granted.

Nas shouts out a lot of his producers, but *Illmatic*'s least acknowledged contributor is one of the most significant: Olu Dara, Nas's father, whose ethereal trumpet comes in at the end of "Life's a Bitch." Later in his career, Nas would do songs that are explicitly about or in collaboration with his pops, "Papa Was a Player," "Bridging the Gap," but here Olu is in the background. Hovering just close enough, you might say, to keep an eye on his boy. And it's the presence of all these benevolent elders—his father and the cadre of big-brother producers steering the album—that empowers Nas to rest comfortably in his identity as an artist and an inheritor of tradition, and thus find the space to innovate.

KC: And it is his art, his cinematic-poetic, which begins to raise the bar for MCs on the tail end of the hyperliterate era of popular hip-hop, when understanding artists like Chuck D, Brother J, and Wise Intelligent meant running to the library to check out alternate histories and historical figures and unknown words. You had to engage in a deep read of Nas's lyrics, too, but in a new way. His portraits and descriptions of places, people, and interactions required a second and a fifth listen. He moved from punch lines and hot lines to whole thought pictures manifest in rhyme form.

AM: You had to rewind a KRS rhyme to dissect whatever new style he was flipping, a Rakim rhyme to unpack the abstraction. A Nas rhyme required situating yourself in the narrative point of view, then working through the density, the emjambment, the combination of realism and metaphysics. I'm thinking of the beginning of "Life's a Bitch," when he says, "I woke up early on my born day, I'm 20 it's a blessing/the essence of adolescence leaves my body now I'm fresh an'/my physical frame is celebrated cuz I made it/one quarter through life." We always link Nas to Rakim, but the differences are also interesting. Rakim is always in control, gliding effortlessly through his physical environment and "thinking of a master plan," whereas Nas admits his vulnerability, tells us how "the streets had [him] stressed somethin' terrible."

Linguistically, while Nas was influenced by Five Percenters, he wasn't deep inside of that community as Rakim was, so their language and philosophy tinge his rhymes but don't dominate; he's inventing more of his own vocab, in some ways. Take a line like "beyond the walls of intelligence, life is defined." It sounds like an MC trying to write a Rakim line, and it ends a verse in a song that uses a Rakim quote for the chorus. So in some ways it has to mesh with Ra's vibe, but it's not quite a Rakim line. The mysticism is there but it floats, unsure of itself. That lack of certainty unlocks a lot of vectors.

Even the idea of a New York state of mind means something different when Ra originates it in "Mahogany." To him it connotes smooth focus, cosmopolitan worldliness. Nas "thinks of crime" and tells hectic, truncated stories about out-of-control situations.

KC: If anything, Nas is knowingly (re)building the tradition of Queens MCs, most notably redeeming the Juice Crew, which was defunct by 1994. In "Memory Lane," the samples of Craig G and Biz Markie point to Nas's lyrical forebears and around-the-way influences. He is repping his borough's hip-hop canon.

AM: *Illmatic* also comes out at a time when twelve-inch singles are still a major site of creativity, a place for B sides and remixes. The producers he was working with were all masters of that lost art, as the richness of Tribe and Main Source and Gangstarr twelve-inch singles prove. And Nas makes brilliant use of the opportunities for public revision. I remember hearing the remix to "The World Is Yours" for the first time, and bugging out at the amendments he'd made: it was spring now, and he switched "suede Tims on my feet" to "Nikes on my feet"; "chipped tooth smile" became "gold toothed smile." He slipped in a line about "Giuliani is 666" that freaked the whole song. It was this way of working against your own text to create new meaning, retaining the exact rhyme pattern but subbing in new words. The shit was fresh. It reflected such an understanding of where his fans were at in their ability to digest his words, and also a whole new confidence about himself. When I think of *Illmatic* as an album, I think about the twelve-inch cuts as well. Not to mention the mixtapes that were out, or the unreleased songs that Stretch Armstrong used to play on WKCR at three in the morning—the version of "It Ain't

Hard to Tell" with completely different lyrics and so forth. *Illmatic* for me is not just ten songs, but another ten remixes and shadow versions, too.

KC: It is more than coincidence that Paul Beatty's seminal book of poems, *Joker Joker Deuce*, was also published in 1994. Seeing and reading Beatty's verse for me was an astounding generational moment, as was hearing *Illmatic*. In Beatty's verse, hip-hop poetics appear on the page for the first time. He was forging and figuring out the poetic response to the sonic and visual and physical aesthetic innovations hip-hop cultural elements provided, in ways similar to black arts writers transcribing a jazz aesthetic a generation earlier.

They're very different writers (Paul is a punner, hilarious, somebody for whom postmodernity is the source of humor and anxiety), but they form the poles of a hip-hop literary aesthetic. They're both second-generation hip-hop listeners whose universes are populated with elements of the young culture. Beatty and Nas emerge together in a collective poetic consciousness, formulating a sincerely innovative *ars poetica* for hip-hop generation writers. From this point on, style, technique, and craft merge with collage/pastiche, braggadocio, stark portrait painting from the margins, frenetic, funny wordplay, and the rupture of linear storytelling schemes. These become tropes in a burgeoning school of American letters that's moving toward an aesthetics of hip-hop poetics or a hip-hop poetica, if you will.

NIGHTTIME IS MORE TRIFE THAN EVER

THE MANY MISUSES OF NAS

JON CARAMANICA

In the late 1980s, people used to argue about what shape the revolution was going to take. Some rode with the gun, arguing that gangster rap told indisputable truths in the tone of hostility they merited. Some crossed their fingers and hoped that a little knowledge would go a long way. But even though the music of, say, Public Enemy and N.W.A. reflected very different ideas about the experience of being young and black in America, they were really just variations on the same theme—at one point, the two groups even toured together. No matter whose records you listened to, though, one thing was clear: conditions were chilly.

Nas was the first MC to fully appreciate that these two worlds of art weren't so different after all. And on his 1994 debut, *Illmatic*, he made a whole from the strains of hip-hop that came before him. *Illmatic* was the great unifier, a seamless hybrid of corner reportage and emotional introspection. It's elegant and deceptive, the rare album that's as rewarding up close as it is from a distance.

But if *Illmatic* was where the roads converged, it also effectively nullified the arguments that came before it. Suddenly, with its arrival, you could claim to be both down *and* superior. It required no compromise. And *Illmatic's* accessibility, at a time of rap's increasing suburbanization, made it an easy entry point for carpetbaggers—it was easy to fetishize the gangster, but it was easier to relate to the thinker. Most importantly, it became a flashpoint for organic intellectuals. If Nas could make hip-hop like this, they reasoned, why couldn't everyone else?

As a result, *Illmatic* became something of a blank slate on which all sorts of rap thought subsets could inscribe themselves. It became what the listener wanted it to be as much as, if not more than, what Nas intended it to be.

Like most writers and thinkers, Nas is as often misunderstood and misappropriated as not. To many, liking Nas was a position statement, and *Illmatic* mobilized a national network of dissidents craving something true to the streets but eager to distance themselves from what was beginning to be perceived as a scourge—gangster rap. It wasn't popular per se; the *Illmatic* album wasn't certified platinum by the RIAA until 2001, and by the end of 2007, it had sold only 1.15 million copies total. (A tenth-anniversary reissue notched an additional 200,000 in sales.) But it's been unusually significant to the intellectual development of the genre, for better and worse.

The negatives are the most interesting. *Illmatic* has been responsible for countless pointless "rap versus hip-hop" debates, a shocking amount of hip-hop self-righteousness, the emergence of the backpack movement as something more than a regional curio, and the persistence of the idea that lyricism is the only standard great rap music should be held to. Very little of this had to do with the intention of the author, though. Fresh out of his teenage years, Nas had crafted a debut beyond aesthetic reproach. But it was so compelling, it couldn't help but cultivate a school of zealots, who would go on to take the album, and its lessons, in vain.

There had been conscientious objectors before Nas. The Native Tongues crew—the Jungle Brothers, De La Soul, A Tribe Called Quest et al.—put New York bohemianism on the hip-hop map, staking a claim to hip-hop turf that had previously been a bit hostile to outsiders. The Los Angeles underground, comprising style wizards and rhyme futurists like Freestyle Fellowship and the Pharcyde, thrived in the long shadow of Compton.

But participation in these scenes coded outsider status, something Nas wasn't interested in. On *Illmatic*'s intro, a friend asks Nas, "What the fuck is this bullshit on the radio, son?" Nas replies calmly, "Chill, chill, that's the shit, God. Chill." The divide—between radio hits and rebel anthems, between *their* music and *our* music—was false. Hogwash.

Why throw stones? Popular acclaim was still something out of Nas's reach; no single from *Illmatic* cracked the Top 10 of Billboard's Hot Rap Singles Chart, and only one, "It Ain't Hard to Tell," appeared on the Billboard Hot 100, peaking at 91. He was not yet a hit maker, but Nas would in time learn this skill—what good was trying to teach if no students wanted to listen?

Instead, *Illmatic* was notable for how insular it sounded. A true rapper's rapper, Nas dazzled with intricate, densely layered rhyme schemes that demanded close inspection. His imagery was both fanciful and morbid: "pointing guns at all my baby pictures" and "burning dollars to light my stove" on "The World Is Yours." That vividness was tempered by a clear-eyed realism. On "Life's a Bitch," he exults in the simple fact of having survived to see his twentieth birthday.

Nas was also the first rapper to consciously explore, and exploit, the gap between perception and experience. (Though

Illmatic has its share of braggadocio, Nas was one of the first streetwise MCs who did not spend an unreasonable amount of time proving his bona fides.) On "Memory Lane (Sittin' in Da Park)," he places himself at a remove: "My window faces shootouts, drug overdoses/Live amongst no roses" and "I hung around other crews as they sling smack to dingbats." Best of all was "One Love," which was conceived as a neat structural trick—a letter to an incarcerated friend detailing what's been happening on the block. It is simultaneously present and distant.

The result was one of the seminal albums of the 1990s, in any genre. Depending who you listen to, it also served as a rebuke to the directions hip-hop was soon to take: the pop crossover, the exuberant production values, the splintering of rap into blithe and concerned wings. *Illmatic*, with its fully cohered, all-encompassing worldview, seemed to argue against all of those developments.

But the truth was less complicated than that. Nas wasn't on an ideological mission—he was just a rapper trying to make a mark. Before *Illmatic*'s release, Nas had already impressed his peers with key guest appearances—notably Main Source's "Live at the BBQ" and MC Serch's "Back to the Grill"—and a handful of his own songs. It was enough to get the genre intelligentsia excited. Such was his reputation that several renowned producers—DJ Premier, L.E.S., Pete Rock, Large Professor, Q-Tip—lined up for a shot at sparring with the prodigy on his debut, producing tracks that were lush and expansive and thoughtful.

For an album that features five different people behind the boards, *Illmatic* is remarkably cohesive (such was the state of New York hip-hop at the time). Soon, though, it became commonplace for rappers to search around for different producers who could enhance their sound. By breaking down the traditional producer-rapper relationship, *Illmatic* took a significant step toward the disintegration of the hip-hop album as art form. Less than a decade later, rap had become a producer's genre. It's ironic that one of the genre's most singular lyricists unwittingly kicked down that door.

Nas has remained a complex figure over the course of his fifteen-plus-year career, simultaneously in the mainstream rap fray and above it. He worked with Sean Combs (back when he was still Puff Daddy) but lashed him to a cross in the "Hate Me Now" video. He has made mindless R&B collaborations ("You Owe Me") and thoughtful uplift anthems ("I Can"). Up until the arrival of Kanye West, no rapper wore his inner conflicts more on his sleeve than Nas. And though he was complicated in the way that most rappers are complicated, the expectations placed on Nas have always been higher. Nas albums weren't mere collections of songs. They were sermons, showered on an adoring faithful. Sometimes it seemed like he had nowhere to go but down.

So maybe it's not surprising that as he got older, he began to suffer from some of the same problems his debut had helped set in motion. Though he was far from dogmatic as an MC, he developed a touch of curmudgeonliness in his later years. When, in 2006, he named his eighth album *Hip-Hop Is Dead*, admirers saw it as an affirmation that the whole genre had gone to swill. But the truth was that New York rap as it was done in the days of *Illmatic* had become a throwback sound— *Illmatic* itself was an elegant museum piece.

In waving a flag for things as they once were, Nas triggered the ire of many, particularly southern rappers like Lil Wayne, Young Jeezy, and Ludacris who noted, quite rightly, that hip-hop wasn't dead at all; it had merely migrated to the South. These were artists who paired strong lyrical presence with radio savvy, who managed to be concerned with matters both carnal and political, who were respected by underground savants (if sometimes grudgingly) and mainstream enthusiasts alike.

In short, these were rappers very much like Nas. *Illmatic* had sowed the seeds of its own undoing, and there was no turning back.

"GENESIS"

IN THE HALL OF MIRRORS

CHARLIE AHEARN

Remember the hall of mirrors in the climactic scene from Bruce Lee's classic kung fu flick *Enter the Dragon*, that mirrored maze reflecting Lee stalking his shifting adversary in multiple slivers of glass? Hip-hop culture is like that, a maze of reflecting sounds and images, an arena for the climactic battle. The culture by its very foundation has been sample based, the DJ weaving past beats and sonic bits, the B-boy moves and the imprints of MCs passed down and the visual styles of graf borrowed and reanimated for the future. *Wild Style* as part of this maze was sampled by many DJs, MCs, and visual artists, but Nas's "Genesis" was one of the early defining moments and perhaps the most inspired.

Nas's opening track on *Illmatic* is an intimate audio self-portrait docudrama dubbed "Genesis." The word, meaning birth or origin, comes from Greek and is of course the name of the first book of the Bible. Nas's obsession with origins led him to fuse *Wild Style* with a scene of himself as a teenage hustler holed up in Queensbridge public housing. Whether this was a flashback or his current life is left up to the listener, but this was Nas representing the real.

A subway rumbles and some dialogue follows: Lee Quinones's iconic graffiti outlaw, Zorro, has returned home from another commando run in the train yards to be caught coming through his bedroom window by brother Hector on leave from the army. His brother's parental challenge to "stop fucking around and be a man . . . there ain't nothing out here for you" is confidently met by Lee's "Yes there is: this!" gesturing to his aerosol bombed ZORO on the wall, followed by the heavy beat of the subway theme from the movie. But a voice interrupts, "Yo Nas! What the fuck is this bullshit?" Nas tells the brother to chill, "that's the shit, God." As the theme music drones in the background, Nas and his partner in arms, AZ, dialog as though someone forgot and left the tape recorder on play; they're stackin' the Jacksons, passing the Hennessey, and making blood oaths to the real, "even without a record contract," because "representing is Illmatic."

Why would Nas, perhaps the most streetwise young MC of the time, open his masterpiece with a tribute to a tiny movie released a decade earlier, buried under the ooze of commercial rap videos? *Wild Style* had not been in distribution for seven years, several lifetimes for a youth from the projects. Nas's "Genesis" was like a voice crying out in the desert; almost nobody was giving props to the pioneers back then, and I feel the track helped spark curiosity in the minds of the youth as to the origins of this thing we call hip-hop. *Wild Style* wasn't rereleased until 1997 on Rhino. That same year Sprite did a series of commercials as homage to the first hip-hop movie, and one of the scenes was Double Trouble's Stoop Rap. They smartly cast the young Nas and AZ in the KK and Rodney C roles, borrowing the simple setup and rhyme cadence of the original. Of course it was still a Sprite TV commercial, but I hoped it might help publicize the movie and refer kids to their roots. All in all, it has been a slow process for youth to rediscover and embrace the culture and its history.

Even though "Genesis" is the first cut heard on *Illmatic*, it was actually the last track recorded. After the album was set, Columbia's A&R Faith Newman visited Nas in his crib and found him playing *Wild Style* on his video deck. He was itching to add one more track and "Genesis" was born. Nas's obsession with the movie may be traced back to the time his father, Olu Dara the trumpet player, took the boy to see *Wild Style* in the movie theater and later supplied him with books and encouraged him to develop himself as an artist. Nas dropped out of school in ninth grade and studied African history, the Qu'ran, and the Bible at home. Nas's fascination with graffiti and hip-hop manifested itself in his adopted pop-locking persona as Kid Wave. He later honed his rhyming skills with partner DJ Ill Will Graham, but Graham's murder in 1992 dashed his hopes before MC Serch from 3rd Bass engineered his signing to Columbia Records. Nas infused his street swagger with deep flow like MC forebears Rakim and early hip-hop pioneer Grand Master Caz.

I was inspired to make that scene in *Wild Style* when I photographed an army recruitment billboard on a Bronx street corner hit with a graffiti piece by Blade, like a dignified "fuck you" to the government's only visible option offered to people hustling in the projects. Hustling, prison time, and death were themes Nas rhymed eloquently about on *Illmatic*, but it was hip-hop and not hustling that saved his ass, and that of countless others of his generation. Or was it Nas that helped save hip-hop? As the prison population swelled, the street corner culture grew into a multibillion-dollar engine and the future of hip-hop, as a cash machine or as a mouthpiece for the people, remained an open question.

BREAK (IS THIS)

SUHEIR HAMMAD

habibi got this complex occupation

nine lyric nines i carry him poetry that's a part of me
sit at a tension checked wa pointed interned direction myrrh smoked
mirror scent rose water all ever saved me was a token a ghetto
loop some hood hoop earrings rolled up bless sweat our lady
of everything is everything

jinn on ice calm cante moro throated nefertiti bust ogun iron
skirted past half time quarter noted collect calls new york upstate
of emergency mind the gap between genesis and now one time
for those ain't here my brothers ready to die coming out of ancient
queens bridged to future space afro asiatic astro destiny maktoub
it's mine it's mine it's mine exu born into a theft disarmed
weapons communicate bodies dispersed forever urban

isis hid herself in pharaoh's torso ana hide self in habibi's gypsy song
accorded notes wa plaited tones wa we still looking for our world

I REMINISCE ON PARK JAMS

AN INTERVIEW WITH BOBBITO GARCIA

SOHAIL DAULATZAI

Rarely is it real talk when someone is called true school. But I can't think of a better description for Bobbito Garcia. My man just is. Whether it be his writing, his DJ-ing, his landmark hip-hop radio show on WKCR in the 1990s, his love of hoops or his taste for sneakers, Bobbito broke the mold. And he's so humble about it too. I've been fortunate to come into contact with Bobbito a few times, mainly through my man Center in New York, and every time we've connected, Bobbito leaves an impression. So you know when it came down to building with someone about *Illmatic* and that moment in hip-hop history, Bobbito was at the top of my list. Not only was his radio show named by *The Source* as the "Best Hip-Hop Radio Show of All Time," but Bobbito has been deeply connected to hip-hop from the jump, even having interviewed Nas for *RapPages* in 1994 in what may be the most incredible and revealing interview Nas has ever done. Thankfully we've included that interview in this collection as well. But as you'll read in the conversation that he and I had, Bobbito takes us back to that era in hip-hop, and when he does he tells it like it just happened yesterday. As always, Bobbito came with incredible insight and perspective, and he did it, like he does everything, with so much passion and flavor. If the '80s are coming back, recognize that Bobbito never left. Def. Fresh. And true school for sure.

Sohail Daulatzai: Let's start real quick at the beginning, man. You've been on the hip-hop scene for a minute, from its inception. And maybe you can talk about how that happened, how you got involved, what led you to get involved in the influential radio show that you and Stretch had.

Bobbito Garcia: I started working for Def Jam in 1989. I was given the opportunity by the rap group 3rd Bass. Pete Nice and MC Serch were friends of mine dating back to 1987 through a mutual friend of ours named Sake, who was a graffiti writer, a basketball player, and a sneaker head. But essentially I started working at Def Jam in 1989. Obviously the cachet of that brand name helped me in terms of networking for *years*, I mean still to this day. And my position there led me to meet a young DJ named Adrian B, who later became Skinny Bones and eventually settled into Stretch Armstrong.

He and I instantly hit it off and we started a radio program on WKCR FM 89.9 in New York City in October 1990. We did it for eight years, and in 1998 *The Source* magazine did its first ever "Best Of" issue—I think it was the one hundredth issue—and we were voted best hip-hop radio show of all time. Part of that was because of the energy we put forth. But the other part of that award was the lane we provided to unsigned artists in that eight-year period, many who became the greatest hip-hop artists of the period, and in some cases, ever. . . . And I'm talking about these artists came to our show when they did not have a record deal and it's the first time anyone's ever heard their voice. Ason Unique, who later became Ol' Dirty Bastard. "Protect Ya Neck" by Wu-Tang was played on our show as a test pressing. Biggie Smalls was unsigned hype by *Source* magazine; first time he ever appeared on a radio show was ours. Big Dog the Punisher was brought up by Fat Joe; he later became Big Pun. Poetical Prophets was unsigned hype by *Source*, and Matty C., the author of that column, brought them up; they later became Mobb Deep. Big L became very cool with us. He brought up a crew called Eight Is Enough/ Children of the Corn. Two of the members were Mace Murda who later became Ma\$e, and then also Killa Cam who later became Cam'ron. An artist named DMX the Great came up in 1990; eight years later he was DMX selling multiplatinum records. Eminem came up to our show in 1998, when I think he had just gotten signed, but not a lot of people knew him. You know, he was still like very much an underground artist. Jay-Z came up to our show a number of times startin' in 1995. Now he obviously had been heard; he was on Jaz's record *The Originators*. But when he came up to our show he didn't have an album deal; he just had a twelve-inch deal. So we have a long list of artists, and those are just the major ones. I could list thirty artists who are on the underground. Company Flow, Juggaknots, Arsonists, Godfather Don, Kool Keith's reemergence, Supernat . . . all these artists that were first on our show who may not have gone on to have platinum careers like the rest of those I mentioned.

So you have all those, and then you have an artist by the name of Nasty Nas. He came up to our show; I believe the first time was February 14, 1991, Valentine's Day, by virtue of our relationship with Large Professor. And if I recall correctly, Large actually wrote his verse for "Live at the Barbeque" in our studio. 'Cause I remember he kicked the verse back in 1990 in the studio, and then the song came out. So when Nas came in 1991, he came with Akinyele and Lord Finesse, and that was the beginning. He would come up to the show two more times; once again in 1992; that was the night when Hurricane G, who was out with Erick Sermon, came up as well, and then again in October 1993, which was *insane*, 'cause if you listen to it [the show] today, you'll hear me interviewing him before he starts freestyling and I'm like, "So, you're not called Nasty Nas anymore; you dropped the 'Nasty' right?" And then I'm like, "You gave Stretch some exclusives, you know, let's hear them." And then, you know, we world premier "It Ain't Hard to Tell," and then he rhymes off the top of his head . . . which I don't think anyone's ever heard him do before or since. . . . [laughs] He doesn't do that [laughs].

So, you catch Nas in a very natural element. The reason why was because Nas, along with Mobb Deep, Jay-Z, and Wu-Tang . . . listened to our show *regularly*. I even have 'em quoted in a *RapPages* interview, which I did in 1994 for Sheena Lester, the editor in chief at the time, where he goes in-depth about how much he loved listening to our show. Nas was a student of rap; it's obvious in the way he presents his lyrics. I mean it's very much a total opposite to what's going on today. A friend told me that this guy named Rich Boy or something had the number-one rap hit, and it was not only the first song that he had ever came out with, but it was also the first rhyme he had ever written. And that just goes to show you the difference of caliber and preparation from 1994 to now; the standards of critique have lowered so much that someone who has no experience can have the number-one song, compared to Nas. When Nas's album came out . . . and the reason why that freestyle session was so special to Stretch and me—and I would say we both feel that that was the number-one appearance in our eight-year history, and I told you we have a long list, Jay-Z, Biggie, I mean, you know, *crazy* performances—is because *Illmatic* was hands down, unequivocally, the most sought-after and anticipated release of the 1990s. No one can argue that. No one can argue that.

SD: Why do you think that was?

BG: The reason why was because it wasn't like Nas was on the underground for three months. Nas was on the underground for *three years*. He appeared on "Live at the BBQ," right? Everybody knew that verse by heart. You know, *everybody*. I remember Stretch playin' that record in clubs, and this doesn't happen anymore, right? Nowadays, people hear rap in the club and you'll basically see them singing along to the chorus. Because that's what's rap has become. It's become a very chorus-driven sing-along form. In the early 1990s, people took pride on the dance floor to sing along to verses. Like yo, I *know* this verse [Bobbito rapping]. . . . *Street's disciple my raps are trifle / I shoot slugs from my brain just like a rifle / Stampede the stage I leave the microphone split / Play Mr. Tuffy while I'm on some Pretty Tone shit.* And Stretch would do dropouts. He would take the crossfader and bring it to the other side and silence the record so that the crowd could sing along to it. This is 1991. Nas doesn't have the album deal; nobody even knows what he *looks* like. So, the fervor starts with "Live at the BBQ." Then he comes out with "Back to the Grill Again," where he's rhyming with Serch and Red Hot Lover Tone. Kills that. *Kills* it. *Kills* it. Right? Then he does "Halftime" for the *Zebrahead* soundtrack. *Kills* it. So you got three appearances where people know every single thing he's got out. So now he's got five verses out, and people know all five by heart. And it's not just a New York thing.

Oh, this is a funny story too. That stuff in the *RapPages* column, the interview I did that Nas didn't like. I was workin' at Def Jam at the time from 1989 to 1993, and part of my job was an A&R rep. And the two demos I really felt strongly about that I went to—well, the first one I felt really strongly about to tell Russell to sign was a group called STP, Simply Too Positive; the group later changed its name to Organized Konfusion. And I remember Russell gave me the cassette. You know demos were on cassette tapes back then [laughs]; they weren't mp3s, they weren't emails. And aw man . . . I *loved* it, I *loved* it, you know. *Wake up to the mathematics of an erratic rap/Rejuvenator of rhyme, that sort of come automatic/Poetical medical medicine for the cerebellum/I divert 'em and flirt 'em insert 'em then I repel 'em/A breakdown, poetical shakedown/Fifty-two pick-up a stick-up so get on the floor facedown/The ammo keep the* . . . I mean I knew that demo by heart. And Russell didn't want to sign it. He was like, "Aw, I don't know if they're gonna sell records. . . ." Whatever, whatever. And he was right. Organized Konfusion's first album came out; it's one of my top ten albums of all time for *any* genre, not just hip-hop. Organized's first album was *incredible.* But unfortunately it only sold forty thousand records, fifty thousand records. So, Russell was right. I mean he was who he was for a good reason. But he wasn't always right. I was *depressed* that he didn't sign Organized Konfusion, and it kind of broke me in terms of trusting that I could bring Russell certain artists and he would give them a shot. So, next I was given the Nas and Akinyele demo. And it might even have been before Serch signed Nas to his production company. The chronology I honestly cannot exactly remember. But yeah, it is right, because Faith Newman, who was the A&R that signed Nas at Columbia, hadn't left Def Jam yet. So yeah, Nas wasn't even signed to Serchlight yet. Large Professor gave me the demos for Nas and for Akinyele. And on that demo was the "It Ain't Hard to Tell" original version, where there's a verse on it that's a little different than what came out. I still have it. I played it on the air like once or twice.

Anyway, I'm jumpin' around. Back to the story. I listened to both demos, and I'm like *Nas is bananas*, but he's gonna be over Russell's head. Ak (Akinyele) was *bananas . . . bananas*. He had punch lines that were *funny*. He wasn't as deep as Nas. He was as gifted, but in a totally different way. [laughs] I bring the Akinyele demo to Russell, but I don't do the same for Nas. And so, in the *RapPages* column he complains. He's like, "Yeah, Bob, you passed on my demo." And I was embarrassed, I was like wow. 'Cause I knew I was gonna transcribe that and print that. Here I am getting called out by Nas to the world for being the dummy that passed on his demo. I had to explain to him, "Naw, you don't understand. I brought the Organized Konfusion, you know, Russell, you know, I didn't wanna waste your time. Or give you false hope. Like I knew Russell would pass on it." And Russell *would* have passed on it, because I'm sure Serch, bein' a Def Jam artist, brought Nas's demo back to him later, and I'm sure he passed on it. Although don't quote me on that. I mean, you can quote me, but I don't know that for a fact.

SD: So Def Jam *did* pass on Nas's album supposedly. I mean, I've heard of him talking about it. So they never got a chance to hear it because of *you?*

BG: Well, it wasn't an album at that point.

SD: Right, it was just a demo.

BG: It was just "It Ain't Hard to Tell," and maybe like half of a song, I don't even remember what it was.

SD: You talk about the anticipation for Nas's album. What was it that Nas was coming with that resonated so much? What was it that cats just kind of felt?

BG: I could break it down. I could break it down.

SD: Go for it.

BG: First of all, it was just as Guru says, the voice. His voice resonated. The motherfucker didn't sound like *anybody*, like *anybody*. He had that raspy deep voice for a sixteen-year-old that didn't even make *sense*. He was *young*, right? So he had that projection, you know. You still hear it in points, but sometimes you listen to his albums years later, and you don't hear that *projection*, that *attack* on the mic. He was a student, not just of rap; it was obvious that he listened to G Rap, Rakim, Kane, and Shan, and any other MC in the late 1980s that really *meant* something. You could *tell* that he had stayed up late night, and he even mentions it on records. Marley Marl, who was on WBLS at the time with his rap show on Friday and Saturday nights. But he was also a student of books; you could tell that he read. So he wasn't just coming forward with light topics. He was mentioning things that were simply *brilliant*. And people at that point in the rap world appreciated genius. *True* genius. I'm not talking like, "Oh, you know, I sold the most records this month so I'm the greatest rap artist ever." Like nah. At that point we didn't care how many records were sold. We were just goin' on like, "Yo, this dude is nice, *nice*." And then it doesn't just stop at that. I mean he was comin' forward with little concepts that were just *insane*. You know, talking about the priests, and I mean it wasn't stuff that we wanted to do or we celebrated. It was just the courage of him to say things like that. He didn't even mean to, you know, *"I'm waving automatic guns at nuns."* I mean it's not like he was really doin' that, it was just wordplay. And we all *loved* it. We loved the wordplay.

Then you have his cadence and his delivery. Which was unlike anybody else's. He came forward with a completely original style. He didn't sound like Rakim. He didn't sound like G Rap. He didn't sound like Kane. He didn't sound like Akinyele. He didn't sound like Q-Tip. He didn't sound like Chuck D. He didn't sound like KRS. He didn't sound like Slick Rick. He didn't sound like any of them. You take any great MC before him, and he's influenced by them, but he doesn't sound like *any* of them. So if you break down in terms of the elements of the MC—delivery, cadence, originality, voice, wordplay, storytelling—he could tell a story; he could also freestyle. And when I say freestyle, I'm not sayin' off-the-head freestyle. I'm sayin' like you can listen to his rhyme, and he's not talking about anything. I mean, one line doesn't relate to the next, but it's still interesting.

SD: It didn't hurt that he had those beat makers underneath him either.

BG: Well, I mean I'm not even goin' on his album. I'm talking about before his album even. You're askin' why people are buggin' out over him. It's like yo, I mean he was comin' to the show freestylin', and we knew his verses by heart.

SD: Right, so do you think that's why those producers are the ones who jumped on him the way they did, because of all the hype that was building around him?

BG: Well, I don't think that's the reason why. I think even if there was no hype, I still think Large Professor, Premier, Pete Rock would have messed with that album. 'Cause *they* knew. Even if the public didn't know. We were like a very tight-knit community back then, and we were *all* geniuses. Seriously, seriously. I mean, I look back on it and I'm not tryin' to be self-aggrandizing, but Stretch and I were geniuses. We didn't think about it like that. We just wanted to put forth the best show we possibly could. It helped that all these artists wanted to be coming on [became] legendary and classic, from our show.

And that's the other thing about why *Illmatic* was so special. *Illmatic* was a two-year process. Maybe even more. It's not like he just went into the studio and did songs in fifteen minutes, and just wrote the verses while he was listening to the beat being made. I mean, you could tell there were months and months and years put into that album. And it shows because you could still listen to that album. . . . *Illmatic* may have eclipsed *It Takes a Nation of Millions to Hold Us Back* as the greatest rap album ever made. It *may* have. I don't know. Some people are too young to understand what Public Enemy meant when that album came out, so when people are talking about the greatest rap albums they can't really judge it properly, 'cause they weren't really experiencing it in its context.

SD: Do you have any favorite tracks on *Illmatic*, and why?

BG: That's an album [chuckles], that . . . normally you have a favorite track on an album because there's a lot of filler, right? So it's easy to pick a favorite track. But how do you pick a favorite track from Nas's album? The *intro* ["Genesis"] is incredible. The *intro* is incredible. The *intro* itself gives me goose bumps.

SD: Let me ask you this, paraphrasing Nas: Is hip-hop dead?

BG: Naw, of course not. Hip-hop is very much alive. It peaked *years* ago. It may have peaked with *Illmatic*. And then leveled off, and then really fallen off. But you know, there's still artists, and there's still songs that come along here and there, very inconsistently, that are still on the level of what happened in rap from 1987 to 1994–1995. You know, those years were creatively the pinnacle, the zenith of what rap could be, and since then whatever's come out that's any good is a ripple of that period. *Or* from artists that actually started during that period. And that's not to say that there's no hope for a younger kid to come out and be on that level, but it's just really difficult because you're only as good as what you're fed. And if a kid who's fifteen years old right now is bein' fed rap and what exists now, he's not gonna know to push the level, 'cause he doesn't know his history, or she.

Stretch and I did the homework for people. I mean, you listen to our show, for that four hours you were given the best hip-hop available in the world, *in the world*, right? We sifted through hundreds of demos and songs and releases and album cuts to make sure that we're really givin' you the illest grief. But now, when people are out there, they're not being told, they're not being, you know, led. . . . I mean it's like anything when you get educated, you have teachers, you have professors to give you history and context, and give you a reading list. I feel like rap artists comin' out should have a listening list. *Required* that you listen to these twenty-five albums, and these hundred singles that you get an idea of what rap really is about before you start rhyming; you have a responsibility. But people don't see it like that.

And I think that's why artists of the stature of Nas can say something like hip-hop is dead. Because that mentorship, because like O.C., when he did "Time's Up," he said "the more emotion I put into it, the harder I rock." He took a year to write that song—it was only two verses, and you could *tell.*

So you know, in some ways, I could understand why he could make a statement like hip-hop is dead. I think it was a call to arms. I think he was tryin' to tell people, "Yo, stuff's gotten wack, let's step it up," and the only way I could do that is if I lit a fire under people, sayin' like "hip-hop ain't dead, I'm gonna come with this stuff."

SD: Where do you think Nas fits into where hip-hop is at to-day? Some say he's out of place in today's hip-hop world. You hear all these things thrown out about Nas. What do you think about that?

BG: When I hear "Made You Look" or "Get Down," where he uses the "Pay the Cost to be the Boss" sample, or "Can't Forget About You," you know those songs resonate with me. Those songs are in a vacuum of time. They could have come out in 1994, they could have come out now. They're timeless. They're beautiful. They're strong. So, is Nas still Nas? Absolutely. Is he still nice on the mic? Yes, absolutely. Does he still give me goose bumps? Yes, absolutely. Does the kid who likes Lil' Wayne, Rich Boy, and you know, whoever else, appreciate Nas the way I do? I don't know. I hope so.

So, I mean to answer those questions, I still love Nas. I think he's the *only* artist I hear that still can do it, you know? To me he's been consistent. Maybe not every album has stood the test of time like *Illmatic* has, but you can take pieces from each album that are *phenomenal*.

SD: Is there anything you wanna say in closing?

BG: Nasty Nas is a rebel to America!

NOTES

1 It Was Signified: Genesis-Nama, by Adilifu Nama

1. See David James, *Allegories of Cinema: American Film in the Sixties* (Princeton: Princeton University Press, 1989), for an interesting characterization of how *Easy Rider* failed to toe the ideological line of counterculture values in the process of film production. Nevertheless, his critique speaks volumes to the film's stature as the emblematic representation of the 1960s generation.

2. See *The Source*, August 2003, pp. 130–133, on where hip-hop has gone from the perspective of one of its most prominent practitioners of body rock, popularly called breaking or break dancing.

3. Also see Amiri Baraka, "The Language of Defiance," *Black Issues Book Review*, September 2001, p. 28.

4. Barry Glassner, *Culture of Fear* (New York: Basic, 1999), critiques American mass media for promulgating a fear of black men. The white public imagination is fed its fear of blackness through images of black men on the nightly news rather than the real-world statistical likelihood of being accosted by a black person. John Fiske, *Media Matters: Race and Gender in U.S. Politics* (Minneapolis: University of Minnesota Press, 1996), also takes on American racial paranoia, recalling how the Willie Horton ad played an important role in the 1988 presidential election campaign.

5. In terms of popular culture, this debate was feverishly engaged with the blaxploitation of the early 1970s and reached its zenith with the *Cosby Show* of the early 1990s. See Herman Gray, *Watching Race: Television and the Struggle for Blackness* (Minneapolis: University of Minnesota Press, 1995); Gray, "Remembering Civil Rights: Television, Memory, and the 1960s," in Lynn Spigel and Michael Curtain, eds., *The Revolution Wasn't Televised: Sixties Television and Social Conflict* (New York: Routledge, 1997); Ed Guerro, *Framing Blackness: The African American Image in Film* (Philadelphia: Temple University Press, 1993); Stuart Hall, "What Is This 'Black' in Black Popular Culture?" in Gina Dent, ed., *Black Popular Culture* (Seattle: Bay Press, 1992), pp. 21–33).

6. See Michael Eric Dyson, *Between God and Gangsta Rap: Bearing Witness to Black Culture* (New York: Oxford University Press, 1996); Dyson, *Holler If You Hear Me: Searching for Tupac Shakur* (New York: Basic Civitas, 2001), for an extended examination of the cultural impact of the slain rapper.

7. See Ron Eyerman, *Cultural Trauma: Slavery and the Formation of African American Identity* (Cambridge: Cambridge University Press, 2001), for a historiography on the relationship between memory and representation in terms of African American enslavement.

8. . See Todd Boyd, *The New H.N.I.C.: The Death of Civil Rights and the Reign of Hip-Hop* (New York: NYU Press, 2001), for a provocative analysis on this political-cultural tension in which his analysis oscillates from trenchant critique of the civil rights movement to celebratory riffing on the power and promise of hip-hop.

9. . See "The Top 115 Artists of the Last 15 Years," *The Source*, August 2003, pp. 138–152, for a listing of top hip-hop artists.

10. See "The CEO of Hip-Hop," *Business Week*, October 27, 2003, marking corporate perception of hip-hop as a mainstream youth market.

11. Nas's *Stillmatic* release is the epitome of this tendency, signaled by the similarity of the title.

2   A Rebel to America: "N.Y. State of Mind" After the Towers Fell, by Sohail Daulatzai

1. I'm using the term "Third World" in its empowering sense—the way we throughout Africa, Asia, and Latin America originally meant it—and not the way that some use it as a term of denigration or hierarchy to the so-called First or Second Worlds.

2. See mtv.com/bands/123/1994/news_feature_010504.

3. Between 1920 and 1970, prison rates in the United States rose relatively equal to the population growth. But the picture dramatically changes beginning during Richard Nixon's first regime and on through Bill Clinton in 2000, so that from 1970 to 2000, while the general U.S. population rose 40 percent, the prison rate skyrocketed over 500 percent. The United States now has more than 2.1 million people in prison, more than any other "civilized" country, and also has the largest number of prisoners per 100,000 people—a number that far exceeds that of any other country in the world. For more info, see sentencingproject.org.

4. According to the Center on Juvenile and Criminal Justice, "Under President Reagan's eight year term, the number of prisoners under federal jurisdiction rose from 24,363 (1980) to 49,928 (1988), and under President George Bush's four-year term, the federal system grew to 80,259 (1992). However, under President Bill Clinton, the number of prisoners under federal jurisdiction doubled, and grew more than it did under the previous 12-years of Republican rule, combined (to 147,126 by February, 2001). By December 31, 1999, a year prior to the completion of his term in office, the Clinton Administration already well outstripped the Reagan and Bush

Administrations with a federal incarceration rate of rate of 42 per 100,000."
For more info, see cjcj.org/pubs/clinton/clinton.html.

5. Eric Schlosser, "The Prison Industrial Complex," *Atlantic Monthly*,
December 1998, theatlantic.com/doc/199812/prisons.

6. Ibid.

4   "It's Yours": Hip-Hop Worldviews in the Lyrics of Nas, by James Braxton Peterson

1. "The world is yours" also appears as graffiti throughout the classic
French film *La haine*, written and directed by Mathieu Kassovitz and released in February 1996. In this film, a group of three friends (one Jewish,
one African, and one Arab) navigate the treacherous terrain of a postriot
suburban French ghetto with hip-hop culture, music, and language as the
backdrop. "The world is yours" graffiti appears several times and is ultimately adjusted to "the world is ours." That instance of "the world is yours"
text is a simulacrum of sorts since we cannot really determine if the line is
borrowed from *Scarface* or from Nas's *Illmatic.*

2. Shout-out to Bakari Kitwana, who initially identified the hip-hop
generation as individuals born between 1964 and 1985. There are at least
two hip-hop generations, maybe more.

3. Many other artists engage in what might be considered racially romantic narratives, including Public Enemy, KRS One, X-Clan, and so on.

4. On the instant classic *American Gangster*, on a song entitled "Igno-
rant Shit," Jay-Z raps, "Scarface the movie did more than Scarface the rapper
to me/So that ain't to blame for all the shit that's happened to me." He juxta-
poses these two figures—one a movie character with a seminal influence on
hip-hop and the other a product of that influence that has in turn become
one of the most well-respected lyricists of the come-up and gangsta/street
narrative genres of hip-hop music.

5. Mark Anthony Neal, *What the Music Said: Black Popular Music and
Black Public Culture* (New York: Routledge, 1999), pp. 145–146.

6. For examples of artists and art forms in the African American oral
tradition from which call and response emerges, the following trajectory by
Priya Parmar is instructive. "Rap music is a contemporary manifestation of
a rich tradition of verbal and percussive orality including but not limited to:
the use of words in the drum rhythms from Jazz musicians like Frankie
Newton and Louis Prima in the 1930s; the irregular rhythms of the snare
and bass drum in bebop beginning in the 1940s; the hipster-jive announc-
ing styles of 1950s rhythm 'n' blues deejays such as Georgie Woods, Jocko
Henderson, and Ewart Beckford, better known as 'U-Roy'; the inclusion of
ritualistic insults or 'the dozens' in songs by blues singers like Bo Diddley,

and in the late 1960s and early 1970s, the political rhetoric of Martin Luther King Jr. and Malcolm X, as well as the Black Power poetry of Amiri Baraka, Gil Scott-Heron, the Last Poets, Sonia Sanchez, and Nikki Giovanni."

7. This critical riff is similar to Gates's notion of critical signification. In *The Signifying Monkey: A Theory of African American Literary Criticism*, Henry Louis Gates defines critical signification by quoting Ralph Ellison: "It might appear . . . as a technical assault against the styles which have gone before and stating: This form of formal revision is what I am calling critical signification, or formal Signifyin(g), and is my metaphor for literary history."

8. *Gandhi*, Columbia Pictures, 1982.

9. Imani Perry, *Prophets from the Hood* (Durham, NC: Duke University Press, 2004), pp. 4–5, 11.

10. John J. Ansboro, *Martin Luther King, Jr.: Nonviolent Strategies and Tactics for Social Change* (Maryland: Madison Books, 1982), p. 5.

11. This shift in Nas's worldview reflected in his lyrics manifests itself in the thematics of *Hip-hop Is Dead* (Def Jam Records, December 2006). Overall the album suggests that the market forces of the music industry have destroyed hip-hop culture and facilitate a certain historical amnesia with regard to the culture and some of its bygone artists.

12. Neal, *What the Music Said*, p. 132.

13. The BET documentary-style news series *American Gangster*, provides several brilliant examples of the illegal drug trade, its effect on communities, dealers, and individuals.

14. Kanye West's track entitled "Crack Music" featuring Game on his sophomore effort, *Late Registration*, is similarly suggestive.

15. I am not the first to assert the powerful, nuanced interconnections between hip-hop culture and the blues. Michael Eric Dyson in his classic *Race Rules* and later republished in the *Michael Eric Dyson Reader* states the following: "Blues music is the style of Black artistry most closely associated with hip hop."

16. In 1994 even the venerable President Bill Clinton singled out rapper/activist Sista Souljah for promoting violence and racial hatred. Of course that's not to mention attacks by Bill Bennett, Tipper Gore, Bob Dole, and C. DeLores Tucker.

17. Bakari Kitwana, *The Hip-Hop Generation: Young Blacks and the Crisis in African American Culture* (New York: Basic Civitas, 2002), p. 180.

18. Vladimir Bogdanov, Chris Woodstra, Stephen Erlewine, and John Bush, eds., *All Music Guide to Hip-Hop: The Definitive Guide to Rap and Hip-Hop* (San Francisco: Backbeat Books, 2003), p. 346.

19. In the fall 2005 I delivered a lecture in Michael Eric Dyson's hip-hop course at the University of Pennsylvania, entitled "Dead Prezence." In

fall 2006 I published this theory with attendant examples in the special hip-hop issue of *Callaloo.*

20. One notable exception to this view is the Internet-spawned protest movement advocating on behalf of the Jena 6. In September 2007 nearly 10,000 hip-hop generation youth descended on tiny Jena, Louisiana, in order to protest the unfair treatment of six black male youths aggressively prose-cuted for an attack on a white youth that by most accounts was provoked by a series of racial incidents, including the hanging of three nooses from a schoolyard tree.

21. Neal, *What the Music Said,* p. 132.

22. Cornel West, *Race Matters* (New York: Vintage/Random House, 1993), p. 20.

23. Michael Eric Dyson, *Race Rules: Navigating the Color Line* (New York: Random House, 1996), p. 136.

24. Todd Boyd, *The New H.N.I.C.: The Death of Civil Rights and the Reign of Hip-Hop* (New York: NYU Press, 2002), p. 91.

25. The other is "One Love."

26. Michael Eric Dyson, *Open Mike: Reflections on Philosophy, Race, Sex, Culture, and Religion* (New York: Basic Civitas, 2003), pp. 260–261.

27. Dyson, *Open Mike,* pp. 272–273.

28. Kitwana, *Hip-Hop Generation,* pp. 138–139.

5 Critical Pedagogy Comes at Halftime: Nas as Black Public Intellectual, by Marc Lamont Hill

1. Main Source, "Live at the BBQ," on *Breaking Atoms,* Capitol Records.

2. I borrow the notion of the public and its problems from John Dewey, whose eponymous book defines a public as a group of people bound together by externalities that are beyond their control (New York: Holt, 1927). For an interesting engagement with Deweyan political philosophy as it relates to the "postsoul" generation, see Eddie Glaude, *In a Shade of Blue* (Chicago: University of Chicago Press, 2007).

3. By referring to the conscious and commercial hip-hop camps as dis-crete spaces, I run the risk of reifying the very binary I am attempting to dismantle. As I mentioned earlier in this chapter, however, I use these labels for heuristic purposes in order to identify the current ideological and artistic factions within hip-hop culture.

4. Jay-Z, "Blueprint 2," on *Blueprint 2* (Roc-a-Fella, 2002).

5. Specifically, I am referring to the pessimism of the Frankfurt School and earlier bourgeois humanist traditions. The generally dim view of popu-lar culture held by the Frankfurt School can be evidenced in the classic work

of Theodor Adorno and Max Horkheimer, *Dialectic of Enlightenment* (New York: Continuum, 1944). The most commonly cited representative of the bourgeois humanist tradition is Matthew Arnold, *Culture and Anarchy* (Cambridge: Cambridge University Press, 1932).

6. Also, skepticism from the black community is not solely a consequence of functioning as a celebrity. In the classic essay "Dilemma of the Black intellectual" (written before he reached celebrity status), West accurately discusses the tenuous relationship between black intellectuals and the black community as the consequence of American anti-intellectualism, "a deep distrust and suspicion" of the their link to community, as well as the lack of immediate impact of their work on society. See Cornel West and bell hooks, *Breaking Bread: Insurgent Black Intellectual Life* (New York: South End, 1991).

7. Cornel West, *Democracy Matters* (New York: Penguin, 2004). For an excellent analysis of their feud, as well as the nature of Cornel West's CD, see Mark Anthony Neal, *Songs in the Key of Black Life* (New York: Routledge, 2003). For a provocative (though highly problematic and unnecessarily ad hominem) critique of black public intellectuals, see Adolph Reed, *Class Notes: Posing As Politics and Other Thoughts on the American Scene* (New York: New Press, 2001). For an equally critical though less visceral critique of black public intellectuals, see Richard Posner, *Public Intellectuals: A Story of Decline* (Cambridge: Harvard University Press, 2002).

8. For a devastating critique of the cultural politics of higher education, see Henry Giroux and Susan Searls Giroux, *Take Back Higher Education: Race, Youth, and the Crisis of Democracy in the Post-Civil Rights Era* (New York: Palgrave Macmillan, 2004).

9. "An Invitation Ruffles Philosophical Feathers," *New York Times*, June 29, 2002.

10. I borrow the term "coopted progressive" from Cornel West's classic essay "The New Cultural Politics of Difference." The notion of intellectuals in exile comes from Edward Said, for whom exile represents a self-imposed marginality that allows the intellectual to function within academic institutions without compromising the humanistic principles that govern the archetypal intellectual life. See Edward Said, *Representations of the Intellectual* (New York: Vintage, 1994).

11. I am not contending that Bill Cosby self-identifies as a neoconservative. However, as Dyson argues in *Is Bill Cosby Right?* Cosby's comments betray a particular belief in individual responsibility, good behavior, and a Protestant work ethic that muffles an engaged analysis of the structural factors that undermine and countervail such practices. The utility of such a

perspective within conservative discourse became apparent in self-described conservative Juan Williams's 2006 book, *Enough*. Williams uses Cosby's speech as an organizing tool for his own assault on the black poor.

12. Antonio Gramsci, *Selections from the Prison Notebooks* (New York: International, 1971).

13. Mark Anthony Neal, "Still a Riot Goin' On: Fela Kuti, Celebrity Gramscians, and the AIDS Crisis," www.popmatters.com/columns/criticalnoire/030226.shtml.

14. For a rich discussion of race music, see Guthrie Ramsey, *Race Music* (Berkeley: University of California Press, 2003).

15. Farred explains that many black intellectuals operate as "vernacular intellectuals" whose "'speeches, lyrics, and social intervention echo, reinscribe, and innovate within the hegemonic discourse." This tradition is an inheritance of the larger African American vernacular tradition. Grant Farred, *What's My Name? Black Vernacular Intellectuals* (Minneapolis: University of Minnesota Press, 2003), p. 22.

16. For an excellent discussion of the links between hip-hop culture and the African American vernacular tradition, see Geneva Smitherman, "The Chain Remains the Same: Communicative Practices in the Hip-hop Nation," *Journal of Black Studies* 28, no. 1 (1997): 3–25.

17. Evidence of this can be found in the generally poor critical reviews that followed the release of *I Am* and *Nastradamus*, the respective albums on which these songs appeared. Neither song was released as a single for radio and video consumption.

18. Jay-Z, "The Takeover," on *Blueprint* (Roc-a-fella/Def Jam, 2001).

19. An excellent example of this came during the release of the Rodney King police brutality videotape and the subsequent public discourse that ascribed to it an "aura of the extraordinary." See Robert Gooding-Williams, ed., *Reading Rodney King/Reading Urban Uprising* (New York: Routledge, 1993).

20. Murray Forman, *The 'Hood Comes First: Race Space and Place in Rap and Hip-Hop* (Middletown, CN: Wesleyan, 2002).

21. Michael Eric Dyson, *Open Mike: Reflections on Philosophy, Race, Sex, Culture, and Religion* (New York: Basic Civitas, 2002), p. 27. For a theoretical and historical treatment of this idea, see Elaine Richardson, *African American Literacies* (New York: Routledge, 2003).

22. For an excellent history of blacks and education, see James Anderson, *The Education of Blacks in the South, 1860–1935* (Chapel Hill: University of North Carolina Press, 1988). For contemporary analysis of the political, economic, and cultural dilemmas of blacks and education, see Mwalimu

Shujaa, ed., *Too Much Schooling, Too Little Education: A Paradox of Black Life in White Societies* (Trenton, NJ: Africa World Press, 1994).

23. I borrow the term "dual degree" from Maisha Fisher's ethnographic study, "Earning 'Dual Degrees': Black Bookstores as Alternative Knowledge Spaces," *Anthropology and Education Quarterly* 37, no. 1 (2006): 83–99.

24. My use of "counterpublics" comes from the Black Public Sphere Collective, which defines them as "sphere[s] of critical practice and visionary politics, in which intellectuals can join with the energies of the street, the school, the church, and the city to constitute a challenge to the exclusionary violence of much public space in the United States." *Black Public Sphere: A Public Culture Book* (Chicago: University of Chicago Press Journals, 1995). For an excellent take on this, see Melissa Harris-Lacewell, *Barbershops, Bibles, and BET: Everyday Talk and Black Political Thought* (Princeton, NJ: Princeton University Press, 2004).

25. I refer to these spaces as *relatively* safe and supportive in order to underscore the ways in which various forms of racial affirmation and uplift within black public and counterpublic spaces often came at the expense of a substantive critique of patriarchy. Such critiques are taken up in Kevin Gaines's *Uplifting the Race: Black Leadership, Politics, and Culture in the Twentieth Century* (Chapel Hill: University of North Carolina Press, 1996).

26. It is important to distinguish these people from those who engage traditional academic texts in out-of-school contexts. Of course, neither tradition is typically taken up exclusively. For example, Michael Eric Dyson discusses Tupac's high level of engagement with the Western intellectual tradition, particularly philosophy and literature, in addition to noncanonical texts such as those of the Black Panther Party. See *Holler If You Hear Me: Searching for Tupac Shakur* (New York: BasicCivitas, 2001).

27. See Ernest Allen, "Making the Strong Survive: The Contours and Contradictions of Message Rap," in William E. Perkins, ed., *Droppin' Science: Critical Essays on Rap Music and Hip Hop Culture* (Philadelphia: Temple University Press, 1995).

28. An example of crude Afrocentric theory is Leonard Jeffries's pseudoscientific melanin theory, which argues for the existence of a proportionate relationship between melanin level and intellectual capacity. This impoverished theory does not excuse, however, the frequently inaccurate and racist counterarguments to Afrocentricity that have come from conservative figures like Diane Ravitch, Arthur Schlesinger, and Mary Lefkowitz.

29. Richard Iton, "Like Water for Chocolate: Common's Recipe for Progressive Hip-Hop," www.popmatters.com/columns/criticalnoire/000505.shtml.

30. Mark Anthony Neal, "Like Hearing for the First Time," www.pop-matters.com/music/reviews/c/common-electric.shtml.

31. Hazel Carby, *Race Men* (Cambridge: Harvard University Press, 2000).

6   "Memory Lane": On Jazz, Hip-Hop, and Fathers, by Mark Anthony Neal

1. Gary Douglas, "Olu Dara; A Lifelong Musical Odyssey," *The Voice*, June 18, 2001, p. 19.

2. Baz Dreisinger, "Nas and His Dad's Jazz," *Los Angeles Times*, December 5, 2004, p. E51.

3. Kwame Toure, "One Son Learns Lessons from a Father," *New York Times*, October 6, 1996, sec. 2, p. 42.

4. Unlike the relationship Nas had with his father, Nas's one-time nemesis Jay-Z talks openly on his most recent recording, *The Black Album*, about the absence of his father during his formative years.

5. Joe Schloss, *Making Beats: The Art of Sampled-Based Hip-Hop* (Middletown, CT: Wesleyan University Press, 2004), p. 79.

6. Guthrie Ramsey Jr., *Race Music: Black Cultures from Be-Bop to Hip-Hop* (Berkeley: University of California Press, 2003), p. 33.

7. Ramsey, *Race Music*, p. 4.

8. Alex Abramovich, "Hip-Hop Family Values," *New York Times*, December 5, 2004, sec. 2, p. 35.

9. David H. Rosenthal, *Hard Bop: Jazz and Black Music, 1955–1965* (New York: Oxford University Press, 1992), p. 63.

10. Mark Anthony Neal, "'A Way Out of No Way': Jazz, Hip-Hop, and Black Social Improvisation," in *The Other Side of Nowhere: Jazz, Improvisation, and Communities in Dialogue*, ed. Daniel Fischlin and Ajay Heble (Middletown, CT: Wesleyan University Press, 2004), p. 212.

7   "One Love," Two Brothers, Three Verses, by Michael Eric Dyson

1. Everett Dyson and Michael Eric Dyson, interview by Soledad O'Brien, CNN, April 2008. All quotes from Everett are taken from this interview.

2. Michael Eric Dyson, *Why I Love Black Women* (New York: BasicCivitas, 2003), p. 202

3. Judith Butler, *Precarious Life: The Power of Mourning and Violence* (New York: Verso, 2004), p. 53.

4. *One in 100: Behind Bars in America 2008*, Pew Center on the States, pp. 5–7.

5. For more on this idea of the "carceral canon" in hip-hop and its connections to black Muslim communities, see Sohail Daulatzai, *Return of the Mecca: Black Radicalism and the Muslim Third World*, forthcoming.

6. Sonia Murray, "Hip Hop Stars Behind Bars," *Arizona Daily Star*, October 10, 2005.

7. Sohail Daulatzai, "Protect Ya Neck: Muslims and the Carceral Imagination in the Age of Guantánamo," *Souls* 9, no. 2 (Spring 2007).

8. Jon Schecter, "The Second Coming," *The Source* 55 (April 1994): 45–46, 84.

8   "One Time 4 Your Mind": Embedding Nas and Hip-Hop into a Gendered State of Mind, by Kyra D. Gaunt

1. "Gender is a set of cultural roles. It is a costume, a mask, a straitjacket in which men and women dance their unequal dance. Unfortunately, the term is used both in academic discourse and in the media as interchangeable with 'sex.'" www.ruralwomyn.net/define.html#source.

2. The Five Percent Nation is a splinter group from the Nation of Islam founded in Harlem in 1964 that has inspired many hip-hop artists, including Nas. Though a violation of traditional Islamic practice, Five Percenters view themselves as their own God. Men in the group are called Gods and women Earths. The name of the group comes from the belief that 85 percent of the population is blind and needs to be led; 10 percent has some knowledge of self but misuses it to control the 85 percent; the remaining 5 percent possesses knowledge of self and the way the world system works and strives to educate and liberate the 85 percent. www.npr.org/templates/story/story.php?storyId=5614846.

3. www.hip-hop-blogs.com/hiphop/2005/04/jon_schecter_mis.html.

4. On the album *Street's Disciple*, Nas refers to his new wife as a bitch before correcting himself on the track "Getting Married."

5. I thank Miss Info (Minya Oh) for bringing this idea of defining misogyny to my attention when we participated on a hip-hop panel together at Black Alumni Weekend at the University of Virginia in April 2005.

6. Large Professor (born William Paul Mitchell) was formerly a member of the hip-hop group Main Source ("Lookin at the Front Door"). He produced *Illmatic* and later *Stillmatic*. His album credits read like a who's who in hip-hop: Eric B & Rakim, *Let the Rhythm Hit 'Em*; Pete Rock and CL Smooth, *Mecca and the Soul Brother*; A Tribe Called Quest, *Midnight Marauders*; and many others.

7. Boys are rarely used as eye candy in hip-hop. The mostly male directors of hip-hop videos consumed on MTV and BET by males between thirteen and twenty-five wouldn't even think of it (analogous to the way di-

rectors and producers of NBC's *Friends* sitcom never thought a show set in the diversity of the Big Apple might include even a peripheral appearance of black or Latino friends).

9 "Represent," Queensbridge, and the Art of Living, by Eddie S. Glaude Jr.

1. Nas captures this violence in a startling moment in "One Love," which eerily calls to mind the fact that during one week in August 1990, four children were killed by bullets intended for someone else. Reflecting in a letter to his friend in prison, Nas recounts a conversation with "shorty doo-wop." "I had to school him, told him don't let niggaz fool him, cause when the pistol blow the ones that's murdered be the cool one. Tough luck when niggaz are struck, families fucked up. Could've caught your man, but didn't look when you bucked up. *Mistakes happen, so take heed never bust up at the crowd catch him solo, make the right man bleed*' (emphasis added).

2. Michael Markowitz, "Public Housing," *Gotham Gazette*, www.gotham gazette.com/article/2003–02–17.

3. See Raymond Williams, *Keywords: A Vocabulary of Culture and Society*, rev. ed. (New York: Oxford University Press, 1983), p. 269.

4. Williams, *Keywords*, pp. 266–267.

5. Imani Perry, *Prophets of the Hood: Politics and Poetics in Hip-Hop* (Durham, NC: Duke University Press, 2004), p. 40.

6. I am taken with Perry's insistence on the moral and political ambiguity of rap music that resists such a reading. She argues convincingly that attempts to interpret rap music in ideological terms often obscure the aesthetic dimensions of the form. Moreover, if politics and moral choices are involved, she rightly notes, there is no guarantee that we may like them. But I insist that we not swing the pendulum in the opposite direction. Art can offer powerful commentaries on a social world, and rap music often does just that.

7. Ralph Ellison, "Society, Morality, and the Novel," in *The Collected Essays of Ralph Ellison* (New York: Modern Library, 1995), p. 695.

8. Ellison, "Society," p. 697.

9. Ellison, "Society," p. 698.

10. This is particularly important given that Nas's *Illmatic*, in the eyes of many, reestablished the presence of Queensbridge in hip-hop after the devastating battles with BDP.

11. Quoted in Samantha Henry, "A Good Rap: Residents of the Queensbridge Houses Make Their Claim to Fame," *Newsday*, Queens Edition, August 5, 2001.

10   "It Ain't Hard to Tell": A Story of Lyrical Transcendence, by Imani Perry

1. Michael Thelwell, *The Harder They Come* (New York: Grove, 1980).

2. Produced by Kip Hanrahan. Recorded in August–September 1983 and released in March 1985. AMCL 1006.

3. Derk Richardson, *San Francisco Bay Guardian*, quoted on the *Conjure* album jacket.

4. Richard Harrington, *Washington Post*, quoted on the *Conjure* album jacket.

CONTRIBUTORS

In 1982 **Charlie Ahearn** directed the hip hop classic movie *Wild Style. Yes Yes Y'all* is an oral history of the first decade of hip hop featuring many photos by Ahearn. His book, *Wild Style: The Sampler,* was published in 2007 on the twenty-fifth anniversary of the movie. He is currently finishing a documentary called *Jamel Shabazz: Street Photographer.* Ahearn resides in New York City.

Jon Caramanica writes about music for the *New York Times.* A former music editor of *Vibe,* he has contributed to the *Los Angeles Times, XXL, Rolling Stone, Spin, the Village Voice,* and many other publications. He doesn't understand why the good remixes didn't make it onto the *Illmatic* reissue.

Kevin Coval is the author of *Everyday People* (EM Press, Nov. 2008) and *Slingshots* (a hip-hop poetica) (EM Press, Nov. 2005) and was named Book of the Year finalist by The American Library Association. Coval's poems have appeared in *The Spoken Word Revolution* and *The Spoken Word Revolution: Redux* (Source Books), *Total Chaos* (BasicCivitas), and *I Speak of the City: New York City Poems* (Columbia University Press), among many other anthologies, periodicals, and journals. Co-Founder of Louder Than A Bomb: The Chicago Teen Poetry Festival, the largest youth poetry festival in the world, Coval is also poet-in-residence at The University of Chicago's Newberger Hillel Center.

Sohail Daulatzai teaches in African American Studies and Film and Media Studies at the University of California, Irvine. He is the author of the forthcoming *Return of the Mecca: Black Radicalism and the Muslim Third World* and is currently working on a graphic novel on *The Battle of Algiers.* He is also a creator and executive producer of *Free Rap,* a benefit album for Jamil Al-Amin (formerly H. Rap Brown). Daulatzai lives in Los Angeles, California.

Michael Eric Dyson, named by *Ebony* as one of the hundred most influential black Americans, is an American Book Award winner, a two-time winner of the NAACP Image Award, and is the author of seventeen previous books. He is currently University Professor of Sociology at Georgetown University in Washington, DC.

Manhattan, NYC, native and world-renowned **DJ Bobbito Garcia** a.k.a. Kool Bob Love is *Bounce Magazine's* Editor In Chief and the critically acclaimed author of *Where'd You Get Those? NYC's Sneaker Culture: 1960–1987*

(Testify Books). In recent years, he has reported for MSG-TV during New York Knicks broadcasts, voiced *NBA 2K* video games, and hosted ESPN'*s It's the Shoes* series.

Kyra D. Gaunt, Ph.D. ("Professor G") is a Brooklyn-based singer-songwriter and Associate Professor at Baruch College–CUNY where she teaches anthropology, ethnomusicology, and black studies. She is the author of *Games Black Girls Play: Learning the Ropes from Double-Dutch to Hip-hop* and winner of the 2007 Merriam Prize for the most outstanding book in ethnomusicology. She is a NEH Fellow, a Ford Postdoctoral Fellow, and a 2009 TED Fellow (Technology, Entertainment and Design).

Eddie S. Glaude Jr. is the William S. Tod Professor of Religion and Director of the Center for African American Studies at Princeton Univeristy. He is the author of the *Exodus! Race and Nation in Early 19th Century Black America* and *In a Shade of Blue: Pragmatism and the Politics of Black America*. He is a native of Mississippi.

Suheir Hammad is the author of *breaking poems* (cypher books, 2008), as well as "ZaatarDiva," "Born Palestinian, Born Black," and "Drops of This Story." An original writer and performer in the TONY award-winning Russell Simmons Presents Def Poetry Jam on Broadway, Suheir appears in the 2008 Cannes Film Festival Official Selection, "Salt of This Sea" and has read her work throughout the world on stage, radio, and screen.

dream hampton is a writer and filmmaker.

Marc Lamont Hill is Associate Professor of Education and Anthropology at Columbia University (Teachers College). He is the author of *Beats, Rhymes, and Classroom Life: Hip Hop Pedagogy and the Politics of Identity*. He lives in New York and Philadelphia.

Adam Mansbach's most recent novel is *The End of the Jews*, winner of the California Book Award. His previous novel, *Angry Black White Boy*, was a *San Francisco Chronicle* Best Book of 2005. It is taught at more than sixty schools, and a theatrical adaptation was named the Best Play of 2008 by the *San Francisco Chronicle* and the *San Francisco Examiner*. His other books include the novel *Shackling Water*, the poetry collection *genius b-boy cynics getting weeded in the garden of delights*, and *A Fictional History of the United States with Huge Chunks Missing*, an anthology of original short stories which he co-edited. An inaugural recipient of the Ford Foundation's Future Aesthetics Artist Regrant, Mansbach is the 2009–2010 New Voices Professor of Fiction at Rutgers University. The founding editor of the pioneering 1990's hip-hop journal *Elementary*, his fiction and essays have appeared in *The New*

York Times, The Boston Globe, The Los Angeles Times Book Review, The Believer, Vibe, JazzTimes, Wax Poetics, The Best Music Writing 2004, Total Chaos: The Art and Aesthetics of Hip-Hop, and elsewhere. He lives in Berkeley, California.

Adilifu Nama is an associate professor at California State University Northridge. He is the author of *Black Space: Imagining Race in Science Fiction Film* (University Texas Press, 2008), the first book-length examination on the topic. He lives in Pasadena, CA, with his wife and two children.

Mark Anthony Neal is Professor of Black Popular Culture in the Department of African and African-American Studies at Duke University. He is the author of several books including *What the Music Said: Black Popular Music and Black Public Culture, Soul Babies: Black Popular Culture and the Post-Soul Aesthetic,* and *New Black Man.* He resides in Durham, NC, with his wife and two daughters.

Imani Perry is a Professor in the Center for African American Studies at Princeton University. She received her Ph.D. in the History of American Civilization from Harvard University and her J.D. from Harvard Law School. Perry is the author of *Prophets of the Hood: Politics and Poetics in Hip Hop* (Duke University Press, 2004) and over two dozen articles in the fields of law, literature, and cultural studies. Her forthcoming book *Righteous Hope* explores the contemporary face of racial inequality and offers solutions to its challenges.

James Braxton Peterson is an Assistant Professor of English at Bucknell University. Peterson's academic work focuses on Africana Studies, Narrative, Graphic Novels, and Hip Hop Culture. He is the founder of Hip Hop Scholars, LLC, an association of Hip Hop generational scholars dedicated to researching and developing the cultural and educational potential of Hip Hop, urban, and youth cultures. Peterson is regular contributor to The Root.com and he has appeared on Fox News, CBS, MSNBC, ABC News, ESPN, and various local television networks as an expert on Hip Hop culture, popular culture, urban youth, and politics. He lives in Lewisburg, PA.

Guthrie P. Ramsey Jr. is Professor of Music History and African Studies at the University of Pennsylvania. He is the author of *Race Music: Black Cultures from Bebop to Hip-Hop* and the forthcoming study *In Walked Bud: Earl Bud Powell and the Modern Jazz Challenge.*

Greg Tate is a writer and musician who lives and thrives in Harlem. He is currently working on a critical biography on The Godfather of Soul, James Brown.

ACKNOWLEDGMENTS

Michael Eric Dyson I'd like to thank Nas for his genius and such an incredible body of work, but especially this remarkable album that we have had the privilege of examining and engaging. I'd like to thank Common for his genius and for his incredible fraternal generosity in penning the preface to this book. I'd like to thank my colleague Sohail Daulatzai for his sheer intellectual brilliance and his never-say-die determination to see this book into print. Without his unfailing commitment and unflagging exuberance for the work, the book you're holding in your hands wouldn't exist. Thanks, my brother, and one love to you for all your hard work. I'd like to thank each writer in this book for their important contributions. And I'd like to thank Basic*Civitas* for its support of our work. Finally, I'd like to thank my family for their love, support, and patience in allowing me to finish this book.

Sohail Daulatzai First off, big up to Nasir bin Olu Dara—whose brilliance keeps shining. I hope we came even remotely close to doing your genius justice. To all the contributors, who without their patience and insight, this never would have happened. To Brandon Proia and the staff at Basic*Civitas*, we did it! Ready for another? To my peoples at UCI and at other spots all over, thanks for the support—and remember, keep your friends close and your enemies closer. Especially when in black or brown face. The wicked a go burn. To Michael Eric Dyson—mentor, brother, juggernaut—who is brolic with knowledge. Keep bench-pressing the standard, and thanks for putting a cat on! One love. To my peoples across seas, behind walls, under ground, trapped in cages, and in war-torn places—though a nomad, I see and breathe your smoke signals. And remember, there ain't an army that can strike back! To the bredren at Ali Mamas—keep smoking the good stuff! To my peoples who stood close and kept the cipher complete: Turtle, Lif Nama, Oscar Michel, Zack de la Rocha, Wesam Nassar, The E (aka Center), Junaid Rana, Vivek Bald, and Loic Howzell—stay chisel, and keep lickin' shots! To the Daulatzai and Amani families, words just can't. So I won't. But just know. Everything is everything. Ameen. And finally, to you, the gift, in whose eyes I see Mecca and in whose heart I found home.

INDEX